WALKIN' THE LINE

50   45   40   35

WALKIN' THE LINE

50   45   40   35

A JOURNEY
FROM PAST
TO PRESENT
ALONG THE
MASON-DIXON

180   175   170   165

William Ecenbarger

M. Evans and Company, Inc.

New York

M. Evans and Company, Inc.
216 East 49th Street
New York, New York 10017

ISBN 0-87131-910-1

Book design and typography by Rik Lain Schell

Printed in the United States of America

9   8   7   6   5   4   3   2   1

CONTENTS

For Susan

ACKNOWLEDGEMENTS

I want to express my deepest gratitude to three members of the Mason and Dixon Line Preservation Partnership—Todd Babcock, Charlie Bitler and Bob Bechtel—those professional descendants of Charles Mason and Jeremiah Dixon who helped me through my ignorance of longitude and latitude, zenith sector and Gunter's chain, meridian and offset.

Special thanks to George W. Dixon and his wife, Lettice, who hosted me at their home in England and offered important insights into his ancestor, Jeremiah.

William H. Williams, history professor, Delaware Tech, Georgetown, Delaware, read my manuscript and made valuable suggestions and corrections.

Hundreds of strangers helped me along in my journey. Most of them are named in the book, but a few are not: Kurt Bell at the Railroad Museum of Pennsylvania; Frances Cloud Taylor, an expert on the Underground Railroad in southeastern Pennsylvania; Charles Gibson at Lincoln University; John Frey at the Washington County Library in Hagerstown, Maryland; and Joe Lake, the historian of Hockessin, Delaware.

George de Kay, my editor and publisher, backed an unusual idea and afforded me maximum editorial freedom. Bert Holtje, my agent, was supportive at the very beginning. Others who deserve recognition are Deborah Whiting and Paul Critchlow.

Among the hundreds of books I consulted, a few need special mention: Hubertis M. Cummings's *The Mason and Dixon Line*; F. Hughlett Mason's compilation and commentary on Charles Mason's Journal; William Still's classic, *The Underground Railroad*; the Maryland Geological Survey's *Report on the Resurvey of the Maryland-Pennsylvania Boundary*; Paul Wallace's books on the Indians of Pennsylvania, and C. A. Weslager's books on the Nanticoke and Delaware Indians.

Finally, I am uniquely indebted to that wonderful American invention and the greatest democratic institution ever created—the public library. All up and down the Line, libraries big and small offered information on local history, suggestions for people to interview and a place to oil a squeaky day.

AUTHOR'S NOTE

It is impossible to walk the entire Mason-Dixon Line. Much of it runs over private property whose owners sometimes don't welcome strangers afoot, and there are unbridged rivers and streams. Nor does it make sense to walk the entire Line. In the west, it goes through uninhabited wilderness, and where there are no people, there are no stories. Therefore, for my purposes, all miles were not equal, and so the lengths of the chapters are disproportionate to the lengths of the sections of the Line involved.

Logic dictated that I structure this book as a geographic progression from the easternmost point on the Line to the westernmost. However, the reader should not conclude that my actual movements followed such a direct path. For many reasons, such as the availability of an individual I wanted to interview, I often found it expedient to jump ahead or to go back.

Working in three- and four-day segments centered around weekends, my travels took about a year. I actually walked about half of the 365 miles covered in this book, following the Line over hills, through cornfields, cemeteries, swamps, parking lots, suburbs, pastures, and even houses themselves.

Although I have tried to inject a measure of spontaneity, most of this book is the result of careful planning. It should be clear that I didn't just happen upon the people and events that fill these pages.

Although it is not legally part of the Mason-Dixon Line, I have included the so-called New Castle Circle because the Circle figured prominently in the drawing of the Line and, moreover, the two connected boundaries have an extensive body of shared history.

For the sake of clarity, I have taken some liberties with the punctuation in Charles Mason's journal; it was correct for the time, but for the modern reader it can be confusing and unnecessarily disruptive.

I struggled considerably with the use of certain words. In the period of some three centuries covered by the book, African Americans have been known as Negroes, blacks, and, now, African Americans. I have tried to use these terms sensibly and sensitively. It seemed awkward to refer to American slaves as African Americans since the term was not in existence at that time. Similarly, the term Native Americans would have been unknown in the eighteenth century to the people who were called Indians (because Columbus mistakenly thought he had landed in Asia). As far as the Europeans who moved into the territory, for want of a better word, I have used "settler"—even though these white people were anything but settling to the Indians they displaced.

I am, by experience and choice, a journalist—not a historian—and I do not present this as a scholarly work but as a popular history. With the exception of Charles Mason's journal, some courthouse records, and the hundred or so people I interviewed, all my sources are secondary sources—books, magazines, and newspapers—about 1,000 in all.

Finally, history is the realm of interesting people, good and evil, and they made fine traveling companions.

INTRODUCTION

The Mason-Dixon Line was decreed, drawn, and marked long before it was named. When Charles Mason and Jeremiah Dixon left America in 1768, theirs was a work that was quickly forgotten. After all, it was merely the effort of two obscure English surveyors; it merely settled a boundary dispute and provided the dividing line between two colonies.

But on March 1, 1780, the Pennsylvania Assembly passed a law calling for the gradual end of slavery, and the longest portion of the Mason-Dixon Line became the boundary not just between Pennsylvania and Maryland, but between freedom and slavery.

It was during the rancorous debates in Congress over the Missouri Compromise of 1820 that the Mason-Dixon Line first came to symbolize the division between the slaveholding South and the free North. Thomas Jefferson immediately saw the new significance of the Mason-Dixon Line, and he wrote to a friend: "A geographical line, coinciding with a marked principle, moral and political, once conceived and held up to the angry passions of men, will never be obliterated; and every new irritation will mark it deeper and deeper."

When the Civil War ended, slavery was abolished but the Mason-Dixon Line was still there, separating North from South. Up and down the Line, the racial hatred that had been seeded two and one-half centuries earlier continued to be carefully watered every day. And the Line is still embedded in the national psyche as a powerful racial symbol.

I had originally intended to tell the story of how the Mason-Dixon Line came to be, and to walk along the Line and talk to people to discover what had happened in the past and what it was like now. But the narrower theme became inescapable—no matter how many ways I shuffled the deck, the race card kept coming to the top. And so I resolved to view the Line through the lens of race and to learn more about this awful thing that runs so deeply in American life.

PROLOGUE

During the heady days of discovery in the seventeenth century, English kings fell into the habit of handing out huge tracts of American wilderness to their court favorites; they did this in true cavalier fashion—that is, without any precise geographical knowledge of the lands they proffered.

So it was that in 1632 King Charles I favored Cecilius Calvert, the second Lord Baltimore and a Catholic, with a large grant north of Virginia. Calvert named the area Maryland in honor of Charles's Catholic queen, Henrietta Maria. The charter set the northern boundary of Maryland as the fortieth degree of latitude.

In 1681, King Charles II gave William Penn a huge tract of land in America whose southern boundary was the fortieth degree of latitude. In a separate grant, Penn also received the so-called Three Lower Counties that now comprise the state of Delaware. The northern border of the Three Lower Counties was to be part of a circle drawn at a twelve-mile radius from the courthouse at New Castle.

The southern border of the main Penn grant (now Pennsylvania) was to extend along the fortieth degree of latitude until it intersected with the circular boundary. This was the big problem—for the fortieth parallel ran some thirteen miles north of the circle and at no point intersected. In other words, it was mathematically, geographically, and physically impossible for both proprietary families to have the land stated in their charters.

At first it didn't matter because no one really knew where the fortieth degree of latitude was. But then sea captains, who had good navigational instruments, came into Philadelphia and warned Penn that the city was in Maryland. Penn had no intention of surrendering his only port.

To establish their right to the disputed border lands by actual occupation, both proprietors began encouraging settlement by German farmers, who had earned a reputation for permanency once they moved in. Penn wrote letters to large property owners who considered themselves to be residents of Maryland and informed them they were residents of Pennsylvania—and should start paying taxes to same. Calvert retaliated with his own letters to those who considered themselves to be Pennsylvanians. But titles were insecure and tax collections were uncertain. When tenants refused to pay taxes, sheriffs were sent out to enforce the law. Soon the border was aflame with violence, bloodshed and, occasionally, death.

The settlers themselves cared very little which colony they were in. If the land was fertile, what difference did it make—and why pay taxes to either wealthy British family?

Meanwhile, the proprietors and their descendants wrangled tediously for three generations. Each side stooped to specious arguments, and no legal straw was too fragile to grab. Finally the king, exasperated by the rising border violence, stepped in and ordered both sides to resolve the issue. Settlement was reached in an English court in 1750. Although the agreement was called a compromise, the Penns clearly came out on top, because Pennsylvania's southern border would run at a latitude fifteen miles south of Philadelphia—significantly below the fortieth degree of latitude.

Commissioners were appointed, three to each side, to work on the specific boundary. Local surveyors were hired, and they began at Fenwick Island on the Atlantic. They successfully ran a seventy-mile east-west line between the ocean and the Chesapeake Bay to establish the Middle Point between the two bodies of water. Here another petty squabble between the proprietors held up work for a decade. It wasn't until 1760 that another team of colonial surveyors took the next step—creating a line heading north from the Middle Point. When the local talent faltered, Penn and Calvert consulted the Royal Observatory, which recommended two English astronomer-mathematicians—Charles Mason and Jeremiah Dixon.

A contract was drawn up in 1763, and it was signed by the grandsons of William Penn and by Frederick Calvert, the sixth Lord Baltimore. Mason and Dixon arrived in Philadelphia on November 15, 1763, and got down to business immediately. For most of the Line, they worked in short bursts of about ten miles, calibrating their position and direction by the stars and then measuring on the ground with rods and chains.

They accepted the Middle Point established by the colonial surveyors some thirteen years earlier, then moved north eighty-seven miles to a point between the thirty-ninth and fortieth parallels (and fifteen miles south of Philadelphia). Here they pushed west 230 miles to a point between western Pennsylvania and what is now West Virginia.

It was a solid piece of work—an achievement of skill and courage. Battling accidents, hostile Indians, snow-covered mountains, dense forests, flooded rivers, wild animals, and nit-picking bureaucrats, Mason and Dixon plotted a boundary that is still accepted by the U.S. Geodetic Survey. The most sophisticated modern equipment shows that they strayed only a few hundred feet one way or the other.

The Mason-Dixon Line was a scientific landmark in the history of geodesy—the science of determining exact positions on large portions of the earth's surface. Until Mason and Dixon drew their Line, geodesy had been largely theoretical; it had not been applied to long boundaries where the earth's curvature could cause complications. The Line became a model for many other surveys in the United States and the British Empire.

The survey was formally approved on November 9, 1768—ending eighty-seven years of dispute between the Calverts and the Penns, who, in one of history's ironies, would lose their land to the American Revolution in eight years.

Mason and Dixon left America on September 11, 1768—four years and ten months after they arrived. They never worked together again. Within twenty years, both men would be dead—long before their linked names became household words and their work became the world's most famous boundary.

What they had drawn is still one of the most unusual boundaries on earth. It is wholly artificial, wholly nontopographical. Most boundaries between states and nations have been determined by land features such as rivers and mountains. But the Mason-Dixon Line does not follow anything palpable; it runs along uneven latitudes and longitudes, and at no point does it touch any prominent landmark. Except for its stone markers, it is invisible—an arbitrary and man-made demarcation, direct and true, but without dimension.

It is, simultaneously, a product of reason and a national landmark.

Chapter One

THE TRANSPENINSULAR LINE
ATLANTIC OCEAN TO MIDDLE POINT —
WESTWARD 35 MILES.

"Traveler, There is no path.

Paths are made by walking"

　　　—Antonio Machado, from *Poesias Completas*, 1917

Rain was turning to snow and temperatures were dropping on December 22, 1750, when a team of four surveyors, two from each colony, gathered at the Atlantic Ocean on Fenwick Island to begin the east-west line across the peninsula. John Watson and William Parsons represented the Penn family; John Emory and Thomas Jones represented the Calvert family. Even though he left the surveying party before the line was completed, Watson was the leader and, in early years, the work was called the John Watson Line. Had they had better equipment, better weather, and better luck, perhaps his name would have become a household word.

The surveyors' task was to run a transpeninsular line due west to the Chesapeake Bay, and then use this line to establish the middle point between ocean and bay. West of the line would be Maryland; east of the line would be Pennsylvania's so-called Three Lower Counties, which by this time had gained a separate identity as Delaware.

The provincial surveyors were instructed to mark each mile with a post and to set up stone markers every five miles. The monuments for marking the five-mile intervals were cut especially for this purpose from native stone. They were rectangular prisms, 4½ by 8 inches, and about four feet long. On one side were inscribed the arms of Lord Baltimore and on the opposite side the arms of the Penns.

According to Watson's diary, they selected as a starting point "a cedar post standing on the northernmost part of the island near to the smallest of four mulberry trees growing together." They presumed the wooden stake was left from an earlier survey.

19

But on December 28 they received a visit from John Bowden, a local resident, who informed them that the marker was not a surveyor's stake at all, but had been placed there by his father twenty years ago to straighten his fishing lines. Despite this new information, the surveyors proceeded as planned—apparently reasoning that any stake on Fenwick Island was as good as any other to start.

Next they built a cabin on the beach to provide shelter while they spent a few days making astronomical observations. Watson recorded that the first night "just as we were composing ourselves to sleep, some asleep and the rest partly so, a spark from the fire kindled in the covering of our cabin, by this time, become very dry, and instantly flashed up into a blaze, each of the company immediately withdrew and bore with us such of our clothing and blankets as we chanced first to lay hands on."

Although they had lost much of their equipment, the survey party left the beach on January 5, 1751, and moved westward. They ran a line about six miles long before a howling blizzard forced them to abandon their work until spring.

After resuming work in the spring of 1751, the survey party moved smoothly due west for thirteen miles to the Pocomoke Swamp, where they encountered one of America's first sit-down strikes. The diary for May 7 reads: "This morning our workmen combined together to extort higher wages from us and all of them except one, had obliged themselves under the penalty of 0 pounds 15 shillings not to work longer with us unless we would enlarge their wages; this stops us some time, but we were fixt as to that point, and after threatening the leaders and speaking fair-to others telling them the dangers of entering into combinations of this kind, several of them upon acknowledging their faults and promising not to do so again were taken again into service."

Getting through the swamp was brutal work, and it took them about ten days. The surveyors' notes recount wading in shoulder-high water, flies and mosquitoes, dangerous snakes, quicksand, poison ivy, and thorn-filled underbrush. There was no stable ground to set up instruments. A resurvey of the transpeninsular line by the U.S. Coast and Geodetic Survey in 1970 showed the surveyors veered off course several times in the swamp. They reached the fifteenth mile on May 14, but were unable to set up a stone and instead noted that a cypress tree stood "at the distance of fifteen miles from the Beginning."

Most of the land beyond the swamp was flat and tilled, and the surveyors moved rapidly. They reached the shore of the Chesapeake on June 15, 1751. It was nearly seventy miles from the Fenwick Island marker. But now the Penns and Calverts began haggling over just where the Chesapeake Bay began. Was it at the west end of Taylor's Island, some sixty-nine miles from the Atlantic? Or was it at Slaughter Creek, which separated the island from the mainland and was only sixty-six miles from the ocean? The Marylanders realized that the shorter the line across the penin-

sula, the better off they would be. Specifically, cutting off three miles by stopping at Slaughter Creek would give them an extra one and one-half miles of territory when the Middle Point was calculated. Not surprisingly, the Pennsylvanians took exception and argued that Taylor's Island was the proper starting point.

They argued for nine more years, until July 4, 1760, when a final agreement was hammered out. The west side of Taylor's Island was designated as water's edge—and once again, the Penns won. The Middle Point was then set at just under thirty-five miles from the ocean, and a white oak was set to mark the precise spot.

FENWICK ISLAND, DELAWARE: ON MILE 0

A halo of yawping gulls encircles the top of the eighty-nine-foot high Fenwick Lighthouse. The steady roar of the wind is broken regularly by the basso *thump!* of breaking waves. Just outside the chain-link fence surrounding the lighthouse stands the first marker placed in 1751 by the colonial surveying team. The round-topped stone is whitewashed and protected by a chain. A sign misinforms me that "this is the marker from which Charles Mason and Jeremiah Dixon started the survey for the Mason-Dixon Line."

A sign on the lighthouse reads, "This structure is maintained by the nonprofit Friends of the Fenwick Lighthouse. For more information contact Paul Pepper." Pepper is tall and lanky, with sparse gray hair, his face a crisscross of wrinkles hammered in over eighty-nine years, and he thinks it's too bad that people move around all the time and don't stay in the same place very long. "I've lived here all my life," Pepper says. "My great-grandfather was the keeper, and my grandfather was the assistant keeper. I was the first president of the Friends of the Fenwick Lighthouse."

The lighthouse was put out of work by the development of on-board navigation equipment; in 1972, the U.S. Coast Guard turned it off. "But we liked seeing the light," Pepper says, "and we all got together, signed petitions, contacted politicians and eventually the state bought it and leased it to the Friends of the Fenwick Lighthouse for one dollar a year. The Coast Guard didn't want us to have the light on because it might confuse ships. We told them it wouldn't be a lighthouse without a light, it would be just another building. Besides, you can't see it from the sea anymore because of all the beachfront hotels. So we worked out a deal, and now it's on from dawn to dusk."

The lighthouse at Fenwick Island, Delaware, on the Atlantic. A round-topped stone in front of it, placed there in 1751, marks the beginning of the line.

Pepper says he likes to think of the Lighthouse as the beginning marker of the Mason-Dixon Line. His eyes narrow in thought. "The Line heads out that way. The next marker's five miles away. Get on West Line Road and look for a pasture. The ten-mile stone is near Selbyville right along the main highway. They didn't put one at fifteen miles because it's right in the middle of the swamp. Then look in Line Mountain Cemetery for. . . ."

I walk due west from the Lighthouse, past the Mason-Dixon Motel. Delaware, to my right, has done a reasonable job of keeping beach development semirespectable, but to my left looms the vast geometry of high-rise hotels, condominia, roller coasters, and Ferris wheels that is the skyline of Ocean City, Maryland

It's the off-season, cold and windy, and the Commander Hotel at 14th Street is empty. It was at this point during the first half of the twentieth century that a wire was strung out into the water and blacks knew that they could swim only north of that wire. They were only allowed on the Ocean City boardwalk for three days every year in September. This time was known as "Colored Excursion Days," and it attracted blacks from as far away as Baltimore and Washington.

At the southern end of Ocean City, Henry's Hotel is boarded up for the winter. The 100-year-old three-story shingle building is now a rooming house, but from the 1920s to the 1960s it was where blacks stayed when they had business in Ocean City. Noted guests included Cab Calloway, Duke Ellington, and Count Basie, who could perform at major hotels but not sleep there.

West of Assowoman Bay the Line goes through sandy soil and scruffy pines. I get directions to the five-mile marker from a convenience store in Williamsville, Delaware, and I quickly find it in thick woods just outside a pasture. It's green with moss but well-protected by trees. Both coats of arms are visible after two and one-half centuries. I walk the Line for several miles where it coincides with West Line Road. There is a field full of cannibalized motor vehicles—the husks of cars, vans, and pickups, the detritus of our motorized society.

SELBYVILLE, DELAWARE: ON MILE 10

The 10-mile marker is just south of Selbyville, along Route 113 (the Dupont Highway) next to an industrial park—just where Paul Pepper said it would be. It was placed here on May 3, 1751, by the transpeninsular surveyors. They noted in their diary that there was a schoolhouse nearby. Today the stone is worn and mossed, but it's flanked by two cypress trees standing erect as pencils. The ground around it is trimmed and neat. At the Mason-Dixon Shopping Center, I talk to five old men sipping coffee at the McDonald's. One of them says the site of the marker is cared for by Boy Scouts and other community groups.

Like many Delaware towns, Selbyville got started before the Revolution as a grist mill and blacksmith shop. The lack of navigable water kept it from growing until 1871, when D. J. Long bought some strawberry plants and started growing them. The railroad came through a few years later and soon Selbyville became one of the strawberry centers of the nation. Blacks began arriving from Southern states to work as pickers.

The strawberry business peaked in 1918 when some 250,000 crates were shipped from Selbyville, but as early as 1910 John G. Townsend, a strawberry broker, became distressed by the railroad freight rates. He told Thomas Coleman du Pont, president of the E. I. du Pont de Nemours and Company, that Delaware needed better roads. Not only did du Pont agree, but he paid four million dollars of his own money to build a road between

Wilmington and Selbyville. When the Du Pont Highway opened in 1924, the stage was set for the chicken business. Today the Delmarva Peninsula is the hub of America's poultry industry, and in the rural areas around the Mason-Dixon Line the chicken house—with its lights shining all night to encourage gluttony via automatic feed pans—is a familiar sight.

In the beginning, blacks filled the lowliest jobs in the industry. They worked as members of "catching crews" that would round up the birds for transportation to the processing plant. They would handle three and four chickens at a time in each hand, and they were entitled to take home for their own use any birds injured in the process. White women held most of the processing plant jobs until after World War II, when they left for better-paying work and were replaced by blacks. Beginning in the 1980s, Hispanics began supplanting blacks in the plants. Cutting and deboning chickens is hard, dangerous work. Knife wounds are frequent, the floors become slippery with blood and poultry fat, and repetitive motion injuries are common.

Just outside the Selbyville processing plant, I find a group of men and women wearing green hardhats, green rubber gloves, and plastic ear coverings waiting for the 8 A.M. shift to start. One of them speaks English and tells me most of the group is from Guatemala. I ask him if he likes working here. A glint of suspicion narrows his eyes, and he says everyone likes the work because the pay is so good. "I can do thirty-eight chickens a minute," he adds.

BERLIN, MARYLAND: SOUTH OF MILE 11

Berlin has a restored Victorian town center—red brick buildings with compatible roof lines, and proportionate windows and doors. The streets are lined with well-maintained magnolias, poplars, and sycamores. The old Atlantic Hotel at Main and Broad still has its full front veranda and rocking chairs. The Globe theater has been spruced up. The first floor has a bookstore, gourmet deli, and restaurant. The second floor balcony, where blacks had to sit until the 1960s, has been converted into an art gallery. These balconies, which were called "nigger heavens," originated in churches and were carried over to movie houses.

Berlin is the hometown of Charles Albert Tindley, who was born into slavery around 1855 and moved to Philadelphia at the age of seventeen to find a better life. He educated himself through correspondence courses, became a minister, and headed one of the largest African American Methodist congregations in Philadelphia. He fought for civil rights, cared for the poor, and found time to write forty-five gospel hymns; his "I'll Overcome Someday," is better known as "We Shall Overcome."

When James Purnell was growing up in nearby Snow Hill, Maryland, his family would come to Berlin to shop and see movies. In the Forties and Fifties, blacks had to park their cars in one designated lot and were restricted to one dirty restroom. When Purnell was twelve years old, he was standing in front of the Atlantic Hotel with his nine year old sister, Patricia; a policeman came along and said, "Niggers, get off the corner!"

"I guess we didn't move fast enough," says Purnell, his eyes going wide with the memory, "because he took out his club and smacked my sister in the stomach." Purnell ran and got his father, who found Patricia doubled over in pain. He went to the police and demanded an apology. He got it, but that wasn't enough. Purnell's father contacted white friends and business associates over the next few days, and pressed his complaint until the policeman was fired.

"That taught me something about being persistent in sticking up for your rights," Purnell said. "Even today you have to keep bangin' on the door and keep it open. If you don't, they'll close it on you and go back to business as usual."

Jim Crow was a constant childhood companion for Purnell. He walked several miles to the segregated school, where he was handed textbooks discarded by the white school. Often there were pages missing. There was no gym, and the basketball team had to practice outside. He recalls going to Ocean City on Colored Excursion Days. "Most of the stores and rides were closed. We were allowed to swim above 14th Street, but the water was usually too cold."

In his mid-forties, Purnell became an activist. He led the fight against a smelly landfill placed in the middle of the black section of town by the white establishment. He marched on the Ocean City boardwalk for better jobs at the beach resorts. In 1986 he became president of the Worcester County branch of the NAACP. He fought a long, bitter legal battle with the county over minority representation on the county commission body— a battle that was finally resolved in his favor by the U.S. Supreme Court. He was elected to the county commission in 1994 and re-elected in 1998 with the help of white votes and white financial support.

At sixty-two, Purnell is nearly bald and built like a Russian war memorial. Clad in a tank top and jeans, he sits in front of a glowing kerosene heater in his home in the black section of Berlin. "There's been some integration, but basically the whites live on the west side of Route 113, the blacks on the east. Up until a few years ago there was a street named Maryland Avenue that suddenly changed into Branch Avenue. We discovered that the town fathers did this so it would be clear exactly where they wanted to exclude blacks from owning and renting. It was right there in the official minutes that way. We got them to change the name officially, but a lot of maps still have it the old way."

Pocomoke Swamp: On Mile 12

I stand near the Line along an unpaved, sandy road in the middle of the Pocomoke Swamp. There are no signs announcing the change in jurisdictions, and I am using a hand-held global positioning system to determine the approximate location of the border. Fog has bleached the landscape. Big ferns lining the roadway give way to a thick forest. There are pine, holly, gum, cedar, and an occasional bald cypress. This spring's rain and last fall's dead leaves give off a putrefaction that is fecund and not unpleasant.

The first European to come here probably was Giovanni da Verrazano, the Italian navigator, who anchored his ship, the *Dauphine*, off Fenwick Island in 1524 while on a mission for the King of France. He led a party of twenty men inland to the swamp, where he marveled at the luxuriant plant life—"wild roses, violets, lilies and many sorts of plants and frequent flowers different from our own," he wrote in a letter to the king. He found the local Indians friendly and the women beautiful.

But a century later, the Maryland charter authorized Lord Baltimore to raise troops and wage war on the "barbarians" and other enemies who might threaten the new colony, "to pursue them beyond the limits of their province," and "if God shall grant it, to vanquish and captivate them; and the captives to put to death, or according to their discretion, to save."

When English colonists began moving onto Maryland's Eastern Shore in the eighteenth century, the colonial government tried to protect the Indians by setting aside land for their exclusive use. But the authorities couldn't control their own land-hungry people, and the Indians kept getting pushed inland. Their frustration boiled over, and in the spring of

1742, the Nanticokes and other tribes gathered in the swamp at a secret place called Winnasoccum to plot against the whites.

Several hundred men, women, and children assembled at the Winnasoccum powwow. Illuminated by campfires, the local chiefs stepped forward one by one and enumerated their grievances. They had been driven from their villages. English hunters killed indiscriminately, and fur-bearing animals were becoming scarce. Pleas to the English authorities to forbid traders from giving intoxicating liquor to the Indians went unheeded. Then an outsider, the Shawnee chieftain Messowan, urged them to join forces with him to drive the English out. It was agreed, and as a first step plans were made to poison the drinking water of the colonists.

But the Maryland authorities learned of the Winnasoccum plot, and the leaders were arrested. A special board of inquiry convened at Annapolis, and new treaties were signed with each tribe. The English would choose the official tribal representatives with whom they would deal. The Indians were forbidden to carry guns and to entertain foreign Indians in their towns. The Nanticokes were singled out for special treatment. They could not assemble to choose an emperor, which destroyed a political structure that had coalesced them for centuries. It was the beginning of the end for the Nanticokes.

Throughout the colonial period, there were white men in the Pocomoke Swamp making cypress shingles that were used for roofs and siding. Much of the hard work, including the felling of the trees, was done by black slaves. By the time of the Civil War, most of the timber was gone, but layers of fallen cypress were found in the peat of the swamp and could be dug out during rainy weather. Because cypress resists the rotting process, these fallen trees were as good for shingles as the living ones. Inexorably, drainage and drought had lowered the water level and, in 1930, a fire raged out of control for months and burned off about ten feet of the now-dry peat, including most of the remaining cypress. It will take several thousand years for the swamp to completely regenerate itself.

The swamp has always been a refuge—for British sympathizers during the Revolution, for Civil War draft dodgers and deserters, for runaway slaves, for criminals, and for moonshiners. The headwaters of the Pocomoke River are in the swamp, and in the fifty years preceding the Civil War it was called a "flowing underground railroad" because it was an escape artery for slaves heading for freedom in the Philadelphia area.

In his 1884 novel, *The Entailed Hat,* George Alfred Townsend wrote some vivid descriptions of the swamp and its use by fugitive slaves. One of the principal characters is the slave Virgie, who flees her master in Maryland and is guided through the swamp on a shingle trail by Hudson, a free black.

> The swamp increased in depth and solemnity as they drew near the rushing sluices of the Pocomoke, and kept along them, the trail being now a mere ditch and chain of floating logs where no vehicle could pass, and the man himself seemed frightened as he led the way from trunk to float and puddle to corduroy, sometimes balancing himself on a revolving log, or again plunging nearly to his waist in vegetable muck; but the light-footed girl behind had the footstep of a bird, and hopped as if from twig to twig, and seemed to slide where he would sink; and the man often turned in terror, when he had fallen headlong from some treacherous perch, to see her slender feet, in crescent sandals, play in the moonlit jungle like hands upon a harp.
>
> He stared at her in wonder, but too wistfully. The cat-briers hung across the opening, and grape-vines, like cables of sunken ships, fell many a fathom through the crystal waves of night; but the North Star seemed to find a way to peep through everything, and Virgie heard the words from Hudson. . . .
>
> "Jess over this branch a bit we is in Delaware!"
>
> The mighty swamp now grew distinct, yet more inaccessible, as its inner edges seemed transparent in the line of fires, like curtains of lace against the midnight windowpanes. The Virginia creeper, light as the flounces of a lady, went whirling upward, as if in a dance; the fallen giant trees were rich in hanging moss; laurel and jasmine appeared beyond the bubbling surface of long, green morass, where life of some kind seemed to turn over comfortably in the rising warmth, like sleepers in bed.
>
> Suddenly the man took Virgie up and carried her through a stream of running water, brown with the tannin matter of the swamp.
>
> "We is in Delaware," he said, soon after, as they reached a camp of shingle sawyers, all deserted, and lighted by the fire, the golden chips strewn around, and the sawdust, like Indian meal, that suggested good, warm pone at Teackle Hall to Virgie.
>
> She put her feet, soaked with swamp water, at a burning log to warm, and hardly saw a moccasin snake glide round the fire and stop, as if to dart at her, and glide away; for Virgie's mind was attributing this kindly fire to the presence of Freedom.

Virgie eventually makes her way to Wilmington, Delaware, and the home of Thomas Garrett, the real-life Underground Railroad conductor who guided fugitive slaves across the Mason-Dixon Line to Philadelphia.

MILLSBORO, DELAWARE: NORTH OF MILE 13

The parking lot outside the Indian Mission Methodist Church near Millsboro, Delaware, is filled, and nearly all the vehicles carry license plates that begin with "NIA"—Nanticoke Indian Association. It's cold and raining, but men and women inside are greeting each other by their first names, shaking hands, hugging, and saying, "Peace be with you." The minister, a white woman, leads the faithful in the Lord's Prayer. There is an unwavering sense of faith here that Moses parted the Red Sea just as the Bible says and that Adam and Eve were historic figures.

The church was founded in 1888 in a dispute within a group that considered themselves to be direct descendants of the original Nanticokes. Some of the lighter-skinned members objected to being considered Negroes and formed the new church. Before the schism, there had been fisticuffs and the threat of gun fights between the rival groups. To further achieve distinction from blacks, the breakaway group incorporated itself as the Nanticoke Indian Association. Today it has some 500 members, but the federal government has refused to recognize them as a tribe because scholars believe them to be a mixture of white, black, and Indian blood.

Until 1962, the group had its own school system through the eighth grade, and to continue their education they would have to go to an Indian school in Lawrence, Kansas. White people regarded the group as Negroes; they could not attend white public schools and were subjected to all Jim Crow laws and traditions. During World War II, two of the members were drafted into the Army and assigned to segregated black units. They objected strenuously and eventually persuaded the Selective Service that they were not Negroes.

Today the minister intones the final prayer and bids the congregation to rise. They open their red United Methodist Hymnals and sing *a capella* a well-known black spiritual: "This little light of mine . . . I'm gonna let it shine . . . let it shine, let it shine, let it shine. . . ." The music swells and fills the room.

In the parking lot, standing beside a car bearing the license NIA-1, is

Kenneth Clark, honorary Nanticoke chief also known as Red Deer. "We are Nanticokes," he explains. "We have nothing against black people. We're just proud of being Nanticokes."

The question of racial identity was difficult and confusing right from the beginning. White men mated almost at their whim with Indian women, and before long fair-skinned children appeared in Indian families. These births were never recorded because a 1695 law required reports to authorities only on children born to white women. Children born to blacks and Indians were not recorded—even if the father was white.

WHALEYVILLE, MARYLAND: SOUTH OF MILE 13

On the southern edge of the swamp, Whaleyville once was a lively center of the shingle industry. Today it's a husk of a town, and I search in vain for the old African Methodist Church that was expanded in 1926 with the help of a white friend, P. Dale Wimbrow, an entertainer who called himself "Old Pete Daley of Whaleyville." Wimbrow later gained a measure of fame as a national radio performer, but in 1926 he decided to help out the church after a hometown recital was attended by "only eight people, including the dog under the stove." Years later, Wimbrow remembered the event fondly:

> Those colored people plastered posters from Curtis's Chapel to Sugar Hill. Every telephone pole shouted in red letters that, "The real Honorable Mister Peter Dale Wimbrow Esquire" would entertain at Whaleyville Schoolhouse—looked as if I was running for sheriff in a Democratic primary. On the night appointed they came from Parsonsburg in buses, from Jenkins Neck in carryalls, from the swamp in oxcarts and one-lung jalopies. They were jammed in the schoolhouse and standing about fifty deep outside. . . .
>
> So I uked—and New York never heard that much uking from me. I sang, danced, whistled, told stories, and did impersonations for a solid hour. When I had to sign off, limp and wet with sweat . . . up came the master of ceremonies, all worried, and whispered: "what we gonna do about all de folks dat couldn't git in?" So I told him to clear the hall and let in another helping. There was a second show from start to finish, and a third. The money they raised not only put the new wing on the church—it painted the whole works.

LINE METHODIST CHURCH: ON MILE 20

The church is in Delaware, but its cemetery is in both states. A highway marker informs me that the land for the church was purchased in 1785 and the present building went up in 1874. The tombstones in the cemetery lean this way and that, jostled by the alternating winter frosts and spring thaws of a century. The first one I see hints at tragedy. "Isaac H. Truitte. Born June 10, 1882. Died March 25, 1883. Budded on Earth to Bloom in Heaven." It takes me fifteen minutes to find the Line marker, which is hiding out among the tombstones. The colonial surveyors placed it here on May 18, 1751, noting that it was "near a hickory." It is twenty miles from the Fenwick Lighthouse. There is a large hickory tree nearby, and I wonder if it's the very one.

A woman is placing fresh flowers on a grave. She straightens up and looks down with unwinking, reptilian concentration. "These are my two boys," she says without me asking. "They died in a house fire. One was two, the other three. Happened in 1977." I extend my sympathy and say such an event must be difficult to accept. "You find a place for it somewhere, and then you go on," she says.

SNOW HILL, MARYLAND: SOUTH OF MILE 20

The manumission of slaves began on Maryland's Eastern Shore in the early nineteenth century, and a free black community developed in Snow Hill. As it grew and thrived, whites became alarmed by the increased numbers of freemen, especially because it belied the cherished theory that blacks could not survive outside the institution of slavery. These blacks owned property and held jobs; many of them worked as oystermen. But in 1835 the Maryland legislature passed a law that said only whites could navigate any vessel working in state waters. This effectively removed the blacks from the oyster industry.

Some black Snow Hill families relocated to New York's Staten Island, where they got back into the oyster business. Others moved to New Jersey and established a town named Snow Hill (which was later renamed Lawnside). Others emigrated to Liberia with the help of the Maryland Colonization Society.

Many blacks stayed, and during this period touring Southern plantation owners came to Snow Hill and other nearby communities to purchase slaves and take them back home. At least once a year some fifty slave dealers came to Snow Hill, carrying thick wads of cash. Newspapers would announce their imminent arrival. Each dealer claimed to offer the "highest cash price" and some bought as many as one hundred slaves at a time. Competition among the dealers was keen. Local slave dealers were everywhere—taverns, county fairs, general stores, auctions, estate liquidations—anywhere slaves might be available.

Farm supply firms carried slaves right along with harrows and lime. Planters going out of business advertised their slaves for sale in newspapers, and fraternal organizations sold slaves by lottery to raise funds.

After the slave trade was abolished in 1808, the fear that the supply of slaves would be exhausted was so great that the Eastern Shore became a systematic breeding ground, and slave holders encouraged mating in every possible way. Experiments in slave rearing were carried on just as intensely as experiments in new irrigation techniques or soil management.

As the Civil War approached and tensions rose over the slavery question, Snow Hill's free blacks were viewed with suspicion and considered the allies of the remaining slave population. For protection, they began to segregate themselves on the southwest side of Snow Hill, and this area became known as Freetown. Ironically, a century earlier, as the number of Indians dwindled, several tribal fragments had banded together near Snow Hill. The area was called Indiantown.

One of the black families that remained in Snow Hill was the Johnsons, and on October 26, 1900, William (Judy) Johnson was born here. He was one of the best baseball players who ever lived, but he spent his career play-

This Quonset hut in Snow Hill, Maryland, was once Outten's Colored Theater. It is now a Masonic Lodge.

ing for teams like the Madison Stars, the Chester Giants, and the Pittsburgh Crawfords. Johnson retired before Jackie Robinson broke the white-only barrier in major league baseball. In 1974 Johnson joined Satchel Paige, Josh Gibson, and Cool Papa Bell as the first Negro League players to be inducted into the National Baseball Hall of Fame.

PITTSVILLE, MARYLAND: SOUTH OF MILE 20

As is often the case, a road coincides with the Line for many miles. When the surveyors came through in 1751, they hacked down trees and brush to facilitate their work. This "visto," or line of sight, evolved first into a pathway, then a trail, and finally a road. I walk the Line for about a mile, then head south towards Pittsville, the erstwhile "Strawberry Capital of the World."

Because of the railroad, strawberries could be picked in Pittsville in the morning and placed on the shortcakes at the du Pont mansions around Wilmington by dinnertime. On a single day in 1923, sixty-one rail cars filled with strawberries—that's about 400,000 quarts—left Pittsville.

Black farm workers were allowed to come into Pittsville during the day, but the farmers warned them to be out before dark or there would be trouble from whites. As more and more blacks moved in to work as pickers, a school was built for their children on Glass Hill Road, but a woman in a store tells me that it's no longer there. "They tore the colored school down. It was falling apart," she says.

DELMAR, MARYLAND & DELMAR, DELAWARE: ON MILE 28

State Avenue, the main street in Delmar, *is* the Mason-Dixon Line, and the civic boast is that it's "the town too big for one state." Grammar school students attend classes in Delmar, Maryland, while secondary school students matriculate in Delmar, Delaware. Each side elects its own town council, and the two bodies meet separately and jointly once a month. There's only one Town Hall, and it's in Maryland. That means that the mayor of Delmar, Delaware, meets with the council of Delmar, Delaware, to conduct the town's business in Maryland. Each side has its own zip code, but there's only one post office. Delmar police have jurisdiction in both states.

Such cooperation wasn't always the case. Until the schools of the two towns were consolidated in 1949, there was intense rivalry. People in Maryland didn't speak to blood relatives in Delaware. There were fistfights when a Marylander strayed over into Delaware at night. They couldn't even agree on the time of day. Maryland observed daylight saving time. Delaware did not. One legacy of these days is that numbered streets don't connect. Heading south on Sixth Street in Delaware, I have to take a short detour east on State Street to find the continuation of Sixth Street in Maryland.

Delmar is an old railroad town that today serves primarily as a bedroom community for larger towns and cities north and south of the Line. The sign over the post office, which is in Maryland, says "U.S. Post Office, Delmar, Maryland-Delaware." Most of the businesses are in Delaware, which doesn't have a sales tax. There are no parking meters downtown, and the business district consists of the post office, a funeral home, barber shop, furniture store, and, with a big OPEN sign, Linda's Railroad Cafe.

Linda herself takes my order for a cup of coffee and brings back a steaming mug. There are big-bladed ceiling fans overhead, and a sign on the counter indicates today's luncheon special is chicken and dumplings plus two vegetables for $3.95. It's too early for lunch though, and I glance over my shoulder at a noisy whirlpool of men—baseball-capped, bespectacled, overalled, suspendered. George invites me over. Fred, Jim, Sam, Dick, Brian, Bill, Bill, and Paul nod their blessing. They are downing 2,500-calorie breakfasts that are the special of the day for $1.99—scrambled eggs, home fries, sausage, toast, and jelly.

"This is the Liar's Club," George says, who wants me to know he's usually called Tweety Bird. "We meet here every morning for about two hours. We've had as many as sixteen, seventeen at this table. We begin arriving at 4 A.M."

"They're waiting at the door before I open," Linda shouts across a row of freshly baked pies on the countertop.

They are all former railroaders. "They're retired; I'm just tired," jokes Dick. One of the Bills points at Dick. "He's an outsider. He's only bin here forty years." Brian says if you get a speeding ticket on the Delaware side, the fine goes to the state, but if it's on the Maryland side, it goes to the county. "As usual, you're almost right," says Sam. "The fine goes to the town, not the county."

There's a five-minute legal argument that ends in irresolution. Then I ask about racial relations in Delmar. A cathedral hush comes over the room. Everyone starts eating with wolfish gusto. The silence stretches tauter and tauter, threaded by the ticking of the clock, and if it goes any longer it will be hard to break. But Paul looks up. "We didn't know we had racial problems until Washington told us. Things were fine until the bureaucrats got into the act. Now we get along pretty well. Some of the white churches have joint services with Negro churches for Thanksgiving and Christmas. There used to be a black guy come in here once in awhile. Not for a couple of years now. . . ." The silence returns and the ticking clock takes over. Tweety Bird rubs his chin. "I forgot to shave this morning."

"Yeah, and you look like shit," Linda says.

Sam Bynum lives in an unassuming house on the Delaware side of Delmar about fifty yards from where he was born sixty-eight years ago. He sits in front of a muted television that is flickering phosphorescent images of the Redskins versus the Cardinals. The living room is filled with photographs of his seven children, and he's not sure how many grandchildren.

"My father was a railroad man. He filled the kerosene lamps they used to light their signals all up and down the line. He'd hop the train to Laurel, then walk back the seven miles filling each lantern. When he wasn't doing that he laid track."

Bynum went through Delmar's segregated school system, but he didn't know how much he had been shortchanged until his children began attending the newly integrated schools in the 1960s. Other aspects of a segregated society were more obvious to him as a child. "We could go inside the train station to buy our ticket, but then we had to wait outside, even if it was raining. Before the family would go out anywhere, mom and dad would make us go to the bathroom because away from home we weren't likely to find one we were allowed to use."

Bynum escaped Jim Crow while serving in the Army in Germany from 1951 to 1953, and when he got back to Delmar he helped form the Dixie Democratic Club, a group of local blacks who began to press for changes. "The white people would say, 'We've given you everything. What more do you want?' But the textbooks they gave us were thirty years old and dragged out of the basements of the white schools. Our high school team played football with any kind of ball—baseball, softball, basketball—and sometimes we used an old sock filled with dirt. That's what they gave us." The changes came grudgingly, but in 1988 Bynum was elected mayor of Delmar by a huge majority that included many white votes.

He was too young to remember the night they lynched Matt Williams in Salisbury, but when he was fourteen and working as a bellboy at the Hotel Wicomico, an older man took him up to the roof and showed him the tree where Williams was hanged.

"I do remember hearing about a nasty white fella. Drank a lot. He cut Williams' toes off and took them home. He used to brag about it and show them to people. One day he got hit by a freight train and died, so I guess he got what he deserved. They cut the tree down a couple of years ago, but the courthouse is still there. Go look for yourself."

SALISBURY, MARYLAND: SOUTH OF MILE 29

Old men, black and white, sit in front of the red-brick Victorian Gothic courthouse, nurturing their idleness. A plaque says it was built in 1878. Just across Main Street is the Hotel Wicomico, where Sam Bynum worked; it has been converted into an office building called One Plaza East.

On December 4, 1931, Daniel J. Elliott, a popular white lumber merchant, was shot and killed in his office in Salisbury. Police quickly arrested Matthew Williams, a former black employee, who confessed that he killed Elliott because "he only paid me 15 cents an hour." Then Williams attempted to kill himself with his gun, but he failed and was hospitalized with a minor wound. As word of the killing spread, a crowd gathered in the courthouse square. With shouts of "Let's get the nigger!" a mob of 300 men surged toward the hospital a few blocks away.

They snatched Williams from his hospital cot and began dragging him to the square. Whenever he faltered, a man would jab him with an ice pick. When they arrived at the courthouse, there was a crowd of 2,000 people standing under battery-operated flood lights. Williams was mutilated and tortured. Men cut off his ears, fingers, and toes and held them up for display. While this was going on, police directed traffic around the courthouse square to avoid any interruption in the lynching. When he was finally

They lynched Matthew Williams in front of the Wicomico County Courthouse in Salisbury, Maryland, on December 4, 1931.

hanged, the crowd applauded as he strangled.

The body was cut down and dragged to Salisbury's black residential section where it was doused with gasoline and burned amid curses and hoorays. Lights went out that night all over the black section, and children were sent to churches for protection. That following Sunday, no clergyman, white or black, mentioned the incident in their sermons.

The Wicomico County Grand Jury investigated the crime, but not a single person could be found who could identify any of the lyncher-torturers. "Absolutely no evidence," said the report of the Grand Jury to Judge Joseph L. Bailey and Judge Robert F. Duer, of the First Judicial Circuit Court, "can remotely connect anyone with the instigation or perpetration of the murder of Matthew Williams."

Chapter Two

THE TANGENT, ARC, & NORTH LINES
MIDDLE POINT TO NEWARK, DELAWARE —
NORTHWARD 87 MILES.

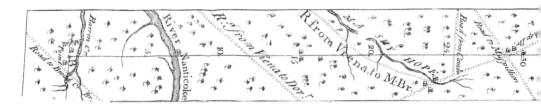

"History, despite its wrenching pain,

Cannot be unlived, and if faced

With courage, need not be lived again."

  —Maya Angelou, "On the Pulse of the Morning," 1993

Once the Middle Point dispute was settled, the colonial survey team turned to the next task—running a north-south line some eighty-two miles so it came to a tangent with the New Castle Circle, a boundary that had been surveyed in 1701 to separate New Castle County from Chester County. It was not a full circle but a circular arc with a twelve-mile radius centered on the town of New Castle. It began on the Delaware River, and it is still a distinctive feature of U.S. maps.

The surveyors had to quit after a few miles because of severe winter weather, and they resumed work on the Tangent Line on May 5, 1761. They labored for the next two years. Their notes are filled with entries about obstacles—mill-dams, rivers, and swamps. There were equipment problems and more bad weather. The first line was about one-half mile east of where it should have touched the New Castle Circle. A second line missed the mark by about 350 yards to the west. These failures drove the Penns and the Calverts to the end of their patience, and they sought help from the Royal Society at Greenwich.

. Although their names achieved eponymous immortality, little is known about Mason and Dixon as persons. No likeness of either man has ever been found. They worked on projects for the Royal Society, and both devoted themselves to the spirit of rational inquiry. Beyond that, few similarities can be found. Mason seems to have

been contemplative and morose, Dixon hedonistic and insouciant. Mason was an Anglican, Dixon was a Quaker—and therefore at the opposite ends of the English religious spectrum of the day. Mason was a widower who would later remarry and father eight children. Dixon was a lifelong bachelor.

Charles Mason was born in Gloustershire sometime in early 1728, Dixon in Durham on July 27, 1733. Although neither was educated at a university, both attended school in their home communities, and both continued their educations under

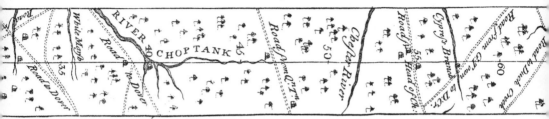

mathematical masters. Mason had a long association with James Bradley, the royal astronomer. Dixon was a self-employed surveyor.

Mason's first wife died of an unknown cause in 1759, and little more is known about his personal life. Dixon was the son of a well-to-do coal mine owner. His usual dress was a long red coat and a cocked hat. He was disowned by his home-town Quakers for "drinking to excess."

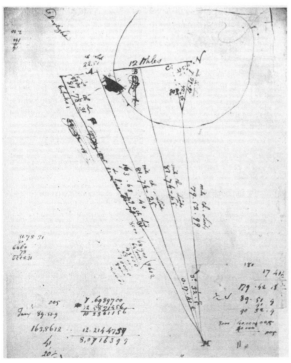

Mason sketched the Tangent Line in his journal.

The unlikely pair attracted the attention of the Penns and the Calverts by distinguishing themselves in 1761 with their work for the Royal Observatory in South Africa, where they observed the Transit of Venus, an unusual, eclipse-like phenomenon that occurs when Venus passes between the sun and earth. For the scientific world of the day, it was a rare opportunity to calculate the distance between sun and earth.

Mason and Dixon planned to observe the transit from the island of Sumatra, but shortly after they left England their ship was attacked by a French man-o'-war

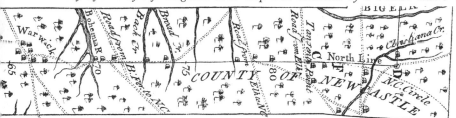

(England and France were at war at this time). Eleven crewmen were killed, thirty-eight were injured, and the ship was forced to return to port for repairs. Because of the delay, Mason and Dixon could get only as far as the Cape of Good Hope in time for the transit. They went ashore, set up their instruments, and stayed there for five months. Their work won them the praise of the international scientific community.

Probably they attracted little or no attention when they stepped ashore and set their feet on the cobblestoned streets of colonial Philadelphia on November 15, 1763. They carried with them five principal instruments—two transits and two reflecting telescopes, which could be used to look at posts in a line for up to twelve miles—and, most important, a zenith sector, a relatively new device designed for astronomical observation. The sector had been precision-crafted by John Bird, a noted English maker of surveying instruments, specifically for the task at hand in America. Simply stated, it consisted of a six-foot brass telescope suspended on a metal framework.

Since the Penn-Calvert agreement called for the southern boundary of Pennsylvania to begin fifteen miles south of Philadelphia, the first job was to ascertain the southernmost point in Philadelphia. After about three weeks and sixty observations of stars, they determined this to be 39 degrees, 56 minutes, 29.1 seconds north. However, to go directly south from this point would have placed the surveyors in New Jersey, so it was decided to move thirty-one miles west before heading south.

It took two days for the caravan of three wagons to reach a farm owned by John Harlan that was thirty-one miles due west of the point in Philadelphia, in the present community of Embreeville, Pennsylvania. The precious zenith sector was carried on a contrivance called a "single horse chair," secured on springs and placed on a featherbed. It was unpacked carefully and set in a special sailcloth tent to protect it from rain and snow. Before nightfall on January 14, 1764, they had established

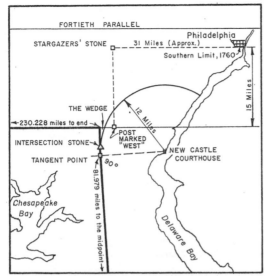

Left: From the Plumstead-Huddle House to the Harlan farm to the Post Mark'd West (dotted line). Below: The Stargazers' Stone, placed here by Mason and Dixon in 1764.

an observatory in a garden north of the Harlan farmhouse. They precisely calibrated their position and marked it with a piece of white quartz about twelve inches square and sticking two feet out of the ground. Night after night, Mason and Dixon were out there gazing skyward, and before long local farmers began calling their marker the Stargazers' Stone.

The Harlan farm would become a home away from home for the two surveyors, and over the next four and one-half years they would return here more than a dozen times—sometimes to rest, sometimes to take more measurements, and sometimes to ride out the winter and plan for the next surveying season.

They completed their initial observations in mid-March, hired a team of axemen, and began moving due south. They used their transits to establish direction over different levels of terrain. The actual measuring was done by chains on flat ground, *and on slopes they used wooden rods to establish horizontal equivalents. To facilitate their periodic sightings and markings, the axemen felled trees and cut a "visto," or rough corridor about nine yards wide, across the landscape. On April 12, they reached a point north of Newark, Delaware, on a farm belonging to Alexander Bryan.*

For the next several months, they busied themselves moving their observatory from the Harlan farm, taking nightly readings in good weather, and meeting regularly in Philadelphia and New Castle with the commissioners from the two colonies who were overseeing their work. Then, on June 12, 1764, they placed a rough-hewn square oak post in a field on the Bryan farm. This was the point exactly fifteen miles south of the latitude in Philadelphia at 39 degrees, 56 minutes, 17.4 seconds north latitude. They called the marker the "Post Mark'd West," and it would be a base and reference point for the project for the next three and one-half years. It would be mentioned almost daily in the journal kept by Charles Mason. Precision here was

Above: The ruins of Alexander Bryan's farm in New Castle County, Delaware. Right: A granite marker was placed here in 1953 at the site of the Post Mark'd West.

crucial. *Each foot that the Post Mark'd West was too far south or too far north would place twenty-four acres in the wrong province. So every attempt would be made to keep the West Line at a latitude of 39 degrees, 43 minutes, 17.4 seconds.*

Mason and Dixon were now ready to begin surveying the main West Line separating Pennsylvania and Maryland, but it would be nearly a year before they would begin. First they had to finish the job started by the colonial surveyors by running the Tangent Line north to touch the New Castle Circle. Moving south with a party of thirty-nine men, including a steward, cooks, teamsters, chain carriers, tent keepers and axemen, two wagons, and eight horses, they reached the Middle Point between the Atlantic and the Chesapeake on June 25, 1764.

Here they began the task that had confounded the colonial surveyors—a northerly line calculated to intersect at a ninety-degree angle with the radius of the New Castle Circle about eighty-two miles away. By June 30 they had progressed some six miles to the bank of the Nanticoke River, which was too wide to measure by chain. Using triangulation techniques, they found the river was 596 feet wide.

The surveyors crossed Marshyhope Creek near the old Nanticoke reservation, then the Choptank and Bohemia Rivers and Broad Creek until they had gone 81 miles and figured they were near the tangent point. On August 25 they sent letters by courier to Governor Horatio Sharp of Maryland and Governor James Hamilton of Pennsylvania notifying them that they were close to their goal. On August 27 they linked the twelve-mile radial line from the New Castle courthouse with the line they had just run. Their predecessors had been off by about 350 feet.

Then they again moved south, perfecting and marking the Line post by post. They were back at the Middle Point by the end of September. Mason had taken a break long enough to visit the Pocomoke Swamp, where the Indians had plotted twenty-two years earlier. Mason was uncharacteristically moved, and his journal for September 13, 1764 reads: "There is the greatest quantity of timber I ever saw. Above the Tallest Oak, Beech, Poplar, Hickery, Holly and Fir; towers the lofty Cedar; (without a Branch) 'till its ever green conical top; seems; to reach the Clouds: The pleasing sight of which; renewed my wishes to see Mount Lebanon."

The Mason-Dixon party spent October moving back north, refining the Line even further. When they reached the New Castle Circle, they found that they had intersected at ninety degrees with an error of only twenty-six inches. On November 21 they met at the river port of Christiana Bridge, just west of the present city of Wilmington, Delaware, with the commissioners, who agreed that the Tangent Line had been established satisfactorily. Five days later, Mason and Dixon were back at the Harlan farm for the winter.

The original stone marking the midpoint between the Atlantic and Chesapeake, placed here in 1765, still stands west of Delmar.

MIDDLE POINT: MILE 0

Along Route 54 between Delmar and Mardela Springs, Maryland, the three-foot limestone marker placed by Mason and Dixon in 1765 stands in a roofed, red brick shelter behind iron bars. That it is here is a small miracle.

Soon after the Middle Point monument was set in place, it was uprooted by treasure hunters who supposed it marked the place where Captain Kidd had buried part of his ill-gotten riches. It was widely believed at this time that pirates had hidden gold and other booty on the shores of the Chesapeake. The stone was reset and forgotten for more than a century. In the twentieth century local farmers realized its significance and took care of the site. But in 1983 vandals tried to steal the marker by towing it with a chain. They broke it off at the base and fled. It was taken to a highway maintenance shed, where it sat until 1985 when it was reseated and rededicated.

A blue Volvo with Virginia plates pulls up to the marker. A man wearing a Chicago Bulls cap and a woman wearing so much makeup she appears taxidermic get out and walk over to peer through the iron bars. "Mason and Dixon," he begins aloud with his history lesson, "were here during the Civil War. . . ."

Just down the highway, on the Maryland side, is Maple Lawn Farm, where Eloise Morrison was born in 1922 and her father was born in 1893. The white farmhouse of calendar-art prettiness is surrounded by well-groomed fields of soybeans. She invites me in with a wink. "Welcome to

Maple Lawn Farm, where three generations of the Morrison family have taken care of the Middle Point marker.

the cat house," she says. Six cats are in various states of languor in the wall-papered kitchen. We sit at a long wooden table and drink coffee.

"The Line has always been an important part of my family's life. We all have a special feeling for it. The land for the monument was given by my parents in Maryland and my uncles in Delaware. When I was a child, my father and my uncle used to take turns cleaning up the stone. That's why it's in such good shape. My father always told the story that when Mason and Dixon got here, they drank a lot of wine to celebrate, and the next morning when they started off they didn't get the ninety degree angle quite right—so Delaware got more land than it should have.

"My son Ridgely did a lot of the work toward getting the stone reset after the vandals broke it off. A lot of people stop to look at the marker. Every time I go by there, someone's stopped. People are always getting married there. One stands in Delaware, the other in Maryland. I guess it's legal. . . ."

MARDELA SPRINGS, MARYLAND: WEST OF MILE 0

Mardela Springs is a tiny crossroads town that began as Barren Creek Mills in the 1660s. Indians showed the English colonists bubbling medicinal springs here, and a century and a half later white people began coming to take to the waters. By 1900 the town lapsed into a somnolence that was broken only briefly in 1992 when a white town councilman referred to

Martin Luther King, Jr., as "Buckwheat." The story ran in the local newspapers, it was picked up by the Associated Press, and quickly it became the slur heard around the world. NAACP chapters throughout the Eastern Shore used it as a rallying cry for membership drives.

Just beyond Mardela Springs is a modest sign along U.S. Route 50 designating this portion of the road as the Harriet Tubman Highway. Tubman was a slave on the nearby plantation of Edward Brodas, and in 1849 she escaped after learning that she and her brothers had been sold to a Georgia slave trader. With the help of Quakers and free blacks, Tubman made it to the other side of the Mason-Dixon Line and went on to become the most famous conductor on the Underground Railroad. Between 1852 and 1857, she crossed the Line into slave territory about twenty times and helped between 100 and 300 people, including her parents and a brother, to freedom.

She avoided detection by constantly changing her routes, by clever disguises, and by surreptitious communication. The fields of the Eastern Shore rang with songs that were coded messages from her. "Swing Low, Sweet Chariot" meant she was here and would be leaving that night; on the other hand, "Go Down, Moses" meant there was danger. Tubman coupled a burning religious faith with toughness and resourcefulness. Once, after a daylong wait in a swamp without food, one of the escapees suggested returning to the plantation and slavery. Tubman, it is told, pointed a pistol to his head and said, "Move or die."

Thomas Garrett, a white abolitionist who worked with her, described Tubman's bold freeing of her parents. "She brought away her parents in a singular manner. They started with an old horse, fitted out in primitive style with a straw collar, a pair of old chaise wheels, with a board on the axle to sit on, another board swung with ropes, fastened to the axle, to rest their feet on. She got her parents . . . on this rude vehicle to the railroad, put them in the cars, turned Jehu herself, and drove to town in a style that no human being ever did before or since. . . . Next day, I furnished her with money to take them all to Canada. I afterwards sold their horse, and sent them the balance of the proceeds."

Within a few years, Tubman acquired legendary status and was called "the Moses of her people."

VIENNA, MARYLAND: WEST OF MILE 3

On the west bank of the Nanticoke River, Vienna was one of the earliest ports of entry in the colonies, and when Mason and Dixon passed nearby it was a major center of trade and shipping—important enough to warrant a shelling from the British Navy during the Revolution.

Today the river bank is devoid of bustling businesses; and its surface ripples like silk in the breeze as it hurries to its rendezvous with the Chesapeake. In the 1800s the Nanticoke was a natural passage for runaway slaves headed north, while at the same time slave catchers rowed captured free blacks downstream into bondage. As cotton gained a foothold in the Deep South, the demand for slaves increased, and the human traffic on the Nanticoke became heavy. There was a slave auction block near Vienna that served as a distribution point for the dealers.

Here it's difficult to know whether I'm in the North or the South. There are grits on many menus. When the local people talk, they stretch their vowels and the words seem farther apart. The letter "g" is dropped from participles, and the sound of the letter "r" almost totally disappears. Though Maryland stayed in the Union during the Civil War, Southern sympathizers shipped supplies to the Confederacy through Vienna. When Union troops came to town and raised an American flag over a dirt sidewalk here, residents crossed to the opposite side of the street rather than walk under it.

Just north of Vienna on Indiantown Road I find the site of the old Nanticoke Indian Reservation, established in 1698 along the river between Chicone and Marshyhope Creeks. Native Americans had a village on this site for 6,000 years, and the village had been the traditional seat of the Nanticoke emperor. In setting up the reservation, the Maryland Assembly decreed that the 5,000-acre tract should be held by the tribe forever at an annual rental of one beaver skin. The government was well-intentioned, but it could not control white colonists, who already were casting yearning eyes on the Chicone lands. Not only were they located between two navigable streams, but the Indians had already cleared the fields to plant their corn.

When the English colonists first arrived, the Nanticokes occupied populous towns all up and down the river. But they were forced from their homes either by trickery or at gunpoint, and by 1711 the Nanticokes were split into two residential groups—one at Chicone, the other at Broad Creek in what is now Delaware. The inexorable white pressure forced them to migrate northward, and by the time Mason and Dixon arrived, most of the Nanticokes were living in New York. Eventually, they were absorbed by other tribes.

A few stragglers who remained behind lived in isolated family groups, nurturing a deep hatred for white people. They lived in wilderness cabins, and fugitive slaves took advantage of these excellent hiding places. The Indians gladly held their doors open to these fellow victims of white racism, and in the natural order of things, black men mated with Indian women, and female slaves with Indian men.

SAN DOMINGO, MARYLAND: WEST OF MILE 5

I follow the Line north across land that stretches out in great vegetative tracts and is so flat it's hard to believe the world is round. Nearly all of the Delmarva Peninsula is on the Atlantic Coastal Plain. Two regular features of the landscape are municipal water towers emblazoned with the name of the town, and Zinmatics—giant, self-propelled wheeled irrigators as long as a football field. Near the site of Chicone is the present-day community of San Domingo, so tiny that entering it and leaving it amount to almost the same thing. During the late eighteenth and early nineteenth centuries, free blacks formed settlements on abandoned Indian reservations, and San Domingo is one of them. William Elzey Brown was born here in 1872.

Brown went to public school until he was ten, but then had to quit to work on his father's farm. At the age of twenty, he went to New Jersey to work, saved his money, and when he returned four years later he bought three acres of land, built a house, tilled the land, and raised a large family. He also educated himself and became a teacher at the grammar school.

When the oldest of Brown's twelve children reached adolescence, there was no way for him to go on to high school because the nearest black school was twenty-one miles away in Salisbury. In August 1930, Brown bought a 1924 Reo bus for one hundred dollars and the next month he began transporting local black children to the high school in Salisbury. By the end of the year he had seventeen regular passengers.

He charged one dollar a week for the service, but few parents could afford it and so the operation lost money. But his major problem was the regular bus company, which had him arrested on charges he was violating its franchise. Brown was jailed several times in this manner in the early years. Each time his older children would get him out of jail in the morning in time to make the school run.

The school district began subsidizing Brown in 1934, and he added more buses. Eventually he had eleven bus drivers working for him. Brown himself continued driving until 1950, when he died of a stroke just after delivering fifty-seven passengers to school.

RELIANCE, DELAWARE: ON MILE 12

Two states and three counties converge here, and geography pulls history in its wake. It was here in the early part of the nineteenth century that Lucretia "Patty" Cannon and her band of kidnappers ran a reverse Underground Railroad by kidnapping free blacks and selling them into slavery to southern plantation owners. Patty worked at odds with the Quakers in nearby communities like Camden and Odessa, who were hiding runaway slaves and sending them north to freedom.

The center of the Cannon operation was a tavern where slavers came to do business. There were rooms on the second floor, and above in the attic there was a "nigger keep" with a bloodstained oak door and wrought-iron rings on the walls where shackled blacks awaited transportation to Mississippi, Georgia, and Louisiana. In the woods out back, there were iron rings on trees where Patty kept her captives in warm weather.

A farmhouse in Reliance, Delaware, has timber and beams from Patty Cannon's tavern.

Patty's house was in Delaware, and the tavern was across the street in Maryland. On the site of the tavern today is a pretty farmhouse painted light green and surrounded by trees and a log fence. Jack Messick, a retired Marine lieutenant colonel, has lived here with his wife since 1982. He sits in front of the fireplace and talks while stroking a big white cat on his lap.

"The timber and beams were used to build the present house about 1880, and it was remodeled in 1954. You can tell the beams were hand-hewn because you can see the marks from the adze. People occasionally knock on the door. Mostly they're interested in history or high school students working on a term paper. Once in awhile somebody's looking for dungeons and bloodstains. There have been a lot of rumors over the years of ghosts in the house, but we have no evidence of that." He forces his face into a smile that is more like a suppressed grimace.

Indeed, as recently as 1979 the Salisbury newspaper carried an article in which the owner of the house claimed to have been visited by evil spirits and heard "bangs on the wall, chains dragging, doors squeaking. . . ."

"There's no doubt that Patty Cannon existed and ran a slave ring out of here," Messick says. "But a lot of the truth has been embellished by legend, and it's hard to separate fact from fiction. The crucial thing was the location on the state line. When a sheriff or some authority came out to arrest her, or even ask questions, she'd just dodge out of his jurisdiction."

The location was critical for another reason. It was illegal to sell slaves out-of-state in Delaware, but interstate slave trading was legal in Maryland. As the demand for field hands on the cotton plantations of the South grew, slaves commanded high prices—$1,000 was not unusual for a healthy black man. Pennsylvania and Delaware experienced a large number of abductions because of the proximity to Maryland and the ease of transportation to Southern states on the Chesapeake. For free blacks in the border areas, life was a daily struggle to avoid capture.

"Patty kidnapped both slaves and free Blacks," says Messick, "but free Blacks were preferred because usually no one tried to get them back, whereas with slaves the masters would offer rewards and often try to track them down."

Sometimes Patty would lure free Blacks to her tavern with promises of a home-cooked meal. Her henchmen would raid fields in which Blacks were working and bring them home at gunpoint. Sometimes they would invade cabins and bring back whole families. The operation reached as far north as Philadelphia, which had a large free Black population. They fitted a ship that would go to Philadelphia and decoy blacks onboard and then take them to the tavern. To this end, she employed an educated and intelligent black named Ransom, who would prowl the waterfront buying drinks and getting his victims drunk. His wife ran a brothel near the Navy Yard where the patrons were given alcohol until they passed out.

Sometimes Patty would kill the slave dealers at the tavern and take their cash, and this led to her undoing. In 1829, as a farmer plowed a field on the Delaware side of the Line right near Patty's Tavern, his horse dropped into a soft place in the soil. He dug and unearthed a chest painted blue. Rather than treasure, it contained human bones. A crowd gathered, and from it emerged an ousted member of the Cannon gang who said the bones were those of a slave dealer named Bell who showed up at the tavern about ten years ago carrying $15,000 in cash. Patty clubbed him to death and took the money. The informant showed authorities two more corpses nearby. He said they were black children murdered by Patty.

Constables from both states showed up at the tavern, and when Patty tried to stay on the Maryland side, she was arrested, dragged across the Line, and turned over to the constable from Delaware, where the bodies had been unearthed. She was placed in the Georgetown jail and charged with murder.

"The story is that she confessed to about fifteen murders," says Messick. "She died in jail about two weeks after her arrest—supposedly by poisoning herself with arsenic. She was buried next to the jail, but somehow somebody got ahold of her skull and now they say it's in the Dover Public Library. I don't know that for sure, though."

I'm at the Dover Public Library the next morning when it opens at 9 A.M. A friendly woman at the main desk greets me.

"Can I help you?"

"I have a strange request. I'd like to see Patty Cannon's skull."

She nods as though I'd just asked for the Dover city directory, wheels, and walks to a back room. She's back in less than twenty seconds with a big red silk hatbox. I open it and stare at a skull. I start to ask a question, but she smiles indulgently and hands me a copy of a letter dated May 2, 1963, from Alfred W. Marsh.

> Just after the turn of the century James Marsh (my Uncle by marriage) was reading law in the office of Robert White of Georgetown, Delaware. Since during this apprenticeship period

there was little income he took the position of deputy sheriff of
Sussex County. While holding this job the bodies of Patty
Cannon and one or two others who had been buried in the jail-
yard of the Sussex Jail were exhumed for reburial in potters field.
The yard now is a parking lot and is south of the old jail which is
now the Sussex County Board of Assessment Building.

In 1827 Patty had taken arsenic and died while being held for
trial for murder.

Somehow while moving these bodies Patty's skull came into
the possession of James Marsh.

About 1907 James Marsh contracted acute tuberculosis and in
an effort to save himself moved to Denver, Colorado. At this time
he gave the skull to my father, Charles I. Joseph of Angola, Sussex
County, for keeping. From that time until the late thirties the
skull hung on a nail in a rafter of my father's barn, by which time
it had become quite a curiosity. To save it from damage or possible theft he put it in a box and stored it in the attic of his home.
At his death in 1946 I took possession of the skull and in 1961
put it on loan to the Dover Library.

Just downstream from Reliance on the banks of the Nanticoke there was
a farm owned by the Twiford family; here Patty Cannon would hold her
victims by manacling them to large trees before they were placed on boats
for the journey south. A "Mr. Twiford" is mentioned several times in
Charles Mason's journal. The two scientists stopped here in June 1764 on
their way to the Middle Point to hire a crew of thirty-nine men. They
returned on December 5, 1765, to pick up the first of the boundary stones
that would permanently mark the Line at every mile point. Up until this
time, they had been using wooden posts, called stobs.

The limestone markers that would signal the limits between two crown-
granted colonies were quarried on the Isle of Portland in Dorsetshire. They
were brought in by ship and unloaded on the river bank where the party
had pitched their tents. Most of them were twelve inches square and three
and one-half feet high, engraved with a "P" on one side, an "M" on the
other. The others were five feet tall and had sculptured shields from the
coats of arms of the Calverts and the Penns. These "crown stones" would be
placed at every fifth mile. They were made very distinctive so it would be
hard to duplicate them for fraudulent purposes. The stones were hauled by
oxcart to their places on the Line, and they could only be set in the presence of a commissioner from each of the colonies.

SEAFORD, DELAWARE: EAST OF MILE 12

Slaves usually lived under the same roof as their owners in Delaware, and therefore separate slave quarters were a rarity in the state. But along the Line near Seaford I find a one-and-a-half-story white clapboard building that once housed the slaves of William H. Ross, who owned a plantation and served as governor of Maryland from 1851 to 1855.

"Ross had 1,400 acres in all," says Claudia Melson, a curator for the Delaware Historical and Cultural Commission. "Most of the land originally was in Maryland, but Mason and Dixon placed it in Delaware."

Above: The plantation house near Seaford, Delaware, owned by William H. Ross, a former governor of Maryland who was a Confederate sympathizer during the Civil War.
Left: The only documented slave quarters in the state of Delaware are on the old Ross Plantation.

Melson heads the local historical group that spearheaded the restoration of the Ross Plantation, including the Italian Villa style mansion, a granary, a carriage house, and Delaware's only documented slave quarters. The building was found abandoned in a nearby woods and moved back to the plantation site. It now rests at its original location and has been restored. It measures 16-by-24 feet. There are two small rooms on the first floor and a staircase leading to an attic.

"Ross had fourteen slaves," says Melson, who is writing her master's thesis on the former governor. "One or two might have stayed in the house, but most of them lived here. They were valued, right along with the land, silver, and livestock, when property taxes were assessed. An ox and a slave were valued about the same."

Melson speaks exuberantly and rapidly—100 words per minute with gusts up to 150. "Ross lent a lot of people money around here, and he didn't always get paid back in cash. He took horses, cows, roof shingles, whiskey, and sometimes slaves. Somebody gave him a female slave named Amey in 1857. She was valued at three hundred dollars. By 1860 Amey was worth only ninety dollars on the property tax assessment." She shows me the official county assessment for William Ross:

1 negro man	Denas	age 64	$ 20
1 "	Zacariah (infirm)	age 55	——
1 "	David	age 40	$150
1 "	Tona	age 30	$200
1 "	Solomon	age 26	$200
1 "	Aaron	age 23	$200
1 "	Ben	age 20	$200
1 "	Jim	age 17	$175
1 "	Abe	age 16	$150
1 negro woman	Harriet (afflicted)	age 42	——
1 "	Eunice	age 20	$ 90
1 "	Amey	age 16	$ 90

After Fort Sumter was fired upon, Ross lamented in a letter to Governor William Hicks of Maryland: "I am among the largest slave holders in this state, and I feel a lively interest in this matter. This Civil War is about to work my ruin, I fear, for some years past I have been investing nearly all my means in Virginia turnpike and Missouri state bonds; they will become worthless, if Negroes have to go next."

After the Nat Turner slave insurrection in Virginia in 1831, Seaford residents became greatly distressed that a similar rebellion might occur among their slaves. The town teemed with rumors of plots and conspiracies. One of the most recurrent held that on election day in October 1831, blacks would stage a violent uprising and try to kill all whites. Hearsay festered into fact. At this feverish point, a group of young white men staged a hoax. They set up just across the Nanticoke River from Seaford where everyone in town could see. They separated into two groups, one of which tied black handkerchiefs across their faces. The "Black" group began firing guns at the whites, who feigned being hit and fell to the ground. It was clear to the people lining the banks on the other side what was happening—the dreaded slave rebellion had begun.

The fainthearted ran to the woods and hid. The stouthearted took up arms. Voting stopped and the election was forgotten. Messengers were sent to nearby communities to spread the alarm, which served to magnify the hoax. People at one polling place were told that an armed band of 3,000 blacks, slave and free, had crossed the Nanticoke from Maryland into Delaware and were murdering whites. Emergency meetings were held in every town and restrictions were passed barring blacks from assembling and owning firearms. Squads of six or seven armed white men patrolled the streets at night for weeks.

The fake insurrection had serious consequences for the blacks, because the paranoia it inspired lived on long after the hoax was exposed. Petitions to the General Assembly late in the fall of 1831 blamed the "unrest" among blacks on nocturnal religious meetings and out-of-state preachers. The legislators responded by passing laws that forbade religious meetings by blacks after 10 P.M., required out-of-state Negro ministers to be licensed, and restricted the use of firearms to blacks approved by justices of the peace on the recommendation of five white persons. More laws soon followed. Free blacks who were not steadily employed could be brought before the justices of the peace or forcibly hired out. Free blacks from other states were forbidden to enter Delaware for any reason. Blacks could not organize camp meetings without white approval. Free blacks protested

these laws vigorously, but William Ross led a petition drive to keep them
on the statute books. They stayed.

Slavery was set in concrete in Maryland by an 1837 constitutional
amendment: "The relation of Master and Slave in this State shall not be
abolished, unless a Bill so to abolish . . . shall be passed by a unanimous
vote of the members of each branch of the General Assembly . . . and [again
by] members of each branch of the General Assembly, at the next regular
constitutional session after [the first vote], nor then without full compen-
sation to the master for the property of which he shall be thereby deprived."
Any one of these three conditions was a long shot—all three together was
an impossibility.

Seaford was a center of Southern sympathizers during the Civil War and
provided many men for the Confederate Army, including William Ross's
son. Though nominally part of the Union, Seaford and surrounding towns
were considered "hotbeds of secession." Rival militia companies drilled in
each town. Seaford's militia had been given guns at the beginning of the
war, but Union leaders soon realized this was a mistake and sent troops to
disarm the local force. William Ross was so suspect that he fled to Europe
for two years after being informed that President Lincoln had sent a Union
officer to arrest him.

The harassment of blacks continued through the war and after. In 1866
a band of whites interrupted a black church service in Seaford, searched
members of the congregation for weapons, and then broke several windows
of the building. William Ross was accused of being one of the ringleaders,
but nothing could be proven. A Union officer conducted an investigation
and found that blacks in southern Delaware needed federal protection
because "their churches are burned, their schools broken up, and their persons and property abused and destroyed by vicious white men with
impunity; and their appeals to the civil authorities are utterly disregarded."

HURLOCK, MARYLAND: WEST OF MILE 12

Like many Eastern Shore towns, Hurlock got started when the railroad
came through right after the Civil War. The railroads had a social as well
as an economic impact on Eastern Shore towns—the tracks themselves
became the dividing line between the races. The cleavage was formidable
and survives to this day in a slightly diluted form.

"This is the black section of Hurlock," says Kay McElvey from the front lawn of her simple frame home. "Today we would say 'predominantly black.' Every town around here still has a white section and a black section, and the black section has always been on the *other* side of the tracks." She smiles wryly, but her eyes are not smiling.

McElvey was a teacher at the local high school in 1972 when she agreed to help a group of students search for information on local black history. Several local histories had been written, but they either ignored blacks entirely or dealt with them only when they were slaves. She began a research project that would last twenty years, carry her into retirement from the classroom, and culminate with her doctoral thesis, "Early Black Dorchester, 1776–1870."

She says I can borrow her thesis for a couple of weeks. "But you can read later. Let me take you on a little tour." McElvey is less than five feet tall, and she has to sit erect to see over the steering wheel as she drives. Soon she is rummaging through the attic of her memory.

"I was bused sixteen miles to Cambridge to go to the black high school. I was lucky to be able to do that. This was the 1930s. A man named Charles Cornish went out and bought a shell of a school bus. There were no seats in it so he filled it with old benches. He charged fifty cents a week, and if a parent couldn't afford that they paid him in chickens and vegetables.

"We had to go away to high school, but the elementary schools were local, and segregation had a good side. The black parents knew that we were being shortchanged in terms of books and equipment, so they went all-out to support the schools with their own money and their own time. They supported us by bringing in school lunches, coming to all the functions. They were involved. They disciplined us to do homework. You don't have that today.

"When integration came, they started with the high schools and worked down. That was a mistake because the younger the child, the less likely there are to be racial prejudices. It takes time for racial hatred to develop in a child. My brother went to one of the first integrated schools in Dorchester County. It was a high school. He went through hell, and so did all the kids that year. It was 1969. They were told that no matter what happened, they couldn't fight back. It was like Jackie Robinson, only it was 20 years later. When my brother got on the bus, the white kids would throw spitballs at him and call him nigger. In school they would put ketchup on his seat and laugh when he sat in it.

"The teacher did very little to stop it. My brother got straight As, but the teacher kept retesting him because she thought he was cheating. Finally, when it became obvious he wasn't cheating, she became angry with the white students. 'No Negro should be getting higher grades than a white student. What's wrong with you!'"

The memory has gotten under her skin and is festering. She pulls off the highway and points to a field. "This place used to be called Ennalls Spring, and the Methodists held big camp meetings here. Once the crops were laid by in August, they'd have a camp meeting. It could go on for several days, even a week. The blacks were welcome, but they were kept separate from the whites. Sometimes they would attend the same services as the whites, but they'd sit in the back of the speaker's platform while the whites were out front.

"The Methodists originally were opposed to slavery, and that's why the blacks joined. But some of the church's richest brethren were slaveholders, and so they eventually broke into white and black Methodist churches. White Methodists did not want black Methodists to have independent churches. A white preacher or policeman had to be present at each service to make sure nothing was said by the black minister that might incite a slave rebellion.

"One of the most unsettling things I discovered in my research was that these black churches themselves divided along skin tone. In some churches they would have a piece of wood hanging from the ceiling that was a certain shade of brown. If you were that shade or lighter, you could go in. But if you were darker, you couldn't worship there."

I sit up in my seat. McElvey is one of the few blacks I encounter along the Line who is willing to acknowledge and discuss the nuances and subtleties of color that exist among American blacks. There has been a historic antagonism between dark-skinned African-Americans and those with light skin.

McElvey winces her ebony-skinned face. "When I was a kid, they used to sing a song that went something like this. 'If you're light, you're all right; If you're brown, stick around; But if you're black, git back!' In grade school, my best friend was lighter than me, and one day she told me, 'You know when we get to high school, I'll be in the "in" group and you won't because you're too dark.' She was right, too.

"We were taught to hate our physical features, our blackness. Whites were always put forth to us as role models. Once I made myself a mask and a wig that I thought made me look like a blond white girl. A white insurance man came to our house and I greeted him at the door. He said, 'You must be an African princess.' I was crushed. He hadn't even recognized that I was trying to be a little blond white girl."

At the village of East New Market, McElvey stops in front of a pretty park, pruned and civic, where three young black children are playing wiffle ball. "We're pretty sure this is where the slave holding pen was. There were bad economic times around here for farmers about 1820, and they began selling their slaves to the big cotton plantations that were springing up all over the Deep South. They kept the slaves here temporarily after the auction."

One East New Market slave trader was John Sterling, whose bills of sale contained precise descriptions of his merchandise. On April 1, 1822, Sterling sold six black children to Jesse Cage of Sumner County, Tennessee, for $1,301. "Mary a tall slim woman of a dark complexion about 18 (years old) . . . Lindy a low chunky woman black complexion about 18 . . . Easter a black girl about nine . . . Bell a girl of dark complexion about 10 . . . Mary a yellow girl about 9 with a black spot on her nose . . . Levin a boy of yellow complexion full face and about 13." Sterling added his own guarantee: ". . . which negroes I warrant to be healthy sensible and sound, clear of any impediment whatever and slaves for life."

There is a description of the East New Market slave pen in *The Life of John Thompson, A Fugitive Slave*. It describes "a room, in the middle of which was a long staple driven into the floor, with a large ring attached to it, having four long chains attached to that. To these were attached shorter chains, to ankles. Men, women and children were huddled in this room together, awaiting the arrival of more victims as the drove was not full."

"There was no railroad back in those days," McElvey says, "and so the newly purchased slave either had to be taken out by boat or on a forced march where they were bound together by leg chains. I studied about one hundred transactions here in the year 1822 and found that the average male sold was fourteen years old, the average female, sixteen."

Just outside of East New Market, she turns down Hicksburg Road, where the Reverend Samuel Green lived. Samuel Green was a free black farmer and Methodist minister who was liked by white people but secretly was a conductor on the Underground Railroad and worked closely with Harriet Tubman. He eluded suspicion until his son, who was a slave, escaped to Canada. Green went to see him, and when he got back the authorities had broken into his house and found a copy of *Uncle Tom's Cabin.* Green was arrested for "knowingly having in his possession a certain abolition pamphlet . . . of an inflammatory character."

"Green was found guilty in 1857 and sentenced to ten years in the state penitentiary," says McElvey. "The case attracted national attention and outraged the abolitionists up North. But he served five years before the Quakers managed to get him a pardon."

We cross the bridge spanning the Choptank River into Cambridge and stop in front of the Dorchester County Courthouse, where slaves were auctioned.

"They brought Kizzia Bowley here for sale in December 1850," says McElvey over the hum of the motor. "She was married to John Bowley, a free man, and she was Harriet Tubman's sister. As she waited to be sold on these steps, the auctioneer took a break for dinner. Her husband grabbed her and hid her in a house nearby. Later they took a small boat to Baltimore, where they were met by Harriet, who got them across the Line into Pennsylvania and then up to Canada."

America's racial divide deepened 117 years later here when H. Rap Brown stood atop a car in Cambridge and called on blacks to take up arms against whites. "Don't be trying to love that honky to death," Brown screamed. "Shoot him to death. Shoot him to death, brother, because that's what he is out to do to you. Do to him like he would do to you, but do it to him first."

The Dorchester County Courthouse in Cambridge, Maryland, where slaves were auctioned from the front steps.

FEDERALSBURG, MARYLAND: WEST OF MILE 15

I cross into Caroline County, Maryland, and a mile west of the Line enter Federalsburg, where I'm looking for the site of an old slave-trading station. I stop in a convenience store to ask directions. Ten or more black people are lined up to buy lottery tickets. A woman hands the clerk a twenty dollar bill and doesn't get any change. I ask a squat, horseshoe-bald man if he knows where the old slave station used to be. He shakes his head negatively, but he doesn't understand my question. A woman turns toward me. "Ain't you heard, Man, slavery's been abolished?" She fixes me with a glare that sticks two inches out my back.

I go to the Federalsburg Library and find a copy of George Alfred Townsend's 1884 historic novel, *The Entailed Hat.* He has a passage about the place I'm looking for: "At Federalsburg they crossed the branch of the Nanticoke piercing to the centre of Delaware state, and saw one large brick house of colonial appearance dominating the little wooden hamlet, and here, as generally within the Maryland line, hunting negroes was the 'lark' or the serious occupation of many an idle or enterprising fellow, who trained his negro scouts like a setter, or more often like a spaniel, and crossed the line on appointed nights as ardently and warily as the white trader in Africa takes to the trails of the interior for human prey."

The novel is as close as I get to finding the trading station. No one at the library knows where it was.

During the Civil War, Maryland adopted a new constitution that abolished slavery, but not all slave owners were ready to give up their cheap labor. Right before the new constitution went into effect on November 1, 1864, the slave owners took refuge in an obscure Maryland law that provided for children to be given out as apprentices if their parents could not support them. It allowed slave owners to summon black children to court by themselves, give them to white overseers, and only later advise the parents of the action. In effect, the scheme made slaves of black children who would become free in a matter of days. In Dorchester County alone, about fifty of these apprenticeships were granted before federal authorities ordered a stop to the practice, and the children were ordered returned to their parents.

HICKMAN, MARYLAND: ON MILE 26

Hickman is a frayed-at-the-sleeve, out-at-the-elbow town that is nothing more than a huddle of slapped-up houses that seem to be sinking under their own weight. It was near here in June 1761 that the original colonial team that preceded Mason and Dixon faltered because the surveyors became ill with a fever contracted in the Pocomoke Swamp. They did not resume work for nearly two months.

The Line passes through small farms with functional houses and neat barns guarding broods and litters. Ruler-straight roads and rectilinear fields sprawl to the horizon. Miles and miles of nothing but miles and miles, broken only by an occasional dreary town. I become a passenger on my own legs, moving unconsciously at footpace. Walking is man's oldest form of transportation, preferred by vagabonds, poets, beachcombers, tramps, drifters, pilgrims, and rolling stones. . . .

In 1864, Caroline was alone among the Eastern Shore counties in voting in favor of the constitution that abolished slavery. This is probably one reason that after the war the federal government selected Caroline to be the site of the Freedman's Bureau, one of the federal offices that were set up throughout the South to help blacks adjust to freedom. The initial jubilation of freedom soon gave way to fear and uncertainty. The former slaves were unprepared economically or socially for freedom. They were surrounded by hostile whites—and, in some cases, hostile blacks such as longtime freedmen who resented new faces in the very competitive job market and considered themselves a step above these upstarts.

The bureau here was abolished in 1872, but the area around it came to be called Bureau, and the two-story wooden building that was its headquarters was used by blacks as a church and school until about 1910. The building began a long downward spiral of decay and neglect. Belatedly, black leaders realized it had historic significance and asked for government help. But on December 9, 1938, it burned to the ground. I walk into the place that used to be called Bureau as night is assembling itself on the western horizon, and in the gray creeping twilight I look for anything tangible—a sign, a foundation—that would recall the past. There is nothing but an open, unmarked field.

This part of the Mason-Dixon Line was only a year old when John Woolman crossed it into Caroline County on his famous "walking journey" through Delaware and Maryland in 1766. Woolman was a Quaker preacher from New Jersey who traveled throughout the colonies, urging his coreligionists to free their slaves. He told them that slavery was wholly incompatible with Quakerism and that alleged Negro "inferiority" was actually the result of slavery rather than any natural predisposition.

His biographer describes his journey through Caroline County:

> . . . the weather was hot, although it was the month of May; and there had been a long drought. Plodding along, ankle-deep in dust, bundle on back, tormented by flies and thirst, stifled in the airless forest stretches, grilled in the miles of cleared land among the parched tobacco fields, when he arrived at his destination he still had the hardest part of his task before him—the personal dealing with the slaveholder. Woolman finally fell ill, and had to delay to rest. He resigned himself, like a good soldier. After all, "we had gone forward much faster than I expected before we came out" and "I saw that I had been in danger of desiring to get quickly through the journey." So he thanked God and took courage and calmed his mind. The very exhaustion to which he had to succumb was an argument in favor of the tedious walk. He had always found that "conduct is more convincing than language." Now when, haggard with fatigue and covered with dust, he presented himself at a wealthy planter's house, and in return for hospitality urged him to throw away his comforts and do without slave labor, his words were supported by the silent witness of his own abandonment of comfort. Now he felt in his body, as far as it was possible for a free man to do so, what it was to live like a slave. That is to say, to live at the very bottom of the social scale "that I might have a more lively feeling of the condition of the oppressed slaves." When he toiled along the road under the hot sun, his eyes dazzled with glare, his nose and throat parched with dust, his body soaked with sweat, his physical sensations were exactly similar to those of the slaves he passed, toiling among the rows of tobacco. . . .

DENTON, MARYLAND: WEST OF MILE 30

It's visiting hour when I walk into the Caroline County Jail in Denton, Maryland. Three young black women are perched on the edge of benches, leaning forward and talking in hushed earnestness to three black men behind a partition. There is a sorrowful huskiness in the women's voices. The men speak in monosyllables, their faces full of stoic grief. Two officers—one black, one white, are behind the desk as I approach.

"Is it true that Wish Sheppard's handprint is on a cell?"

"We've both heard that story, but we don't know if it's true," says the white officer.

"Can I go in and look?"

"Nope. 'Gainst regulations." He closes the conversation and sits on the lid.

An old man standing nearby taps me on the shoulder. "It's true. I've seen it with my own eyes. They closed off the cell and haven't opened it since 1938."

Wish Sheppard was a black man who was convicted of the brutal murder of a young Denton girl in 1915. In its coverage of the trial, the local newspaper described Sheppard as "a negro about twenty years old, of exceedingly repulsive features, with very thick, protruding lips, flat nose and retreating forehead, his big, bold, rolling eyes being conspicuous by the white in them, suggesting brutish instincts."

As he was being carried from his cell to be hanged, local tradition holds that Sheppard put his hand on the wall. In subsequent years, the story developed that Sheppard had come back to haunt the jail and that his hand print kept reappearing on the wall despite all efforts to obliterate it. Dozens of prisoners came forth at different times to report seeing apparitions and of hearing footsteps and voices.

The jail in Denton, Maryland.

Interviewed in 1990 for an oral history project, retired Sheriff Louis Andrew said: "There is a handprint on the wall of Wish Sheppard's old cell. I painted over it several times since I've been here, but it comes back. The legend is he put his hands on the wall to hold himself back when he was carried out to be hung at the bottom of the hill. The handprint is on the wall of the old part of the jail. When they remodeled the jail in 1981–1982, they left the door that Wish Sheppard came out of, and as far as I know, that door has not been opened since 1938. They say the door will not open."

Not far from the jail is the Denton market, which was established in 1818. Today local farmers are selling produce from the beds of their pickup trucks. A mono-bosomed woman with middle-parted hair passes a bag of carrots and a smile over the counter. Everything from apples to zucchini is available—lettuce, tomatoes, broccoli, chickens, turkeys, ducks, rabbits, smoked hams, apple butter, watermelon pickles, fresh horseradish. And one other commodity was available here in 1818.

Back in colonial days, tobacco was the main crop in Maryland. Indeed, tobacco was king, and a man's wealth was reckoned by the acres of tobacco he tilled. Tobacco came to be used as money to pay bills, taxes, salaries, and debts. A pound of tobacco could buy three pounds of beef. Tobacco was used to buy slaves, who could in turn produce at a low cost even more tobacco for the owner. But tobacco abused the soil, and by 1820 it was dethroned. Many slaves were no longer needed, and they were sold to Southern plantation owners here at the market in Denton.

Free blacks could not leave Maryland without permission from the clerk of the county court, and in the Caroline County Courthouse I find a certificate issued on March 14, 1826, by County Clerk Joseph Richardson.

> Whereas application has been made to me by a colored woman named Mahala Scott for a certificate of her freedom agreeably to the Act of Assembly in such case made and provided by which said Act, free negroes and mulattoes are permitted to travel out of this state, upon the obtaining of a certificate of being free born. And whereas also upon the oath of Sarah Williams, of Caroline County, that the said colored woman named Mahala Scott, for whom this certificate is made, was free born. I do therefore grant her said application and hereby certify that she is seventeen years of age, or thereabout, about five feet high, of a complexion nearly black, was born and raised in Caroline County, and has a large

scar of a burn across her right wrist, and a scar of a cut on the
inside of her right wrist-joint, another scar on her left cheek
directly under the eye and no other notable mark or scar that I
have discovered.

WYE MILLS, MARYLAND: WEST OF MILE 34

Beyond Denton I make a detour west, and after a fifteen-minute drive I am
standing under the 107-foot Wye Oak, one of the largest in the United
States. It is the oldest living thing in Maryland—450 years old, a woody
blueblood. I marvel at everything that must have passed under it before
me. Indians and slaves, preachers and murderers, and, almost certainly in
1764, Mason and Dixon.

The state bought the Wye Oak and the land around it in 1939 and made
it into a state park, but between 1664 and 1907 it was on land owned by
the Lloyd family. Colonel Edward Lloyd III presided over a pillared plantation and hundreds of slaves between 1749 and 1770. Mason's journal merely mentions the side trip to see him without explanation, but Lloyd helped
in the colonial survey of the Line in 1762, and this is the apparent reason
he was visited by the two English surveyors.

I'm most interested in seeing the Wye House, but it's a private residence
with a closed entry gate. Wye House was built by Col. Lloyd's son, Edward
IV. Around 1818, one of the Lloyd slaves, Harriet Bailey, gave birth to a
son and named him Frederick Augustus Washington Bailey. The father was
a white man, probably Captain Aaron Anthony, who was the overseer for
the Lloyds' empire, which at that time numbered thirteen farms and some
550 slaves. At the age of about six, the boy was brought here to the main
house to work for his master.

When he was about twenty years old, he escaped from slavery by using
forged papers that identified him as a free black man and taking a train and
then a boat from Baltimore to Philadelphia. He changed his name to
Frederick Douglass, and within a few years he was a fiery abolitionist.
Douglass wrote a narrative of his life in 1845, and he became a prominent
speaker at abolition meetings. His writings and his oratory were bitter.
"Slavery," he said, "is alike the sin and the shame of the American people."

Douglass never learned who his father was or the date of his birth.
"Genealogical trees did not flourish among slaves," he wrote later in life.
"A person of some consequence among freemen, sometimes designated

father, was literally abolished in slave law and slave practice. It was only occasionally that an exception was found to this system. As to the time of my birth, I am equally indistinct. Indeed, I seldom knew a slave who could tell exactly how old he was, for slave mothers knew nothing of the months of the year or the days of the month. There was no family record among them. They measured the ages of their children by spring-time, harvest-time, winter-time, and planting-time, and naturally, little by little, even these designations became obliterated."

A mellower Douglass returned to his birthplace in 1877, and in a speech before an integrated audience, he said:"I am an Eastern Shoreman, with all that name implies. Eastern Shore corn and Eastern Shore pork gave me my muscle. I love Maryland and the Eastern Shore." Four years later, he visited the plantation house where he had worked as a boy and drank wine on the veranda with the descendants of his former master.

WHITELEYSBURG, MARYLAND: ON MILE 34

The sky releases a rain of Old Testament intensity, and I trudge water-logged and muddy into Whiteleysburg, Maryland, which hugs the Line. It is a place of dilapidation and impoverishment, suggesting unwed mothers and unfed children. Cars and trucks are going to canker and rust, and right on the Line is an abandoned store with the remnants of a gas pump. The sagging porch supports an RC Cola machine and a clawfoot bathtub. At the outbreak of the Civil War, the U.S. marshall received an unsigned letter advising that if he showed his face in Whiteleysburg, he should bring along a grave digger and a coffin. The correspondent vowed it would take half of "Abe's nigger army" to arrest anyone here and that the Confederacy was "bound to shine" in the new war.

BRIDGETOWN, MARYLAND: WEST OF MILE 39

I visit the grave of Massy Fountain, who was a prominent businessman, politician, and landowner in the first half of the nineteenth century. He was also a slave dealer. *The History of Caroline County,* published in 1920 to give the white schoolchildren a feel for local history, describes him: "Tradition has it that he was one of Patty Cannon's crowd of kidnappers, but we find no proof of this and he was never accused of the other crimes of which she was instigator. Certain it is, however, that he bought and sold slaves. Maryland slave owners, feeling it a disgrace to deal openly for negroes, would secretly bring them to Fountain, who in turn would sell them to southern dealers. The cellar of the Fountain home was used as quarters for the darkies until convenient for the dealers to move them south. This being 'sold south in to Georgia,' as the slaves termed it, was the greatest terror of their lives."

MARYDEL, DELAWARE
& MARYDEL, MARYLAND: ON MILE 45

Marydel is another of the Line's split-personality towns where telephoning your next door neighbor can be a long-distance call and bosom-buddy play-mates go off on different school buses. Delaware Route 8 suddenly becomes Maryland Route 311, and the two roads are stitched together by slightly askew dotted lines. Back-to-back signs welcome me to Maryland ("PLEASE DRIVE GENTLY") and Delaware ("HOME OF TAX-FREE SHOPPING"). Not surprisingly, nearly all the businesses are in Delaware.

The marker is a crown stone, forty-five miles from the Middle Point, set in concrete and surrounded by flowers and neatly trimmed shrubs and grass. It was placed here by the Mason-Dixon party in 1765, and it remained here until 1904, when Maryland officials who wanted to make a good showing at the St. Louis Fair removed the stone and made it part of the state exhibit. After the fair it was taken to the state capitol at Annapolis, where it was put on display, and then to a branch library in Baltimore, where it ended up in a little-used storage shed. No one noticed the stone was missing until 1954. The Marydel Lions Club led a deter-mined search and found it. The crown stone came back to Marydel in 1964.

Just across the street from the marker in Delaware is Karen's Treasure House, which sells Beanie Babies and other collectibles. Karen Sanders has been here since 1986 and makes it her personal responsibility to care for the stone. "I plant the flowers, clip the shrubs, mow the lawn, and on good weather days I run up the two state flags. Not that many people stop, but the motorcycle clubs have it as one of their locations where you can earn some points, and so they stop here and pose for pictures to prove they've been here."

Right: The crown stone at Marydel was missing for sixty years before it was discovered and set back in place in 1964. Below: The Line goes through the middle of Karen Sanders' house in Marydel.

Sanders's house is next to her shop, and the Line goes right through the middle of it. She pays property taxes in both states. Rusting railroad tracks are just a few yards away. "When I moved in I noticed that it had a lot of very small bedrooms. Then I was redoing one of the rooms and found some red velvet wallpaper. With a little research I discovered that it started out as a bordello for the railroad workers. It was built around 1800. You can tell because they were using wooden pegs instead of nails."

Unlike other Line towns, the railroad tracks do not separate white from black in Marydel. "As far as I know, there have never been any black people here. We have a lot of Guatemalans, though. They work in the poultry plants. They live in trailers on the Maryland side of town. The landlords charge them by the head because they pack ten or eleven into a single trailer. We've had a few minor incidents, but there are no big problems with the Guatemalans. They're hard workers."

The trailer park is just off Route 311. I try to count them but give up at one hundred. Tejano music pours forth from inside many of them. Men sit outside in drugstore lawn chairs stone-eyed with boredom. Two mothers carrying babies on their hips talk to each other. Older children run and shout in Spanish, laughing and celebrating this precise moment in their lives. I try to talk to a group of men, but they throw up their hands in incomprehension. I leave frustrated, a prisoner of my own language.

It was on the Mason-Dixon Line in Marydel that an illegal, bloodless duel was fought in 1877 between James Gordon Bennett, the owner of the *New York Herald*, and Frederick May, whose sister said she had been insulted by Bennett. The participants chose the Line as a way to avoid interference from the law.

May was somewhat well-known as a New York socialite, but Bennett was a world-famous journalist in the manner of Ted Turner or Rupert Murdoch today. It was Bennett who assigned reporter Henry M. Stanley to search for Dr. David Livingstone, the explorer and missionary who was believed lost in Africa. Upon finding him in 1871, Stanley uttered his famous line, "Dr. Livingstone, I presume?"

The combatants arrived unannounced in Marydel by train accompanied by their seconds. Local residents heard two shots, and when they got to the scene along the railroad tracks all four men were preparing to leave by separate carriages. No one was injured. Bennett felt so humiliated that he lived the rest of his life in Europe and on his yachts, returning to New York only for brief periods.

A few miles east of Marydel is Mt. Zion, where black camp meetings were held throughout the first half of the twentieth century that attracted people from all over the eastern seaboard. A tradition evolved called "White People's Night" when the residents of Marydel were invited to attend the services.

CHESWOLD, DELAWARE: EAST OF MILE 52

Though it's home to fewer than 1,000 souls, Cheswold has two Methodist churches one-half-mile apart on Main Street. At Cheswold United Methodist Church, the congregants are all white, but at Immanuel Union Methodist Church the skin colors range from white to deep brown.

There are fourteen pews at Immanuel, and on this Sunday morning they are packed four generations deep. Flickering candles illuminate faces pinched in prayer. Clutching their dog-eared Bibles, they rise and sing *a capella*: "Me and Jesus got our thing goin'; me and Jesus got it all worked out; Me and Jesus don't need anybody to tell us what it's all about." After an hour, they emerge bathed in religious spirit and the noonday sun. I ask a very old woman if she is a Moor.

"Yes, I am."

"What is a Moor?"

She looks at me as though I'd just asked what a human being was. Then her words come out squeezed by the inanity of my question. "I don't know what you mean. We're Moors. We've been Moors for hundreds of years. . . . "

The people who called themselves Moors first appeared in the Cheswold area several decades before the Civil War, and the first official record of them came in an 1855 trial in which a man named Levi Sockum was charged with selling guns to a black named Isaac Harmon—an illegal act at the time. Sockum's defense was that Harmon was a Nanticoke Indian, not a Negro. A witness for the prosecution, Lydia Clark, testified that Sockum and Harmon were the descendants of a black Moroccan prince who had been sold into bondage to a Delaware white woman named Regua. Mistress and slave fell in love, married, and had children. Their children intermarried with the local Nanticokes, and their offspring came to be called Moors. It was a dubious tale, but it was widely accepted until the 1940s when the research of C. A. Weslager, a Delaware historian, estab-

A memorial to Lydia Clark, who died in 1856 and was the last person to speak the Nanticoke language.

lished that the Moors were a mixture of three races.

The Moors found themselves shunned by the white community, and they distanced themselves from the black community. They turned inward and married one another. Even today it is not uncommon for it to be unnecessary for a woman to change her name at marriage because she and her husband already have the same last name. Part of their ancestry goes back to the Nanticokes who were denationalized after the failure of the plot at Winnasoccum in 1742; part of it goes back to the Lenni Lenape tribe; part of it goes back to the white colonists who drove the Indians out; and part of it goes back to the slaves and free blacks of antebellum Delaware.

From the beginning, the Moors were determined to keep their racial identity. In the days of school segregation, they were barred from white schools and refused to attend Negro schools. In 1881 a law was passed allowing them to run their own school system. At one point the state of Delaware was maintaining separate schools for whites, Negroes, Nanticokes, and Moors. In 1950 they persuaded the state to give them their own racial designation on their driver's licenses. For a few years, Delaware licenses were marked "W" for white, "N" for Negro, "O" for Oriental, "R" for red—and "M" for Moor.

The Moors observed a color line with blacks as rigid as any Southern plantation owner. Pity the Moorish girl who had anything to do with a common black man. First she would be warned, and if she persisted she would be disowned by her parents and shunned by her community. In the 1890s the Moors asked the state to send them a teacher for their school, but specifically asked that it not be a black. Three days later a Virginia man came to Cheswold who appeared to be Negro. There were indignant protests, and he was sent packing back to Virginia. The Moors reiterated their request for a teacher and said he could be a Moor, a white or an Indian—but not a Negro.

For their part, the Moors suffered unremitting discrimination from whites, who made no distinction between them and blacks. They could not attend the white public high school in Dover, they could buy food in white restaurants but had to eat it outside, and before they set up their own church they were obliged to sit in the balcony of the Methodist church in Cheswold. The joke among whites was that "Moor" meant "more or less a nigger. . . ."

John L. Gaines is the lay leader at Immanuel Union Methodist, and on the church steps he and his wife Charlotte have me in a crossfire of words—

the ends of one sentence are colliding with the beginnings of the next.

"I went to the drugstore in Dover and bought a Coke. They told me I could have it but had to drink it outside. . . ."

". . . He was a welder in the Navy, but when he got out he couldn't get a job. It was whites only. . . ."

". . . I was admitted to Kent General Hospital and had to go on a floor with the blacks. . . ."

". . . When I graduated from high school, the only jobs available for young women were to clean house for white people. It didn't matter if you were Negro, Native American, or Moor, if you weren't white the jobs were closed. . . ."

". . . We thought we were Moors because that's what we were always called. As we got older, we realized we were Native Americans. . . ."

". . . Our parents knew they were Indians, but Indians had no rights then. . . ."

". . . We now consider Moor to be a derogatory term. . . ."

". . . We are Lenni Lenape. . . ."

". . . Yes, we are the Lenni Lenape Tribe of Delaware. . . ."

". . . But at the white church down the street they still call this the Moor church. . . ."

". . . A lot of people are getting their birth certificates changed. They used to say 'Moor.' But four years ago the state passed a law allowing us to change 'Moor' to 'Native American.' . . ."

". . . If a Native American marries a Negro in Cheswold, they are shunned by the other Native Americans. . . ."

In 1994 the people who used to call themselves Moors applied to the state to be recognized as the Lenni Lenape tribe of Delaware. They were turned down on the ground that there was insufficient documentation of a historical connection.

CALDWELL CORNERS, DELAWARE: ON MILE 63

In the pre-dawn dark I come to the intersection of Caldwell Corner Road and Vandyke-Greenspring Road, about twenty yards east of the Line; only a change in the color of the rain-rutted road surface indicates the location of the boundary. The town consists of an abandoned mobile home on one corner and three small houses on the other corners. One of them has a sluttish lean to it, and a thread of smoke curls from the chimney.

For a few miles Maryland Line Road coincides with the Line itself, arrowing through farm fields. Dawn elbows its way onto the scene, and a bank of clouds over Maryland slowly turns purplish pink. I find an original marker at the edge of a plowed field, protected by three guard rail-type beams driven perpendicularly into the ground. It's tilting northward. The "P" is clearly visible, but the "M" has been worn and chipped away.

A mile beyond the ground turns spongy, and in a swampy area on the Delaware side rests a small mountain of garbage—a dreadful stinking pile of bones and rinds, plastic and paper, gunk and junk, a sofa, two refrigerators, a dozen broken storm windows, a whole motor pool full of tires. I will encounter many such piles—illegal dumping seems to be the leading law-breaking activity along the Line in modern times.

East of here is Middletown, Delaware, where a Quaker named John Hunn helped runaway slaves and referred to himself as "the superintendent of the Underground Railroad from Wilmington down the peninsula." I stop for coffee and ask the waitress if she knows where he lived. She asks a breakfasting group of men. No one's ever heard of him. But at Odessa I find the little red brick Appoquinimink Meeting House, a favorite stopping place for Harriet Tubman and her charges. The building is only twenty feet square, but it has a pitched roof that conceals a loft where the runaways hid until it was safe to move North.

A farm field near the Line in Middletown, Delaware.

THE CHESAPEAKE AND DELAWARE CANAL: ON MILE 75

Gaunt, scavenging gulls wheel and mew overhead. On the canal a sailboat inhales the stiff breeze as it cruises toward the Chesapeake. Since it opened in 1829, world-faring ships have taken this shortcut between the Chesapeake Bay and Delaware Bay. Some Delaware historians call the canal the state's "own Mason-Dixon Line" because it demarcates two distinct sections of the state. The land begins undulating in gentle hills north of the canal, and plantations were impractical. The farms were small and a family could handle the work. But south of here the plantations developed, and slave labor was needed to run a profitable operation.

With good reasons, Delaware has been called "a northern state with a southern exposure, and a southern state with a northern exposure." It has always been ambivalent about race. Though it did not secede during the Civil War, there was little real support for the Union cause south of the C&D Canal, and many southern Delawareans defected to the Confederacy or helped it clandestinely. South of the canal, the notorious Patty Cannon and her accomplices kidnapped blacks and sold them to unscrupulous slave dealers, while north of the canal in Wilmington, Thomas Garrett and his fellow Quakers shepherded slaves to freedom on the Underground Railroad. The two divergent operations were only sixty miles apart.

Historically, slaves made up a small portion of Delaware's population. On the eve of the Civil War, there were only about 1,800 slaves in the entire state. White fear centered not on the slaves, but on the free blacks, who constituted about 20 percent of the population. When it came to clamping restrictions on blacks, Delaware took a back seat to no state. For example, in the first half of the nineteenth century, any white person could arrest any black suspected of being a fugitive slave; the services of an unemployed free black could be auctioned off for a year; and no more than twelve free blacks could assemble after dark unless "three respectable white men" were present.

Delaware's "southerners" controlled the legislature, which became a font of anti-black laws for nearly a century. During the Civil War, Lincoln offered a generous program of reimbursing slave owners in exchange for freeing all of Delaware's slaves, but the plan was rejected by the Legislature. In 1865 the state's lawmakers rejected the 13th, 14th, and 15th Amendments outlawing slavery; guaranteeing life, liberty, and property to all regardless of race; and guaranteeing the right to vote regardless of race. It was not until 1901, thirty-six years after they had taken effect, that the Delaware Legislature got around to ratifying the three Amendments; by this time, it was a whimpering, meaningless gesture.

North of the canal, agriculture has surrendered the soil to business, industry, and suburbia. All that is raised on this land today is taxes. There's no sign of the cow pasture about a mile east of the Line where, on July 31, 1965, some 2,500 people watched the local Ku Klux Klan burn a forty-two-foot cross in the name of white purity. The crowd moved slowly around the cross while speakers played a recording of Tennessee Ernie Ford singing "That Old Rugged Cross." The speaker of the evening was Robert Shelton, imperial wizard of the national Klan, who assailed President Johnson and told Negro-dialect jokes. Because of its racial symbolism, the Line has been a magnet for Klan rallies since the 1920s.

ELKTON, MARYLAND: ON MILE 77

There's a little red and white bungalow housing a secondhand clothing store where the Line intersects with U.S. 40. Jane Deford says she's only open on weekends, but the location is good for business because people stop to take pictures at the Line and then come in and browse. When Mason and Dixon passed by here, the road was a wagon trail blazed by colonists moving west from the Delaware River. During the Depression, Route 40 became the through road to San Francisco and was known as the "Fastest Route West." Route 40 was the main link between Washington and New York, and in the 1950s African diplomats making the trip complained repeatedly of being refused service and insulted at restaurants and gas stations along the way. They received only official apologies.

Route 40 became a second-stringer with the opening of Interstate 95, which is just a mile north. President Kennedy stood on the Mason-Dixon Line on November 15, 1963, and cut a blue-and-gray ribbon opening the final link of the north-south interstate. Civil rights picketers strolled in front of him as he spoke. One sign said, "MR. PRESIDENT, YOU'VE OPENED HIGHWAY NO. 95. NOW, HELP US OPEN PUBLIC ACCOMMODATIONS." But seven days later, Kennedy was dead.

Elkton, Maryland, rubs up against the Line, and I find the Historic Little Wedding Chapel conveniently located across Main Street from the Cecil

The historic Little Wedding Chapel in Elkton, Maryland.

County Courthouse. It's the only survivor of dozens of chapels that were here during Elkton's heyday as wedding capital of the world in the 1920s and 1930s. There was no waiting period for eager couples, and a single preacher with a mail-order divinity degree could perform up to 4,000 ceremonies a year. Joan Fontaine, Willie Mays, Babe Ruth, Burt Lahr, Pat Robertson, and John and Martha Mitchell all took quickie vows here.

I step inside and am greeted by a man wearing a black tuxedo who says he's already performed four marriages today. It's about 1 P.M. on Friday. His telephone rasps. "May second? Two o'clock is gone, but I can give you one. . . ." With a wave of his hand, he invites me to look around. The tiny chapel has three pews and an open Bible. Next to it is a parlor with a velvet sofa and a huge splash of plastic flowers.

I cross the street to the courthouse and find an old bill of sale for slaves auctioned off at a sheriff's sale to satisfy an unpaid debt in 1821:

> Know all men by these presents that I, William Moffitt, Sheriff of Cecil County in the State of Maryland, for and in consideration of the sum of Twelve hundred and forty-four Dollars current Money of the United States, to me in hand paid by Charles Oldham of Cecil County in the State aforesaid, the receipt whereof I do hereby acknowledge, have bargained, granted and sold, and by these presents do grant, bargain and sell unto the said Charles Oldham, his heirs and assigns, the following Negroes, to

Wit: Negro Isaac, aged about twenty seven years, black colour and has a scar on his nose; Negro Philip, aged about twenty years, very black colour, and has a very small scar near the corner of his right eye; Negro Hannah, aged about fifteen years, black colour; Negro Mary, aged about twelve years, black colour; To Have and To Hold unto the said Charles Oldham, his heirs and assigns for and during the natural lives of the said Negroes Isaac, Philip, Hannah and Mary, and which said Negroes were taken in execution by me and sold by virtue of a Writ of Venditionas exponas issued out of Cecil County Court against a certain George David of Cecil County in the State of Maryland at the Suit of the Elkton Bank of Maryland and sold by me at public sale on the thirteenth day of this Instant to the said Charles Oldham. In Witness whereof I have hereto set my hand and Seal this fourteenth day of July Eighteen hundred and twenty One — William Moffit, Shff

CHRISTIANA, DELAWARE: EAST OF MILE 82

Christiana is an orphan of modernity, cut off on all sides by highways, shopping malls, and industrial parks. Even Mason and Dixon would have difficulty finding it today, but during their time in America they were frequent visitors to the town, which was then called Christiana Bridge. There were regular meetings here with the boundary commissioners appointed by the Penns and the Calverts to review programs and make plans. Mason's journal contains more than a dozen references to Christiana Bridge, but there is no mention of where they stayed. It is highly likely, however, that it was the Shannon Inn, which today is collapsing on the corner of Main Street and Old Baltimore Pike.

Although much of the inn was remodeled in 1842, the structure was on the road here in colonial days when it was on the most direct route between Philadelphia and Baltimore. George Washington exhorted his soldiers from the front of the inn, and Lafayette set out from the inn's livery stable to apprehend Benedict Arnold in Virginia. In the twentieth century, it was abandoned as a commercial enterprise and, after a few decades of serving as a private residence, it was abandoned altogether. Joe Harper, a retired math teacher, bought it in 1975 when he read about plans to raze it in favor of a convenience store.

An old black pickup trailing a blue vapor of exhaust fumes wheezes up

Joe Harper, current owner of the Shannon Inn, inspects a crumbling wall. Mason and Dixon probably stayed here several times.

to the curb and stops. The door opens and before his foot hits the pavement Joe Harper is already talking in a voice that shatters the silence like a bronze gong. "The only thing that's changed in this building is what the thieves and the vandals have done. I bought the thing to keep it. So it wouldn't be destroyed. I wanted to develop it into a restaurant, but the plans showed it would cost $550,000, and the best rate I could get from the bank was 20 percent. That made it a million-dollar project. . . ."

He pauses to catch his breath and redirect his anger, shifting his toothpick from one side of his mouth to the other. His rumpled attire makes him look like an unmade bed. A Spencer Tracy shock of white hair hangs from his forehead. "I've gotten nothing from the state and the county but bullshit and fines. No support of any kind. Now they want me to tear it down. They say it's an eyesore." He rolls his eyes heavenward and smites his brow. "Well, maybe it is. I'm getting old, and I'm an eyesore, too. But I've still got a lot to offer and so does this building. . . ."

He fumbles in his pockets. "I'm almost certain Mason and Dixon stayed here. The Shannon was advertised in the Philadelphia newspapers in the 1760s as having the finest food in the Colonies. Do you want to see the inside? Why not, I own the damn place." He puts a key in the padlock.

He steps inside and crunches broken glass. "This is the original wood flooring. . . . They stole the mantle from the fireplace. . . . Feel this doorway. . . ." He runs his hand over it lovingly. "That's original, hand-planed, never been painted. . . . See those nails? Blacksmith-forged. . . . The architects want to tear down this wall and that wall. . . . Hell, that's not restoration. That's destruction." He pulls on a bannister. It's absolutely rigid. He pats it paternally. "That's original, too."

Outside, he walks over to a stone that sits in a corner and brushes dirt away with his foot. "That's the stepping stone they used when the carriages came in. George Washington stood on it when he addressed the troops. . . ." His eyes go glassy, and he seems to disappear into his own thoughts. "You know, I have great plans for this place, but I know they won't get done. The truth is, when I kick the bucket, this inn will be no more."

A few paces from the inn is the bridge over the Christiana River, and near here a slave named Sabrina was tied up and whipped by her master for some unknown offense. So severe was her beating that she died a short time later. Her master was indicted for manslaughter, but later the charges were quietly dropped.

Whipping was the most common discipline measure for slaves, and it also had been on the law books in Delaware since 1717 as the official punishment for a variety of crimes committed by blacks and whites. "The punishment of whipping shall be inflicted publicly by strokes on the bare back, well laid on," stated a law that was not repealed until 1972. Prisoners were manacled to the post bare-backed, and struck with a cat-o'-nine tails, which was a short-handled lash consisting of nine strands of rawhide eighteen inches long. The last government-sanctioned whipping occurred in 1952.

Officially, the state defended its whipping law as a necessary deterrent in a small rural state between Philadelphia and Baltimore that had to keep big-city hoodlums away. Unofficially, much of Delaware said the whipping post helped keep the Negro in his place.

Just off the Old Baltimore Pike is the charred hulk of Public School 111-C—the "C" stands for colored—better known as the Christiana Colored School, which was destroyed by fire in 1990. There was a drive to rebuild the historic school as a community center, but it ran out of steam several years ago.

Delaware was alone among the states in segregating not only schools, but school taxes. Whites paid for white schools, blacks paid for black schools. In the decades after the Civil War, most Delaware blacks were laborers and tenant farmers and paid too little to provide quality education through taxes. The government failed to respond to this inequity, so philanthropist Pierre Samuel du Pont gave $2.5 million so the state could build eighty-nine schools for black children in the 1920s. With indoor toilets, they were considered state-of-the-art.

Colored School 111-C was one of them. I walk through the open-ended shell of the building, which now houses only the wind. It is unfloored, unroofed, unwindowed, unmourned. Off in a corner, I spot the toilet.

NEWARK, DELAWARE: EAST OF MILE 83

Home of the University of Delaware, Newark brushes up against the Line on two sides, the west and the north. The Deer Park Tavern has been here since 1851, and before that this was the site of St. Patrick's Tavern, where Mason and Dixon set up a headquarters in 1754 and then returned in 1765 to ride out a late winter snowstorm. In his *History of Cecil County, Maryland,* published in 1881, George Johnston gives this account of their first stay: "The surveyors and those in their employ are said to have been a jolly set, and to have lingered long at the northeast corner of the county, near which may yet be found some fine springs of cool water, to enjoy the pleasure of drinking the apple-jack and peach brandy for which that part of the county was famous. Tradition says they had a pet bear which they always took with them, and that the curiosity and apprehension of the simple country people, who called them 'the star gazers,' were much excited by the habit they had of viewing the heavenly bodies at all hours of the night. Many of the country people viewed them with holy horror as necromancers or soothsayers whom it was not safe to meddle with." Several other local historians state that the surveying party consumed prodigious amounts of peach brandy at the inn.

Today the Deer Park Tavern is a dark cavern of stale smoke inhabited by pouchy-eyed men. Video game monitors with names like Megatough and Global Touch are strung along the bar every ten inches or so. At the far end of the bar two muted televisions are aglow, one with a golf match, the other with a basketball game. Over the tavern-murmur of male voices, the strains of rock music trail in from another room. The barmaid is sitting at the other end reading Camus and bobbing her head to the music. She sees me and comes over. She's a pretty young woman with a tattoo on her upper left arm that looks like a bruise. She's wearing faded jeans with holes at the knees and a leopard skin patch at the buttocks. She has a white towel draped over her belt like an NFL center. I order the house special salad.

On June 12, 1963, the Reverend George F. Brown, a black, came in to the Deer Park and sat down to have lunch. After being ignored for about half an hour, Brown went to the bar and asked to see a menu. He was brought a special menu that offered sandwiches for one hundred dollars and coffee for fifty dollars. He refused to leave the restaurant and was arrested for trespassing. He appealed but lost the case in the Delaware Supreme Court, which ruled on November 9, 1963, that there was nothing unconstitutional about the 1875 state law that said: "No keeper of an inn, tavern, hotel or restaurant, or other place of public entertainment or refreshment of travelers, guests or customers shall be obliged, by law, to furnish entertainment or refreshment to persons whose reception or entertainment by him would be offensive to the major part of his customers, and would injure his business." The following year the law was overturned by the federal Civil Rights Act.

The waitress returns in a few minutes with a bowl of iceberg lettuce, shredded carrots, and winter tomatoes and a bottled French dressing. Just outside the window, a Conrail freight train rumbles by on the old Baltimore & Ohio Railroad tracks, which are so close I can feel the room vibrating. Fifty years ago and more, this was the route of the Chickenbone Special, the daily whistlestopper between Tampa and New York that was part of the massive migration of young black people from the South to the big cities of the North. Its name came from the fact that worried mothers, knowing their sons and daughters couldn't afford the railroad dining car, fixed brown bag lunches that unfailingly included fried chicken, which was eaten along the way.

The migration of the Southern blacks to Northern cities was one of the greatest population shifts in American history, as significant as the pioneers' movement to the West. Richard Wright, the great black novelist, wrote of it: "Lord in Heaven! Good God Almighty! Great Day in the Morning! Our time has come! We are leaving! We are angry no more; we are leaving! We are bitter no more; we are leaving! We are leaving our homes, pulling up our stakes to move on. We look up at the high southern sky and remember all the sunshine and rain and we feel a sense of loss, but we are leaving. We look out at the wide green fields which our eyes saw when we first came into the world and we feel full of regret, but we are leaving . . . we feel glad, for we are leaving . . ."

Langston Hughes celebrated it in the poem, "One-Way Ticket":

> I am fed up
> with Jim Crow laws
> People who are cruel
> And afraid
> who lynch and run
> who are scared of me
> And me of them
> I pick up my life
> And take it away
> On a one-way
> Ticket
> Gone up North
> Gone out West
> Gone!

The catalyst for the migration was World War I, which depleted the white male work force and prompted Northern industries to recruit in the South. Blacks were promised that on the other side of the Mason-Dixon Line they would find better jobs, better wages, better schools, and better treatment. But for millions of blacks, the dream of the Promised Land was shattered by the reality of the ghetto. Another black writer, Ralph Ellison, described it: "In relation to their Southern background, the cultural history of Negroes in the North reads like the legend of some tragic people out of mythology, a people which aspired to escape from its own unhappy homeland to the apparent peace of a distant mountain; but which, in migrating, made some fatal error of judgment and fell into a great chasm of maze-like passages that promise ever to lead to the mountain but end ever against a wall."

By the 1990s, the flow had been reversed. "Atlanta is to black America what Harlem was to black America during the great migrations earlier in the century," said Raymond Winbush, director of the Race Relations Institute at Fisk University. "The willing return of blacks to a region that once had the harshest racial segregation laws in the country reflects dramatic improvements in race relations, at least among the middle-class professional blacks and whites who are moving there."

Three sets of tracks bristle with overhead wires near Newark where the roadbed of the old Pennsylvania Railroad, now Amtrak, crosses the Line. A train flashes by—a red, white, and gray blur—the faces of its passengers pasted to the windows. Just north of the tracks is the Tangent Point—the spot where Mason and Dixon's north-south line from the middle of the Delmarva Peninsula touches the New Castle Circle boundary. I walk along Dixie Line Road, past neat suburban houses surrounded by deep green hyper-fertilized lawns. I find a marker at the side of the road. It's chipped, but the "M" and the "P" are still visible.

There are actually three separate lines between the Middle Point and the intersection with the West Line at 39° 43' 17.4" latitude—The Tangent Line, which runs just under eighty-two miles from the Middle Point to the tangent; the Arc Line, which follows a part of the circular boundary for about 1.4 miles; and, finally, the North Line, which runs about 3.5 miles from the Arc Line to the 39° 43' 17.4" latitude. The Arc Line and the North Line were completed by Mason and Dixon in June, 1766, in less than a week.

The North Line created a pie-shaped, 714-acre piece of land that ran southward in an ever-diminishing width until it ended in a sliver of nothingness at the Arc Line. Here generations of children would amuse themselves by jumping from the state of Maryland, over the state of Pennsylvania, into the state of Delaware. But for residents of the Wedge, the situation would create a state of confusion that would last a century and a half, spilling much ink and a little bit of blood.

Chapter Three

THE NEW CASTLE CIRCLE
NEWARK, DELAWARE TO DELAWARE BAY —
SOUTH AND EAST 22 MILES.

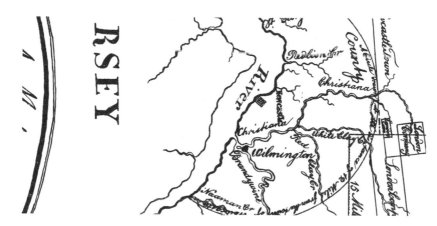

"We are each of us, like our little blue planet,
hung in black space, upheld by nothing but
our mutual reassurances, our loving ties."
                                    —John Updike, *Rabbit at Rest,* 1990

The circular boundary separating the present states of Pennsylvania and Delaware is one of the oldest surveyed lines in America, and it owes its unique shape to a royal whim.

When William Penn received his grant in 1681, the area that is now Delaware was owned by the Duke of York and already occupied by English colonists, who had organized the land into three counties. With some difficulty, Penn persuaded the Duke, who was his godfather, to give him jurisdiction over the so-called Three Lower Counties—but it was stipulated that the newcomers must stay at least twelve miles away from the capital city of New Castle.

It soon became apparent that the people of the Three Lower Counties wanted no part of Quaker rule, and so Penn granted them self-government while continuing to own the land. To delineate the two areas in accord with the Duke's stipulation, it was agreed that the boundary would be a part of a circle drawn with a twelve-mile radius from New Castle. The 120-degree arc would begin at the Delaware River and extend to a point in the general area of the still undetermined Maryland-Pennsylvania border.

On September 26, 1701, Isaac Taylor and Thomas Pierson began running a crude survey of the curved line. They used only a chain and compass, and they marked their work with axe slashes in trees. The whole job took only ten days. From 1702 until the time the Declaration of Independence was written, Pennsylvania and the Three Lower Counties functioned as separate colonies under the Penn family. Then they became separate states—and, over the years, the tree notches disappeared. The location of the boundary became a matter of local tradition, opinion, and conjecture.

Mason and Dixon surveyed a small part of the arc in 1764, but because they had been hired only to mark the boundaries between the lands of the Penns and the Calverts, the New Castle Circle was not an issue that directly concerned them.

MILE 0

I walk along Route 896, the old New London Road, and cross the north-south Mason-Dixon Line from Delaware into Maryland. After about 300 yards, I cross the east-west Mason-Dixon Line from Maryland into Pennsylvania. I retrace my steps, looking for the stone that will mark the juncture of the three states.

Back in Delaware, I find an old farmhouse surrounded by greenhouses and a sign, "Teeter's Horticraft Enterprises." Enolajane Teeter is inside one

Enolajane Teeter has lived near the Wedge all her life.

The Initial Stone marks the point where the West Line begins.

of the greenhouses watering plants. She is wearing rose sweatpants, a gray sweatshirt, unlaced boots with lolling tongues, and a dark blue watch cap. I knock and wave. She opens the door, which comes off its hinges. She carefully rests the door against the wall.

"You're in Delaware right now," she explains. "Pennsylvania and Maryland are just down the road. The marker's on private land, but I can take you to it."

She leads me past a white ranch house and down a winding, double-track dirt road. Summer is rusting into autumn, and the trees are flared bright red and gold. The stone lies on flat ground amid leaves and twigs. It is not a Mason-Dixon stone but was placed here in 1849 as part of a resurvey of the Line. The original stone disappeared sometime during the Revolution. It's called the Initial Stone, and it's about eighty-seven miles north of the Middle Point. Today it marks the point where the northeastern corner of Maryland, the northwestern corner of Delaware, and the southern border of Pennsylvania come together.

However, the four-sided stone is engraved only with two "Ms" and two "Ps" because when it was placed here the land was not in Delaware. At least not legally.

"This was part of the famous Wedge," explains Enolajane, amusement lurking in her eyes. "It was a pie-shaped piece of land that no one knew who owned for a hundred years. It was a no-man's land, and my father used to tell me stories. . . ."

Maps drawn in the second half of the nineteenth-century show

Pennsylvania with a tiny tongue of land jutting down between Maryland and Delaware. This was the Wedge, and while geographers thought it was part of Pennsylvania, the one hundred or so residents fervently believed they lived in Delaware, where they paid taxes, served on juries, and voted. The village of Mechanicsville sat within the Wedge. One Wedge-dweller, William Henry Smith, who lived a half-mile on the Pennsylvania side of the circle, was elected to the Delaware House in 1846 and then to the Delaware Senate in 1850, where he was addressed by his colleagues as "the gentleman from Pennsylvania." During his legislative career, there were several unsuccessful proposals to abolish slavery—one of which failed by a single vote. Smith, a Democrat, always voted against them.

Because of its nebulous status, the Wedge became a site and refuge for lawlessness. "There were cockfights, bulldog fights, and prize fights," says Enolajane. "All these things were illegal. The idea was that if the sheriff showed up, they could claim they were in the other state. It became a kind of island of wickedness. Pennsylvania tried to collect taxes and exercise jurisdiction, but the residents would have none of it."

An Elkton newspaper, the *Cecil Whig,* carried an account of a boxing match in 1867:

> One of those disgraceful brute exhibitions took place at Mechanicsville, Pennsylvania, on Wednesday last, between Bill Kelly, of New York, and Sam Collyer, of Baltimore. The bet was $1000, Collyer winning the fight the hundred and tenth round, after an hour and a half of hard pummeling. A party of the roughs, with one of the principals, stopped at Elkton, on Tuesday night last, where they remained till Wednesday morning. They were very orderly, creating no disturbance, such as is reported to have existed at Newark, Delaware, where the roughs took posses-sion of the Washington House, beat the proprietor and clerk, cre-ating a perfect hell of the village. The spot selected for the ring was in New Castle county, Delaware, near Newark, but the Sheriff made his appearance, and stepping into the ring said he would arrest the first man that attempted to fight. The brief speech from one **held** man who stood in the midst of that circle of roughs, without uttering another word, and unsupported by a posse, as was erroneously reported by the daily press, seemed to strike the crowd of cut-throats with blank amazement; and after regarding the stern officer of the law for a few moments in silence, they

pulled up stakes and marched off for the nearest point on the Pennsylvania line, accompanied by the Delaware Sheriff, who escorted them out of his State. Here, no Pennsylvania officer being present, the exhibition took place. A large number of our Elkton citizens joined the crowd and witnessed the mill, some of them showing their appreciation of the "manly art" by cheering their favorite champion, thus identifying themselves with, and becoming a party to, the disgraceful affair. A number of extra fights were extemporized before and after the prize set to, with the usual pocket-picking, watch stealing, etc., etc., which make up the grand total of such affairs.

A joint commission was created in 1892 to study the problem of not just the Wedge, but the entire New Castle Circle extending some twenty-two miles to the Delaware River. The recommendation was that the Wedge be given to Delaware but that another section be given to Pennsylvania. Thus, farmers with roots in Delaware suddenly found themselves surveyed into Pennsylvania while others with ancestral ties to Pennsylvania awakened as residents of Delaware. The uncertainty dragged on until 1921 when the U.S. Congress finally ratified the 1892 recommendation. The Wedge became part of Delaware—*de jure* as well as *de facto*.

WHITE CLAY CREEK: MILE 1

The Circle bisects the White Clay Creek Preserve, a 2,100-acre natural area in the Brandywine Valley that was donated by the du Pont Family to Delaware and Pennsylvania in 1984. About 600 yards north of the Line is the site of Minguhanan, where Lenni Lenape Indians lived for some 12,000 years before the land was sold to William Penn by Chief Machaloha on October 18, 1683.

Penn was impressed by the Lenape, and in a letter that year he described them as swarthy, tall, and handsome men and women who "tread strong and clever and mostly walk with a lofty chin." White men called them Delawares because they lived near the shore of that river, but they called themselves Lenni Lenape, which translates approximately as "Original People."

They were peaceful agriculturalists, who were often attacked by other tribes. Their great chief, Tammany, was revered for his wisdom, virtue, and kindliness and was believed to be in direct contact with the Great Spirit.

Some of the earliest American settlers are buried in the graveyard of the London Tract Baptist Meeting House, built in 1729.

Only long after Tammany's death did that name come to be associated with corrupt politicians in New York.

Penn believed that the two races could live together harmoniously, and during his lifetime all land transactions and disputes were resolved amicably. His treaties with the Indians are an early example of American tolerance for minorities. But when his sons took control they duped the Lenape out of 1,200 square miles of land in the infamous Walking Purchase of 1737. The Penns got the Lenape to agree to give them as much land as could be covered in a day and a half of walking—and then hired three fast runners who covered fifty-five miles in the allotted time.

A cycle that would last 130 years began. The Lenape would move to a new place, be promised by the government that it would be their permanent home, and then be uprooted by white settlement. Each time the movement was westward, and today about 10,000 Lenapes live near Bartlesville, Oklahoma. A few straggling Lenapes remained in the Brandywine Valley, and they were in constant danger of being seized by slave traders.

The original surveyors of the New Castle Circle showed Minguhanan on their 1701 map, but by the time Mason and Dixon got here, the village was gone and the London Tract Baptist Meeting House had been erected on the site. The meetinghouse, which was built in 1729, now serves as park head-quarters, and Gay Overdevest works here for the Pennsylvania state park system. Her official title is environmental interpretive technician, but she says "I just kind of look after things, try to answer people's questions, and

The site of Mason and Dixon's Post Mark'd West is now marked with a more recent stone.

maybe suggest a nature activity."

Some of the area's earliest settlers rest in the adjacent stone-walled ceme-tery. Overdevest guides me to the most famous grave, the Ticking Tombstone. "The story goes that a local surveyor who was hired by Mason and Dixon swallowed a chronometer while working on the survey. It con-tinued ticking inside of him throughout his life, and when he died and was buried here. . . ." She puts her ear to an unmarked stone. "You can't hear it now, but I have heard it tick." She pauses, reads my eyes for reaction, then adds, "It's probably an underground spring."

Armed with a handwritten map from Overdevest, I set out for the site of the reference marker set up by Mason and Dixon three miles east of the Initial Stone. In their notes, they called it the "Post Mark'd West." On June 12, 1764, the Mason-Dixon party placed a square, rough-hewn oak post near a small stream on a farm owned by Alexander Bryan. All their calcu-lations of latitude and distance for the West Line were based on this post.

Narrow paths, once trod by moccasined feet, wriggle across gentle hills and fields that remind me of the English countryside, and I half expect to bump into a gaunt, eccentric vicar out for his morning stroll with a well-mannered dog. The early colonists must have felt the same way. There are wild orchids along the trail, and beavers have dammed up White Clay Creek and built lodges. The site of the Post Mark'd West is now occupied by a handsome Brandywine granite marker that was placed here in 1953. About one hundred yards to the north, across a flat green field, I can see the foundations of the Bryan farmhouse.

93

FRANKLIN TOWNSHIP, PENNSYLVANIA: NORTH OF MILE 1

North of the New Castle Circle, the terrain steepens and is ill-suited for agriculture. It is on such marginal land that blacks, emancipated by their Quaker masters in the 1700s, set up communities. Later they would be joined by fugitive slaves from south of the Line. Still later these settlements would become stations on the Underground Railroad. Often they had no legal status or name, and were centered on churches.

Union Church was the focus of a black settlement two miles north of the Line in Chester County, Pennsylvania, and about sixty of the former residents are buried in the adjacent cemetery, which is the only vestige of the community. For nearly 100 years even the cemetery was hidden by brambles and vines that climbed around locust trees.

On a dreary, drizzling Sunday morning, thirty or so people—some white, some black—are hacking away with machetes, digging into the wet soil with shovels. Gas-powered weed trimmers shriek through the chilly air. A chainsaw coughs, coughs again, and then roars to life. Robert Maxfield points a work-calloused hand to the top of a hill.

"The church was up there. We have old newspaper clippings that refer to it as the African Methodist Episcopal Church. My grandmother told me that on holidays they'd have to come in shifts so there would be enough places for everyone in the church. There were camp meetings here at the end of the harvest. They'd come here and party for a few days and then go to church service on Sunday."

This land, about seventeen acres in all, has been in Maxfield's family for at least four generations. He still lives in a 200-year-old house that was originally a log cabin. College students and local residents have formed a volunteer group to clear the cemetery.

"Here's the most interesting thing we discovered," Maxfield says, kneeling and brushing mud from a tombstone to reveal the engraving. "Colonel Harry Harris. Co D. 3rd US Inf USCT." There's another nearby. "Amos J. Boyd. Co D, 8th Regiment, USCT. . . ."

On May 22, 1863, the U.S. Department of War issued General Order No. 143, which established the Bureau of Colored Troops. The units of black soldiers recruited to fight the Confederates were called the United States Colored Troops, or USCT. By the end of the war, some 178,000 freedmen and former slaves had enlisted and participated in 449 engagements and thirty-nine major battles.

By and large, the Black troops acquitted themselves well in supporting roles—despite the fact that they were given substandard equipment and supplies. Initially, there was a pay differential under which a white private was paid thirteen dollars a month while a black private received only seven dollars. The 54th Massachusetts Regiment served a year without pay rather than accept the discriminatory wages, and the pay was equalized in 1864.

HOCKESSIN, DELAWARE: SOUTH OF MILE 7

As a lifelong resident of Hockessin, Delaware, and its retired postmaster, Ed "Monk" Gormley is the man who knows where everybody lived in his hometown. He answers the phone on the third ring. "Bulah? Hmmm. Bulah. Bulah. Oh, yeah. Fred Bulah. Wife's name was Sarah. It's out there on Limestone and Valley, heading toward the Pennsylvania line, catty-corner to Tim's Liquor Store. A small chicken farm. There's not much left of it now. . . ."

In fact, there's nothing left of it except a pile of rubble that is being pushed to one side by a grunting yellow bulldozer on a weedy lot a half-mile from the Line. There is no historic sign—nothing to commemorate this site as an important one in American civil rights history.

It was here that Sarah and Fred Bulah had their truck farm, earning a poverty-level income by selling tomatoes, strawberries, eggs, and chickens. In 1944, a brief story appeared in the Wilmington *News-Journal* about a one-year-old black girl who had been found abandoned in the hallway of a white apartment house. The Bulahs adopted the child and named her Shirley Barbara. It would be Sarah's only child, and she vowed to give her the best of everything.

Shirley started school in 1949, and every day Sarah Bulah drove her daughter two miles each way to attend Hockessin School No. 107, the colored school. And every day she watched the yellow school bus pass by the farm carrying children to Hockessin School No. 29, the white school.

One day she waved the bus driver to a halt and asked if Shirley could ride to school. He said to contact the school superintendent, who said to contact the Hockessin school board, who said to contact the governor, who referred her letter to the attorney general, who referred her letter to the

Hockessin School No. 29, which was integrated by Shirley Bulah in 1952, is now a church.

state board of education, which said no, citing a state law that forbade white and black children to ride on the same school bus.

Sarah Bulah sought help from a prominent black Wilmington lawyer, Louis L. Redding, who had just won a battle to integrate the University of Delaware. Redding said he wouldn't fight for Shirley's right to ride the white bus, thereby perpetuating segregation, but he would fight for her right to attend the white school. She agreed, and Redding filed a suit on her behalf challenging the provision of the Delaware Constitution that required the segregation of black and white children in schools of equal quality.

Sarah Bulah knew the schools were not equal. The black school had one room and one teacher. The white school had four rooms and four teachers. The black school had no running water and outdoor toilets. The white school had complete indoor plumbing. The white school had a nurse. The black school had a first aid kit. Unlike the white school, the black school had no auditorium, no dancing classes, no basketball court, no landscaping. Shirley's desk was missing a leg and was propped up by a cinder block. When she was in the second grade, Shirley could not write the letter "B" properly.

After the suit was filed, sales at the Bulah's truck farm dropped dramatically, because white customers no longer stopped. Even many of Hockessin's blacks were opposed and some whispered that the Bulahs didn't want Shirley to associate with black children because she was light-skinned. Other black children refused to sit near Shirley in Sunday school, and a boy spat in her face.

Hockessin Colored School No. 107 is now a community center.

A vocal opponent of the Bulah suit was the Rev. Martin Luther Kilson, pastor of the Chippey African Union Methodist Church, which was next door to the black school. "These folks around here would rather have a colored teacher," he said. "They don't want to be mixed up with no white folks. All we want is a bus for the colored."

No other Hockessin parents would join the suit, but the parents of eight black children from Claymont, Delaware, did. Redding said he chose Hockessin and Claymont for the test case because they were on the Mason-Dixon Line—and therefore peaceful integration was more likely than farther south.

The case went to the Court of Chancery and Judge Collins J. Seitz, who handed down his opinion on April 1, 1952: "I conclude from the testimony that in our Delaware society, State-imposed segregation in education itself results in the Negro children, as a class, receiving educational opportunities which are substantially inferior to those available to white children otherwise similarly situated."

Seitz ordered that Shirley Bulah and the eight Claymont children be admitted to the white schools in their communities immediately. For the first time in American history, a court ordered white public schools to admit black children. Thurgood Marshall, the NAACP attorney who would become a U. S. Supreme Court justice, exulted: "This is the first real victory in our campaign to destroy segregation in American elementary and high schools."

The state of Delaware appealed the ruling to the U.S. Supreme Court, and there it was joined by Washington, D.C., and the states of Virginia, South Carolina, and Kansas. The cases were consolidated into the landmark 1954 decision, *Brown vs. Board of Education.*

Shirley Bulah entered Hockessin School No. 29 in the fall of 1952. Her mother drove her there the first day. She was afraid, but her teacher put her at ease by welcoming her and allowing her to pick out her desk. That afternoon, as usual, the bus came by the Bulah farm, but this time it stopped.

Today, the farmlands of Hockessin have given way to pricey subdivisions and townhouses. The churches are modern, sprawling, and unsteepled. The pile of rubble where the Bulahs lived seems dangerously close to toppling. The red brick school that Shirley Bulah integrated a half-century ago is now the Hockessin Baptist Church, but "Hockessin School 29" is still inscribed over the door. On the other side of the railroad tracks, Colored School No. 107 is now the Hockessin Community Center. Rusted playground equipment is still in the back, and a swing hangs by one chain, swaying gently in the wind.

Shirley Bulah graduated from an integrated high school in 1962, studied to become a nurse for a time, and then joined the Army, where she met her husband and became Shirley Bulah Stamps. They had one son. She is now an ordained minister in the African Union First Colored Methodist Protestant Church, lives in Wilmington, and is an assistant pastor at a church in Marshalltown, N.J. . . .

The electronic voice clicks on. "This is Reverend Shirley Stamps. Please leave a message, and God bless you." She calls back the next day. "I remember that first day of school like it was yesterday. I was scared, but I was too young to understand what was really going on. I didn't realize the significance of what happened until my parents took me to an NAACP meeting when I was eleven or twelve. Thurgood Marshall came over and patted me on the head and thanked me for my courage."

A century before Shirley Bulah stepped on the white school bus, Hockessin was a gateway to freedom for fugitive slaves. Hundreds of exhausted, frightened blacks sought out the big white house sitting on a hill at a right-angle to the Newport and Gap Turnpike. It was built by the

Strathworth estate was the last stop for runaway slaves before crossing the Line.

Jacksons, a Quaker family, in 1763, and named "Strathworth." The top floor garret window had a commanding view of the main road into Pennsylvania, and a guard was posted to give the alarm if a sheriff's posse or bounty hunters showed up. Slave catchers usually searched the house first, so the fugitives were hidden in the barn.

Strathworth is now part of an estate, and there's a big "For Sale" sign in front of it. Only a small pile of gray stones remains on the site of the barn. On the turnpike, a long worm of traffic winds up the hill toward the big blue sign that announces, "PENNSYLVANINA WELCOMES YOU."

In the years before the Civil War, a guard was posted at the Line and the road was blocked by a gate. At night runaway slaves would cross into Pennsylvania off the road. By day, they reached Pennsylvania in the secret compartments of wagons built by the Quakers. Usually, these wagons had heavy cargoes, like bricks, which would be difficult to remove in a search for human cargo. Most of the slaves came here with instructions from Thomas Garrett, a white merchant in Wilmington.

KENNETT SQUARE, PENNSYLVANIA: NORTH OF MILE 7

The Quakers of Chester County were among the first to extend white helping hands to runaways, and the busiest traffic center was Kennett Square, known in the antebellum years as a "hotbed of abolitionists." However, not all Quakers were abolitionists, and the Longwood Meeting House was formed in 1854 by Kennett Square Quakers who were disowned by their co-religionists for anti-slavery activities.

The meetinghouse is now the headquarters of the Brandywine Tourist Information Center, and it has an exhibit about the Underground Railroad. In years past, these walls reverberated with the impassioned oratory of the giants of the American abolitionist movement—William Lloyd Garrison, John Greenleaf Whittier, Susan B. Anthony, Sojourner Truth, and Lucretia Mott. Harriet Tubman frequently worked out of Kennett Square, saving enough money to finance another trip into Maryland.

A group of black children, ranging in age from five to sixteen, have come here by bus from the Immanuel Baptist Church in Elmont, New York, and they are being lectured on the Underground Railroad. They are fidgeting, smuggling whispers to each other, patting yawns back into their faces, teetering on the edge of their chaperones' patience. Finally the lecturer injects a note of finality in her voice and says, "And now I have someone I'd like you to meet. . . ."

A young black woman comes out singing "Amazing Grace." She is costumed in a long skirt, white blouse, and a bright red bandanna on her head. "Hello, my name is Harriet Tubman," she begins. "I was born in Maryland as a slave. I don't remember much about my mother and father because they were always off working in the fields. When I was six, my master began hiring me out to work for local people. Some of them were cruel. One day I found out that my brothers and sisters and I were going to be sold to a slave dealer from Georgia and taken there in a chain gang. That's when I decided to escape. . . ." She draws her audience in, and soon the whole room seems to be standing at attention. After twenty minutes, she asks if anyone has questions; there is an interrogatory hailstorm: What work did you do as a slave? Did you get to see your brother and sister after they were sold off? Did it make you angry to be a slave? Did you like any white people? Did you ever kill anyone? Did you go to church? Did you ever get married? What kind of clothes did you wear? Did you go to school? Did you have your own room? . . . An adolescent girl is awestruck, as though she had lived her entire life for this moment.

Longwood Meeting House stands along U.S. Route 1, which once was the main route to Philadelphia from the south and the west. Nearby is the home of John and Hannah Cox, who concealed hundreds of escapees in their attic and under hay in their barn. To commemorate their fiftieth wedding anniversary, Whittier wrote a poem, "Golden Wedding at

Longwood," which said, in part, "Blessings upon you. What you did for each sad, suffering one/So homeless, faint and naked, unto our Lord was done." Farther along Route 1 is "The Pines," which was the home of Dr. Bartholomew Fussell and his wife, Lydia. Ivy now covers the door leading to the root cellar where slaves could be concealed and, if necessary, escape through a shallow well connected to the room.

One of the great abolitionist families of Kennett Square was the Pennocks. The home of Moses and Mary Pennock is on Route 1 between Longwood Gardens and the town. Their children, especially Samuel, grew up to become anti-slavery activists and were active in the Underground Railroad. Later another family member, Herb Pennock, became a famous baseball pitcher who played for the New York Yankees in the 1920s and was a teammate of Babe Ruth and Lou Gehrig. Pennock went on to become general manager of the Philadelphia Phillies and was elected to the Hall of Fame.

The Kennett Square Historical Commission started raising funds in 1998 for a statue to honor Pennock, but the project was put on ice after it was charged that Pennock was a racist during Jackie Robinson's integration of major league baseball in 1947. A book written by Harold Parrott, an executive with the Brooklyn Dodgers at the time, tells of a conversation between Pennock and Branch Rickey, president of the Dodgers. "You just can't bring that nigger here, Branch," Pennock is quoted as saying. "We're just not ready for that sort of thing yet."

By many accounts, Pennock was a class act, and his defenders point out that Parrott is the sole source of the story. Nevertheless, it is true that Pennock's Phillies were more vicious toward Robinson than any other team—so offensive that fans wrote letters of protest to the baseball commissioner. And there is no evidence that general manager Pennock did anything to stop it. That in itself is enough for Mabel Thompson, a longtime black activist in Kennett Square. "It's difficult to get at the truth. But overall, I believe he was a racist. At least we know for sure that he supported racists."

HAMORTON, PENNSYLVANIA: NORTH OF MILE 11

For slaves fleeing up the Kennett Pike from Wilmington, the first stop across the Mason-Dixon Line was the red brick home of Isaac and Dinah Mendenhall. It was topped by a cupola with windows on all four sides and an excellent view down the main road towards the Line some two miles away. The Mendenhalls designed a sub-cellar in their basement where slaves could be hidden and refreshed before being passed on to the next station. Usually, they were sent here by Thomas Garrett of Wilmington, who instructed them to follow the North Star and "go on and on until you reach a stone gate post and turn in."

I turn in at the stone gate post and am greeted by William and Nancy Barlow, a retired couple who now own the house. They show me a stone over the front door that is inscribed, "I And DM." The Barlows take me to the basement and point to the sub-cellar. "The stairs fell down several years ago with me on them," he says. "There was a tunnel that went under the road and came out in a well across the street. There was a barn there and they could hide in the haymows. The tunnel has been boarded off."

The Mendenhalls built this house in 1859 and called it "Cottage Rest." William says, "We want to come up with a different name. Maybe the Ten Mile House because it was ten miles from Thomas Garrett."

MILE 11

The Kennett Pike used to be a toll road, and right at the Line a small two-room toll house was built in 1780. Charles Twaddell bought the land in 1814, expanded the tollhouse, and opened a tavern called the Spread Eagle. It changed hands several times and came to be known as the Line House. Since authorities from both states would rarely show up at the same time, the tavern's location permitted a certain amount of illegal activity.

The Line House is an old tavern, and the Line runs through the front door.

It was later converted to a private residence, and today Dave Garrett answers my knock at the front door. "The Line runs right through the front door. You're standing in Pennsylvania, I'm in Delaware." Garrett, a retired lawyer, is dressed in a dark blue suit, white shirt, and yellowish silk tie; he's on his way to teach a public administration class at the University of Delaware. He hands me a flashlight and takes me to the basement, where he lifts an iron ring on a wooden trap door. Six wooden steps lead down to a 12-by-6-foot room with stone walls and an arched ceiling. It's damp. "There was a tunnel that used to lead from this room into Pennsylvania. We sealed it off to keep out various creatures. The Line House is on the National Register of Historic Places, and it's mentioned in some of the accounts about Harriet Tubman."

It is believed that Tubman went by here on her initial flight to freedom, and some biographers record her reaction: "I had crossed the line of which I had so long been dreaming. I was free. I looked at my hands to see if I was the same person. There was such a glory over everything. The sun came through like gold through the trees and over the fields, and I felt like I was in Heaven."

WILMINGTON, DELAWARE: SOUTH OF MILE 13

A modern, built-by-the-lowest-responsible-bidder red brick building is at the corner of Fourth and Shipley, and a sign notes that the home of Thomas Garrett stood near here at 333 Shipley Street. Garrett was one of the Underground Railroad's most active conductors, and the many black friends of the Quaker merchant stood guard here nightly to protect him from slave-owners infuriated by the loss of their property.

It was from here that escapees made their final, frantic dash for the Line. Most of them tried at night because any white person who encountered a suspicious black had the right to make a citizen's arrest on the spot. Trains and roads were carefully watched, and Garrett employed many different stratagems. He would give a runaway a rake or shovel to carry as if he were going to work. Several women fugitives crossed the Line in his personal carriage dressed in his wife's clothing. In his written communications to the Mendenhalls and other agents, he referred to the impending arrival of "bales of black wool."

Harriet Tubman regularly stopped at 333 Shipley, and Garrett came to

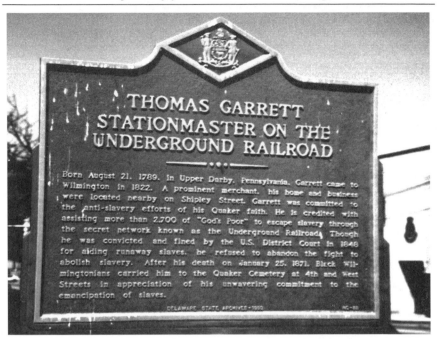

A historic sign marks the site of the home of Thomas Garrett in Wilmington, Delaware.

have deep fears for her, which he expressed in a letter: "There is now much more risk on the road than there has been for several months past . . . yet, as it is Harriet, who seems to have a special angel to guide her on her journey of mercy, I have hope."

But it was Garrett who got caught trying to help a freedman smuggle his family across the Line to Philadelphia in 1848. He was tried in federal court, where one of the judges was Roger B. Taney, who as a Supreme Court justice nine years later would write the Dred Scott decision, ruling that blacks had no constitutional rights. Garrett was convicted and ordered to reimburse the slave owners for the lost property. It left him bankrupt, but he told the court: "I have assisted over 1,400 in twenty-five years on their way to the North, and I now consider the penalty now imposed might be as a license for the remainder of my life. If any of you know any slave who needs assistance, send him to me."

Garrett got his business restarted and resumed his illegal activities. In his lifetime, it is believed that he helped some 2,700 runaways reach the Line.

The U.S. Congress has been considering legislation that would create a network of Underground Railroad sites to be managed by the National

Park Service. Pinning down many of these sites will be difficult because the Underground Railroad is long on legend, short on documentation. Sometimes it seems that every 200-year-old house north of the Mason-Dixon Line had a root cellar or a spring house or a crawl space or a secret compartment or trapdoor or a corncrib that sheltered fugitive slaves.

Over the years, the legends have expanded, rumor has percolated into fact, and the impression has been created that the entire white population north of the Line was opposed to slavery. But in truth the abolitionists were a tiny minority, and often they had to conceal their activities from their white Northern neighbors. There was even racism within the Underground Railroad. Fugitives sometimes were not permitted inside the homes of conductors and were shackled until they moved on. Historian Larry Gara warned of these distortions in his 1961 book, *The Liberty Line.*

> The characteristic outlines of the traditional version reveal that it is largely derived from postwar abolitionist reminiscences. The abolitionists' accounts tended to neglect the role of the fugitive slaves themselves in the escape drama, gave the impression that all successful escapees were passengers on the mysterious line, and implied that the 'railroad' was a nationwide abolitionist organization which operated in secret. In reality, it is probable that fugitive slaves succeeded, if at all, mostly by their own efforts. Such help as they received came sometimes from abolitionists, sometimes from other groups, and was often casual and temporary.

Nevertheless, there was a small, voluntary, and spontaneous group of white and black people who worked to usher black runaways to freedom, and thousands of enslaved men and women escaped by riding an imaginary railroad across an imaginary line.

Coded spirituals were used by slaves plotting an escape. The River Jordan sometimes meant the Line; the Promised Land was Pennsylvania. After the Fugitive Slave Law of 1850 allowed slave owners to pursue runaways into Northern states and only Canada offered safe refuge, the singing shifted to "O Canaan, sweet Canaan, I am bound for the land of Canaan."

"Follow the Drinking Gourd" was the code spiritual for the North Star, which was found in the Big Dipper—the same North Star that Mason and Dixon had watched night after night a century earlier. Escapees were instructed to follow the North Star. The slaveholders were aware of this and frequently raged at the star and vowed to tear it from the heavens. The anti-slavery poet John Pierpont wrote a mocking poem from Boston in 1843 called "Slave holders Address to the North Star."

> Star of the North, thou art not bigger
> Than is the diamond in my ring;
> Yet every black, star-gazing nigger
> Stares at thee, as at some great thing!
> Yes, gazes at thee, till the lazy
> And thankless rascal is half crazy.
> Some Quaker scoundrel must have told 'em
> That, if they take their flight tow'rd thee,
> They'd get where "massa" cannot hold 'em;
> And, therefore, to the North they flee.
> Fools! to be led off, where they can't earn
> Their living, by thy lying lantern. . . .
> . . . Men who have faces firm as dough,
> And, as we set their noses, go—
> To these, we'll get some scribe to write,
> And tell them not to let thee shine—
> Excepting of a cloudy night—
> Any where, south of Dixon's line.
> If, beyond that, thou shin'st, an inch,
> We'll have thee up before Judge Lynch:—
> And when, thou abolition star,
> Who preachest freedom, in all weathers,
> Thou hast got on a coat of tar,
> And, over that, a cloak of feathers,
> That thou art "fixed" shalt none deny,
> If there's a fixed star in the sky.

The first stationmasters were Quakers, whose denomination was formally known as the Religious Society of Friends, and thus the traditional announcement of the arrival of "passengers" was "a Friend with friends." Because travel was usually at night and therefore slower, the stations were relatively close together—about ten to twenty miles apart.

Though today it is often viewed as a racist caricature, the traditional black lawn jockey was used as a marker along the railroad. Green ribbons were tied to the arms of the statue to signal safety, red ribbons meant danger.

CHADDS FORD, PENNSYLVANIA: NORTH OF MILE 13

About a mile north of the Line on Bullock Road is a pile of rubble that once formed an octagonal building that was a school before the Civil War. It was closed for lack of pupils in 1890, and the following year Lydia A. Archie bought the building and began holding religious services for the local black community. "Mother Archie" lived next door until she died in 1932. When Andrew Wyeth, the artist who lived nearby, learned it was to be sold in 1952, he went out in the snow and painted it. The work, "Archie's Corner," is now in a private collection.

MILE 17

The Line runs diagonally through a stone farmhouse that was built in 1742. It was originally part of a 212-acre farm owned by Richard Sanderson, but when he died in 1769 he split it into three parcels and left a thirty-acre tract to his slave, James Cherry, whom he also granted his freedom. About 1834 the farmhouse was purchased by the Ebright family and became an Underground Railroad stop.

The house now is an office for the Winterset Farms Mobile Home Park, a family business operated by Sheila Moran, who was born here. "My grandfather bought it from the Ebrights," she says. She takes me to the basement and shows me a brick alcove about five feet high and four feet deep. "They would hide in here until nightfall, and then move North. This is on the Delaware side of the house."

A stone marker, placed here during the 1892 resurvey, is about ten feet from the back door. "Before my family moved in, two Ebright brothers lived here. They were both bachelors. They set up the kitchen stove so the line ran through it, and when they made breakfast they liked to say that the eggs cooked in Pennsylvania and the coffee perked in Delaware. Then they'd sit down to eat in different states."

MILE 21

From a hill in a rundown neighborhood that seems inhabited only by black people, Amtrak's main line and three sets of tracks dwindle off toward Philadelphia. There have been rails here since 1837. Before the Civil War they were used by the Philadelphia, Wilmington and Baltimore Railroad, and many slaves escaped by this route.

However, the railroad was not sympathetic. Faced with lawsuits from slave owners, they imposed tough identification requirements for blacks, and at the President Street Depot in Baltimore, this sign was posted: "Notice to Colored People—All Colored People (Bond or Free) wishing to travel on the Philadelphia, Wilmington and Baltimore Railroad, will be required to bring with them to the Ticket Office, President Street Depot, some responsible white person, a citizen of Baltimore, known to the under-signed, to sign a bond to the company before they can proceed. . . ."

Nevertheless, hundreds escaped on the train. The most notable was Frederick Douglass, who traveled the route on September 3, 1838, using forged seaman's papers that enabled him to pass as a free black. He remembered his fear before the journey.

> To accomplish my escape seemed a very difficult thing. The railroad from Baltimore to Philadelphia was under regulations so stringent that even free travelers were almost excluded. They must have free papers; they must be measured and carefully examined before they could enter the cars; and could go only in the daytime, even when so examined. . . .
>
> I was well on the way to Havre de Grace before the conductor came into the negro car to collect tickets and examine the papers of his black passengers. This was a critical moment in the drama. My whole future depended upon the decision of this conductor. Agitated though I was while this ceremony was proceeding, still, externally, at least, I was apparently calm and self-possessed. He went on with his duty—examining several colored passengers before reaching me. He was somewhat harsh in tone and peremptory in manner until he reached me, when, strange enough, and to my surprise and relief, his whole manner changed. Seeing that I did not readily produce my free papers, as the other colored persons in the car had done, he said to me, in friendly contrast with his bearing toward the others: "I suppose you have your free papers?"

To which I answered: "No sir; I never carry my free papers to sea with me."

"But you have something to show that you are a freeman, haven't you?"

"Yes, sir," I answered; "I have a paper with the American Eagle on it, and that will carry me around the world."

With this I drew from my deep sailor's pocket my seaman's protection, as before described. The merest glance at the paper satisfied him, and he took my fare and went on about his business. This moment of time was one of the most anxious I ever experienced. Had the conductor looked closely at the paper, he could not have failed to discover that it called for a very different-looking person from myself, and in that case it would have been his duty to arrest me on the instant, and send me back to Baltimore from the first station. When he left me with the assurance that I was all right, though much relieved, I realized that I was still in great danger: I was still in Maryland, and subject to arrest at any moment.

William and Ellen Craft, husband and wife, traveled from Baltimore to Philadelphia on the Philadelphia, Wilmington and Baltimore Railroad in 1848. She was light-skinned and disguised herself as the male owner of her husband. She had her head bandaged and her arm in a sling to provide her with an excuse for not signing the requisite paperwork for slave passage. In 1856 Henry Brown packed himself in a 2-by-8-by-3-foot crate in Richmond, Virginia, and had himself shipped on the PW&B—and thereafter was known to all as Henry "Box" Brown. That same year Charlotte Giles and Harriet Eglin rode the PW&B to freedom by dressing in black, covering their faces with veils and passing as women in mourning.

Of course, the PW&B was just as likely to be the route back to bondage accompanied by a master or bounty hunter.

After slavery was abolished, rigid segregation on trains was imposed by law, custom, and railroad policy in Delaware and Maryland. This was the era of steam power, and the Jim Crow car usually was placed nearest the engine and absorbed most of the smoke and soot. Often only half a car was used, with baggage placed in the other half. Railroad employees were insulting to black passengers, and newsboys placed their bundles on the seats, even if black passengers had to stand. Although blacks could not enter the white cars, whites had free access to the Jim Crow car and frequently used it to smoke.

Rail terminals had separate entrances, waiting rooms, ticket windows, lunch counters, and rest rooms, and the black facilities were invariably inferior. Because the sleeping cars were owned by the Pullman Company rather than the railroads, blacks could get a sleeping berth—if they had someone purchase the ticket in the North and then mail it to them. Even then, the white passengers were given blue blankets while pink blankets were handed to blacks—just to assure whites they would not get one that had been racially contaminated.

Some trains denied blacks access to the dining car, but they were allowed to order from the menu at full price and eat in their seats. More often, seating in dining cars was segregated, sometimes by a curtain, which was removed once northbound trains crossed the Line. Novelist Toni Morrison describes it in *Jazz*.

"Breakfast in the dining car. Breakfast in the dining car. Good morning. Full breakfast in the dining car." He held a carriage blanket over his arm and from underneath it drew a pint bottle of milk, which he placed in the hands of a young woman with a baby asleep across her knees. "Full breakfast."

He never got his way, this attendant. He wanted the whole coach to file into the dining car, now that they could. Immediately, now that they were out of Delaware and a long way from Maryland there would be no green-as-poison curtain separating the colored people eating from the rest of the diners. The cooks would not feel obliged to pile extra helpings on the plates headed for the curtain; three lemon slices in the iced tea, two pieces of coconut cake arranged to look like one—to take the sting out of the curtain; homey it up with a little extra on the plate. Now, skirting the City, there were no green curtains; the whole car could be full of colored people and everybody on a first-come first-serve basis. If only they would. If only they would tuck those little boxes and baskets underneath the seat; close those paper bags, for once, put the bacon-stuffed biscuits back into the cloth they were wrapped in, and troop single file through the five cars ahead on into the dining car, where the table linen was at least as white as the sheets they dried on juniper bushes; where the napkins were folded with a crease as stiff as the ones they ironed for Sunday dinner; where the gravy was as smooth as their own, and the biscuits did not take second place to the bacon-stuffed ones they wrapped in cloth. Once in a while it happened. Some well-shod woman with two young girls, a preacherly kind of man with a watch chain and a rolled-brim hat might stand up, adjust their clothes and weave through the coaches toward the tables, foamy white with heavy silvery knives and forks. Presided over and waited upon by a black man who did not have to lace his dignity with a smile.

During World War II, black and white soldiers on troop trains bound for training camps in the South would be separated at or near the Line. Bernadine Flanagan, a Northern black, joined the Women's Army Corps. "We had our own barracks and white Wacs had their own barracks. We had our own training facilities and they had their own training facilities. I was surprised because in New London, Connecticut, where I grew up, everything was integrated. I left New London with white girls to travel to Fort Des Moines. We got on the train going south, and we were separated when we got down to the Mason-Dixon Line. I was told that I had to move to another section of the train. . . . The whole military service was a shock to me because I had no idea it was segregated. I don't know what I was thinking about. But being from an integrated town, I just didn't think that way."

Jim Crow permeated nearly every aspect of life in Maryland and Delaware—buses, airports, restaurants, schools, hotels, sporting events, theaters. Littleton Mitchell, a Delaware NAACP leader, remembered growing up in the 1950s. "When I went downtown in Milford, I had to say 'Sir' before I could get waited on in the stores. We never got to see Santa Claus because Santa Claus went to the volunteer firehouse, and blacks weren't allowed in there. When we went to baseball games, we had to sit down beyond the third base area, sort of out in left field on the line. So there were many things. When we went to the movies, we had to sit upstairs way up there in the back of the balcony. Our whole life was made that way—to grow up angry."

In such ways did one group of people in a society tell another group of people that they are inferior—and make them feel inferior.

MARCUS HOOK, PENNSYLVANIA, AND CLAYTON, DELAWARE: MILE 22

The end of the Circle is a fingernail across the eyeball. An industrial skyline smudges the bright face of the day—smokestacks, tanks, towers, hissing valves, and roaring flare—a vast petrochemical wasteland, sulfurous

The Line bisects a refinery in Marcus Hook, Pennsylvania.

and pungent. The Line goes through a steel mill and a refinery on its way to the Delaware River.

Marcus Hook was a quiet village in 1902 when the Sun Oil Co. decided it was an ideal location for its east coast refinery. The operation mushroomed, other industries came to town and 5,000 people worked here.

In the early 1700s, Marcus Hook was a busy port twenty miles south of Philadelphia that attracted cargo ships, which in turn attracted pirates, including Edward Teach, better known as Blackbeard. A local historian gave this account: "Brutal, bloodthirsty and utterly depraved, this hideous monster cruised along the coast, capturing and sinking merchant ships after gutting them of their valuable cargoes. He knew no mercy and always compelled the helpless crews of captured vessels to walk the plank or else hacked them to pieces."

A blockhouse to shelter colonists from Indian attacks was built on the south side of the Line in 1654 at the direction of Johann Rising, who was the last governor of a Swedish colony here. Subsequently, it came under the control of the Dutch, the English, and the Americans. Its walls are two feet thick, and the loopholes through which muskets were fired are still visible. Just now it is surrounded by yellow caution tape, and workmen are shoring up the stone foundation.

In Mason and Dixon's time, there was a house and mill next to the blockhouse that had been purchased by Thomas Robinson in 1749. A few years later he was killed fighting Indians, and his family opened an inn.

The Robinson House was on the main road to Philadelphia, and its roster of guests included George Washington and the Marquis de Lafayette. Today it stands, muted and vacant, looking on the Philadelphia Pike like an old prima donna facing the audience. A milestone in front reads, "20M to P."

The spot where Marcus Hook and Clayton meet at the Line was a favorite site for dueling in the first half of the nineteenth century. Many military officers, at least one congressman, and at least one newspaper editor fought here on forgotten points of honor. More than one hundred men died here from their wounds.

Runaway slaves came up the Philadelphia Pike, and if they were lucky, they did not stop at the home of Hannah Pennock, a free black woman who lived just across the Line in Pennsylvania. She would lure the fugitives into her house with promises of helping them get to Philadelphia, but then deliver them over to bounty hunters to be returned South. She became wealthy and died in 1897 at the age of 105.

A uniformed security guard meets me at the refinery gate. She's cordial and helpful, but uncomprehending. She drives me to a squat, one-story building near the water's edge. It's a fire prevention substation that takes water from the river. The marker, placed there during the 1892 resurvey, is begrimed but arrow-straight. There are puddles all around it. Styrofoam, driftwood, cardboard, and other debris have washed up on the rocky shore. A big tanker is anchored in the middle of the river.

"This is the chemical part of the plant," she explains. "We make a lot of ethylene oxide, which is used in heavy-duty soaps and detergents."

DIVERSION: PHILADELPHIA, PENNSYLVANIA

Under the Penn-Calvert agreement of 1760, the northern boundary of Maryland was a parallel of latitude fifteen miles south of the southernmost point in Philadelphia. With the help of maps and local officials, Mason and Dixon determined that this point was near a house occupied by Thomas Plumstead and Joseph Huddle on Cedar Street, which is now named South Street.

The area was called Southwark and was peopled by shipbuilders, rope and sail makers, dockworkers, and craftsmen. Across the street was a busy market that stretched for several blocks. Fruits and vegetables were available in season, and year-round vendors offered fish and meat, including raccoon, possum, and bear bacon.

At Second and Chestnut, across the street from First Presbyterian Church, was the slave auction, which was regularly advertised in Benjamin Franklin's Pennsylvania *Gazette*. When Mason and Dixon were here, one in every 10 residents was a slave—some 1,500 in all. Franklin himself sold slaves here, once advertising: "To be sold: a likely negro wench, about thirty-five years of age; is an exceeding good cook, washwoman and ironer, and is very capable of doing all sorts of housework. Inquire of the printer."

Another slave owner was Benjamin Chew, who was a judge and one of the Pennsylvania commissioners overseeing the work of Mason and Dixon. Chew kept slaves on a plantation in Kent County, Delaware. One of them, Richard Allen, purchased his freedom, moved to Philadelphia, and founded the African Methodist Episcopal Church.

Robert Morris, who would later sign the Declaration of Independence, operated a company that imported thousands of slaves from Africa for sale in America between 1760 and 1766. Morris' business partner, Thomas Willing, also was a commissioner for the Mason-Dixon project. In 1761 the firm advertised the sale of 170 Negroes who had just arrived from Guinea. Morris amassed a fortune, and used part of it to help underwrite the American Revolution.

Today Southwark is called Queen's Village, and it's a pleasant area of small shops, restaurants, and townhouses. The market, which opened in 1745, has been restored in red brick, and it is a National Historic Landmark. The site of the Plumstead-Huddle House is now occupied by an

The Plumstead-Huddle House, which Mason and Dixon found to be the southernmost point in Philadelphia.

Italian restaurant, but no historic marker tells of its earlier significance.

Soon after they arrived, Mason and Dixon hired a carpenter to build an observatory near the Plumstead-Huddle House, and on the clear, cold night of December 19, 1763, they made their first astronomical reading in America. They continued until January 4, 1764, when they determined that this point was at a latitude of 39 degrees, 56 minutes, 29.1 seconds. Later observations with better equipment would find this to be only 2.5 seconds in error. They spent two days double-checking, for every other boundary they set in America would be tied to this calculation.

Since going directly south from this point would place them in New Jersey, their plan was to move west some thirty-one miles, set up a point at latitude 39° 56' 29.1", and then move south fifteen miles to Maryland. On January 6, Mason wrote in his journal: "Set out from Philadelphia with a Quadrant to find (nearly) a Place in the Forks of Brandiwine having the same Latitude as the South Point of the city of Philadelphia."

Chapter Four

THE WEST LINE
NORTHEAST CORNER TO THE
SUSQUEHANNA RIVER — 23 MILES.

"Sufficient attention has not been paid to the difference between slavery, such as we have kept it in our colonies, and slavery as it was generally established among the ancients. A white slave, in ancient times, had no other cause of humiliation than his present lot; if he was freed, he could mix straightway with free men and become their equal . . . But in the present case, it is not only the slave who is beneath his master; it is the Negro who is beneath the white man. No act of enfranchisement can efface this unfortunate distinction."

—Marquis de Chastellux, *Travels in North American the Years 1780, 1781 and 1782*

Mason and Dixon returned to the Harlan farm on Brandywine Creek in early December, 1764, to ride out the brutal Pennsylvania winter. Throughout his time in America, Mason took a keen interest in his New World surroundings. On February 11, 1765, Mason took an excursion on horseback to New York City. He crossed the frozen Delaware River into New Jersey and was at Princeton on February 14, where he wrote in his journal about "the most Elegant built Colledge I've seen in America." He rode into New York the next day, but he left no impressions whatsoever in his journal, and he was on his way back to his scientific labors by February 21.

His journal comes to life on February 24, a Sunday, near Mount Holly, New Jersey. "Met some boys just come out of the Quakers Meeting House, as if the De--l had been with them." They blocked his way, and he tapped his horse on the head with the whip, which brought the animal "to the ground as if shot dead." Mason went sprawling from his mount, "I over his head one way, and wig and whip anoth-

er." *Mason struggled up and walked his horse past the Meeting House, "the Friends pouring out very serene, as if all had been well." He nursed soreness and bruises the next day, and rejoined Dixon at Harlan's by the end of the month.*

On March 1, they began planning for the West Line, which would begin at the Northeast Corner of Maryland along at latitude 39° 43' 17.4". Their measurements would be made from the Post Mark'd West, which was three miles east of the Northeast Corner at the same latitude. They were delayed for more than a month by bad weather—first cloudy skies that obscured the stars, and then by a blizzard that dumped three feet of snow. They finally set off on April 5.

The long West Line presented a special problem because a parallel of latitude is not a straight line but follows the curvature of the earth. To stay on a parallel of latitude on the surface of the earth, they were obliged to keep changing direction—slightly. Thus, the surveyors kept drifting off the true parallel—as they knew they would—and stopped every dozen miles or so to recalculate their position and offset

The bulk of Charles Mason's journal is filled with notes on stellar observations like these.

the error to get back on the true parallel.

And so it was that after moving westward for about twelve miles, crossing Little Christiana Creek, Great Christiana Creek, and the Elk River, they stopped to check on their latitude. They had five consecutive fair nights that enabled them to study carefully the positions of Alpha Lyrae, Capella, and Alpha Cygni. Using this stellar information, they found they had deviated about 129 feet north of the parallel; they made a slight correction in latitude, and on April 29 again pushed westward.

They continued the Line for the next two weeks, crossing the serpentine Octoraro River three times in about a half-mile on May 9. About twenty-three miles from the Northeast Corner, they stopped again on May 12 — only about 500 feet from the Susquehanna River. Mason and Dixon spent nearly two weeks reading the stars, calculated the deviation at 382 feet northward, and made the adjustment. They then went to the east bank of the Susquehanna, whose width at that point they figured at about 4,500 feet.

AVONDALE, PENNSYLVANIA: NORTH OF MILE 0

William Miller built a farm on what is now Ellicott Avenue about 1730, and in 1812 he added a stone barn that has a twenty-eight-foot tunnel and was used to conceal runaways. An arrow pointing north is chiseled into the crossbeam at the top of the tunnel. The area next to the tunnel was used to exercise horses, which obliterated the footprints of the slaves. The slaves were then taken north at night in a wagon.

KEMBLESVILLE, PENNSYLVANIA: NORTH OF MILE 3

A hall on the property of the Kemblesville Methodist Church was rented on December 19, 1923, for a Ku Klux Klan rally. Some 600 Klansman from Delaware and Pennsylvania crowded into the hall to hear Dr. J. H. Hawkins, a Protestant minister from Atlanta, Georgia, who was frequently interrupted by hissing from outside hecklers. When Dr. Hawkins questioned whether Catholics were good Americans, a melee broke out. There were no serious injuries, and the next day the West Chester newspaper observed: "It was the liveliest evening the little village has experienced in many years, and there are many sore heads being cared for as a result of the battling."

One of Maryland's few remaining covered bridges is near the Line at Fair Hill.

FAIR HILL, MARYLAND: SOUTH OF MILE 5

Hundreds of fishermen line the banks of Big Elk Creek in the 7,000-acre Fair Hill Natural Resource Management Area, which once was the private fox-hunting preserve of William du Pont Jr. He built tunnels and bridges across roads and creeks so riders and foxhounds could move freely.

A sign, "MOVIE SITE," directs me to a field that holds a replica of a nineteenth century farmhouse, barn, privy, spring house, corn crib, and smokehouse. It was the set for the Disney movie *Beloved*, starring Oprah Winfrey and Danny Glover, based on Toni Morrison's novel about the struggles of an escaped slave and her family seeking to adjust to emancipation. There are flashbacks to a slave ship crossing, a Georgia chain gang, and a cruel overseer in Kentucky.

Morrison depicts slavery as a family-destroying institution in which fathers and sons, mothers and daughters, husbands and wives, and brothers and sisters are routinely and abruptly separated forever. Families were separated by sales, not deaths, and slave sale days were more solemn occasions than funerals.

DIVERSION: EMBREEVILLE, PENNSYLVANIA

The Harlan farmhouse "at the forks of the Brandywine," which Mason and Dixon used as their center of operations from 1764 until 1768, is at the corner of Embreeville Road and Star Gazer Road. Woodsmoke is pluming from the chimney. Dr. Kate Roby greets me at the door, but beckons me toward a grassy sward some one hundred yards north of the house where a rose-and-gray rock, about one foot high, is surrounded by a protective stone wall. There is the smell of honeysuckle and freshly mown grass.

"It's amazing that the stone survived," she says. "It was sitting in a cornfield that was farmed for hundreds of years, but it was never knocked down. The historical society dug up the stone, set it in concrete, and put the wall around it in 1908," she says. "It's white quartz and was very ordinary in those days. There were thousands of such stones along the Brandywine. This was John Harlan's vegetable garden. Very few people stop to look at it, but it's a very important part of American history."

Mason and Dixon placed the stone here in 1764 to mark the point where they made astral observations that would be a reference point for the entire Line. It is on the same parallel of latitude—39° 56' 29.1"—as the Huddle-Plumstead House in Philadelphia and thirty-one miles to the east. From here they measured fifteen miles south to find the Maryland-Pennsylvania border. There was nothing special about the distance of thirty-one miles—it could have been thirty, or thirty-two or thirty-five. The only requirement was that they go west far enough so that when they turned south fifteen miles, they would be within easy measuring distance of the line from the Middle Point to the New Castle Circle.

"They had a tent built specially to house their equipment," Roby says. "They were out here every clear night, looking up at the heavens. The local farmers started calling them the Star Gazers, and this became the Star Gazers Stone.

"There's a stream not far from here called Punch Run, and the story came down through the Harlan family that when Mason and Dixon got out here from Philadelphia, they had a wild party and a lot of punch was spilled into the stream. . . ."

The Harlans were among the first Quaker families to follow William Penn to the New World. They built the farmhouse along the Brandywine about 1724, and added to it in 1758. Roby, a veterinarian, bought the fieldstone farmhouse in 1983 with the help of her brother, who's a historic preservationist. They are restoring the building and researching its history. Sitting at the rustic kitchen table, Roby opens a file folder with deeds and land records.

"The farm was built by George Harlan, but his son, John Harlan, lived here when Mason and Dixon were here. John died sometime before 1768 by drowning in the Brandywine. The Harlan family lived here until 1956.

We're only the third family to own it. The house has been reconfigured since Mason and Dixon were here, but the original walls are intact."

When the stone was turned over to the Chester County Historical Society in 1908, Henry K. Harlan, a lineal descendant of John Harlan, said that each succeeding generation had been instructed that the stone was historically significant and should never be moved.

Roby points to one of the remaining features of the house, a walk-in fireplace. "The Harlans used it for cooking. Years later, Indian Hannah used to come here. She'd sit right there by the fire place in a rocking chair. Her grave is just up the street. . . ."

A half-mile down the road from the Harlan farm a dirt lane leads onto the grounds of what once was the Chester County poorhouse, where Indian Hannah died in 1802. She was believed to be the last Lenni Lenape in the Brandywine Valley.

Hannah was born near Kennett Square about 1730. She spent her life wandering the countryside from farm to farm, selling brooms and herbal medicines. She also made baskets from oak and ash plants, which she decorated with bright paints she concocted herself. Today they are considered museum specimens. When sales fell off, she sewed, performed minor chores, and told fortunes. Hannah was known to everyone, and she was respected for her dignity and wisdom.

She ended her days in the poorhouse, and she was buried without ceremony. But around 1920 a Quaker poet, John Russell Hayes, researched Hannah's life and persuaded the county to place a marker at her gravesite that is still there: "HERE RESTS INDIAN HANNAH. THE LAST OF THE LENNI-LENAPE IN CHESTER COUNTY WHO DIED IN 1802." Hayes' poem about Hannah begins:

> Last of her race,
> She sleeps in this lone grave
> Lowly and lone
> And dim and half forgotten.

LEWISVILLE, PENNSYLVANIA: AT MILE 5

The miniature Lewisville Post Office is just north of the Line, and the postmistress is amiable and voluble. "The Line goes right through the side of the building. You can see where it veers off. It's not at a right angle to the road. We live right next to the cemetery. We tried to maintain it for a while, but it was too much. Now a man with a tractor from the church cuts it a couple times a year. You can go back there."

My boots and cuffs get wet in the high, dewy grass. Oak trees soar all around me with 200-year grips on the soil, holding out against the odds. The iron gate is unhinged and leaning up against a rubble that was once a stone wall. About half the tombstones are tipped over. The Old Stone Graveyard was an appendage to Rock Presbyterian Church, which was founded here in 1724. The Line is about one hundred yards away. The first burial was in 1733, and the register lists 109 others—the last in 1872.

Philip Tanner was killed by a panther in 1751, and the stonemason etched the figure of a panther on his tombstone, probably as a warning to others. David Warry was killed by an Indian, and the profile of an Indian is on his stone. Jane Hathron made her departure on December 16, 1748, when a bolt of lightning flashed through a room where she was playing cards. Her stone shows a hand holding the four of diamonds as a warning about the sins of gaming. Such "sermons in stone" were fairly common in the eighteenth century.

Rock Presbyterian Church, on the Maryland side of the Line, and its Old Stone Graveyard on the Pennsylvania side, were here when Mason and Dixon came through.

Rock Church, which is on the Maryland side of the Line, originally was called "Church Upon Elk River," and it was nothing more than a log hut with a dirt floor. The present handsome stone church was built by Scotch-Irish settlers in 1761, and the name was changed in 1801.

HOPEWELL FARM: SOUTH OF MILE 6

In the early 1700s, there was a great migration of Scotch-Irish (lowland Scots who lived for several generations in northern Ireland) to America. Among them were members of the Mackey family, who settled along the Line within a forty-mile radius of the point where the three states now meet.

Robert Mackey, an elder at Rock Presbyterian Church, built a fieldstone farmhouse on a 300-acre tract in Maryland about 500 yards from the Line in 1761 and called it Hopewell. Eight generations later it is superintended by Tucker Mackey, who is trim and fit at seventy-six and could pass for Carl Sandburg. He tethers a part-this, part-that dog to a tree and invites me in for a glass of iced tea.

"You've probably noticed a lot of building activity around here," he says. "Farmers are selling out to developers left and right. There's too much money involved. I don't want to see that happen to Hopewell. Once it's gone, it's gone. Nobody's buying subdivisions and converting them to farms."

Hopewell Farm, about 500 yards south of the Line, was built in 1761.

Mackey is among hundreds of Maryland farmers who have attempted to preserve their land by selling the development rights to the state and placing their farms in a perpetual preserve. Similar programs are in place in Delaware and Pennsylvania.

They may be too late. All along the Line, rural America is being chopped into five-acre pieces. Down come the barns and silos, up go housing developments, where the only fertilizer is Scott's Turfbuilder. Piersons Ridge, Meetinghouse Meadows, Hunters Crossing, Hunters Ridge, Hunters Farms, Tennyson, Runnymede, Carriage Run, Morgan Hollow, Surrey Hills, Fox Brook, Wingate Farms, Horseshoe Hills. . . . Farm-to-market roads have been transformed into cheap necklaces dangling fast food joints and muffler shops. The down-to-earth beauty of rural areas and their link to America's past is endangered, and there is a real question of how much longer there will be a countryside worth living in and looking at.

LINCOLN UNIVERSITY: NORTH OF MILE 8

A small army of outsiders is whipping Lincoln into parade-ground neatness in preparation for its 140th commencement. Grass is being mowed, flowers are being potted, chairs are being set out in neat rows, signs are being repainted.

I stop for directions at the Kwame Nkrumah (Class of '39) Visitors Center. A student worker directs me past the Thurgood Marshall (Class of '30) Living-Learning Center to the Langston Hughes (Class of '29) Library. . . .

Where Lincoln University now stands once stood Hinsonville, a scattered community of a half-dozen black families established by Emory Hinson in 1830. Fugitive slaves crossed the Susquehanna at Havre de Grace or Conowingo and made their way along the Elk River and crossed the Line to Hinsonville, where they found temporary refuge.

On December 31, 1851, Thomas McCreary, a professional slave catcher from Baltimore, came to the Pennsylvania farm of Joseph C. Miller and forcibly abducted Rachel Parker, a seventeen-year-old free black girl who was apprenticed to Miller. McCreary took the girl by carriage across the Line to Perryville, caught a train to Baltimore, and placed her in his slave pen for sale to the South. When Miller learned of the kidnapping, he went to Baltimore and, with the help of a sympathetic Quaker, obtained a court order delaying any sale of Parker.

Miller then boarded the train home, but never showed up. He was found hanging from a tree at a station a few miles outside of Baltimore. Local authorities ruled it a suicide by hanging, but two Pennsylvania physicians examined him and concluded he had died from a large dose of arsenic.

John Miller Dickey, a Presbyterian minister in Oxford, Pennsylvania, took up the case of Rachel Parker, using his own money and his considerable contacts on both sides of the Line. It became part of the national debate over the new Fugitive Slave Law. Dickey organized a group of some sixty witnesses who testified that Rachel was a free-born Pennsylvanian— not a fugitive slave from Elkton, Maryland, as McCreary alleged. After an extended legal battle, Rachel was returned to Pennsylvania as a free person in January 1853, some thirteen months after her abduction.

His success emboldened and inspired Dickey to make blacks "a race of men enlightened in the knowledge of God" in order to "light them to an elevated position, social and civil, among the people of the earth." The best way to do this, he reasoned, was to free American blacks from slavery and return them to Africa. To this end, he wanted to create a school to train the brightest among them for positions of leadership in the new African nations.

Thus, in 1854 he founded the Ashmun Institute at Hinsonville, and the world's first institution to provide higher education for blacks was established—with the idea of returning blacks to Africa. The first building was dedicated on December 31, 1856—the fifth anniversary of the kidnapping of Rachel Parker.

The first class had four students, and Dickey was forced to mortgage his home to keep the school going. There were periodic harassing raids from whites on the other side of the Line. During the Civil War, there were threats and raids from across the border. Muskets were issued in June 1863, when Robert E. Lee was heading for Gettysburg and it was feared he might come all the way to Philadelphia. On April 15, 1865, the day after Abraham Lincoln's assassination, the school was renamed Lincoln University.

Under the guidance of a faculty of stern, white professors, Lincoln quickly gained a reputation for academic excellence and for producing professional blacks—ministers, physicians, lawyers, and teachers. Alumni were known as "Lincoln men," and this was a ticket to money, influence and prestige.

But Lincoln remained steadfastly under white control. When the white trustees gathered to choose a new president in 1926, the alumni association pressed for the election of a black man. But the majority held that Lincoln University was "the white man's work for the Negro" and that the election of a Negro president would erode public confidence in the institution.

The trustees' final choice that year was Dr. Walter B. Greenway, pastor of the Bethany Temple Church in Philadelphia, who had delivered a sermon a few months earlier urging that the Ku Klux Klan be permitted to parade as part of the city's sesquicentennial celebration. When news of his election broke, the black press around the country reacted scornfully. "Under such a head," the *New York Age* speculated, "there would probably be a department devoted to Ku Klux ethics and etiquette . . . ministerial students would be instructed in the correct way to behave gracefully when robed Klansmen entered their churches. . . ." The trustees rescinded their action but then chose another white man.

Lincoln got its first black trustee in 1929, and in 1932 Joseph Newton Hill became the first black faculty member. When the white president announced his retirement in 1945, the board of trustees was half white and half black, but the opposition to a black president remained—even among some of the black trustees. There was concern that the change would affect fundraising from white sources and that white faculty members, who occupied most of the department chairmanships, would object.

Carter G. Woodson, the black scholar, looked at the question from a different perspective. "If, after three generations, the Negro colleges have not produced men qualified to administer their affairs, such an admission is an eloquent argument that they have failed ingloriously and should be immediately closed."

The trustees relented, and Dr. Horace Mann Bond, Lincoln Class of '19, head of the Fort Valley (Georgia) State College, became the first black president of the oldest institution for the higher education of blacks in the world. With him Bond brought his wife and three children, Jane, James, and Julian, who as an adult recalled the train trip from Atlanta to Philadelphia.

"The trains were segregated then, and the Jim Crow cars were just horrendous. The windows didn't close; or if they did close they didn't open, and if they opened the soot came in. If they were closed, they were boiling. They were overcrowded, the people were standing in the aisles. . . . I knew something was going on that I didn't quite understand. There was one point where there was a change and you got to ride in these nice cars. . . ."

When they arrived in Pennsylvania, the three Bond children were enrolled in the Oxford, Pennsylvania, public schools and assigned to all-black classrooms. The elder Bond sued to end segregation, and Julian and

James were named as plaintiffs. School authorities quietly agreed to consolidate the schools. In this manner, Julian Bond, now chairman of the NAACP, began his civil rights career in 1948 at the age of eight.

All along the Line in southeastern Pennsylvania, Jim Crow was established as a local custom rather than a legality, but black GIs returning from World War II and entering Lincoln chafed against segregation in nearby Oxford. In 1950, they began sitting in at the Oxford coffee shop, which refused to serve blacks, and at one of the two movie theaters. These were among the first examples of the civil rights activism that would explode in the sixties. The demonstrators were supported by Horace Bond, who filed a lawsuit that culminated in a desegregation order.

"They were segregating my children, and I had come north from Georgia expecting something a little different," Bond said. "Segregation was clearly against Pennsylvania law, but we were five miles from the Maryland border, and there was a strong Ku Klux Klan operating nearby. People drove by my house and threw giant firecrackers. And there were harassment calls. Some dear lady called and said, 'Don't you know God ordained that your people should be hewers of wood?' I had no answer. . . ."

Bond left Lincoln in 1958, and as a temporary successor the trustees appointed a white faculty member, Dr. Armisted O. Grubb, who had actively opposed Bond's attempt to desegregate Oxford's public schools on grounds blacks didn't pay enough taxes to justify their complaints against segregated schools. During his few months as acting president, Grubb continued to be a major fundraiser for a whites-only swimming pool in Oxford.

The little red brick Hosanna Church is out on Route 1—originally the old Nottingham Road trod by Mason and Dixon—just off the Lincoln campus. It was built by local blacks in 1829 as the focus of the Hinsonville community, and it was called the "African Meeting House." In 1843 it became the African Union Methodist Protestant Church. It was an Underground Railroad station and an abolitionist meetingplace. Frederick Douglass and Harriet Tubman spoke here.

The cemetery is erupting in violets, dandelions, and clover. Tiny American flags decorate the gravestones of seventeen veterans of the 54th

Frederick Douglass and Harriet Tubman spoke at Hosanna Church, which was built by local blacks in 1829 near the present site of Lincoln University.

Massachusetts Infantry Regiment, perhaps the most famous black unit in the Civil War. One of them reads, "WILLIAM JAY, CO B, 5TH REG, MASS INF VOLS, DIED 1893."

OXFORD, PENNSYLVANIA: NORTH OF MILE 10

A Pizza Hut is on the site of the movie theater where Lincoln students were ordered out of the white section, but the Oxford Hotel, built in 1754, is still in the center of town and has been reincarnated as an office building. I stand on the veranda and look through the window to the desk in the lobby where Jacques and Gauraud Wilmore, Ben F. Holman, and Ralph Anderson, Lincoln students, were told there were no rooms available. Minutes later, Dick Winchester, a white history professor, asked for a room and was handed a key.

CHROME, PENNSYLVANIA: NORTH OF MILE 11

Termites, weather, and neglect are conspiring to bring the old Chrome Hotel to ruin, and today the only guest is the wind. Its windows gape like eyeholes in a skull. A girl with bobby-pinned hair at a farm market across the street says two women lived there for many years, but they sold it last year and it's been vacant ever since. It was built between 1715 and 1720, and although Charles Mason didn't mention it in his journal, the surveyors must have stopped here when they passed by less than a mile south on April 29, 1765. And it was here on the night of December 31, 1851, that Thomas McCreary, the slave catcher, turned south and sent his buggy careening over frozen roads carrying seventeen-year-old Rachel Parker to a slave pen in Baltimore.

Beginning about 1830 this area along the Line produced the world's supply of chrome. Cheaper ore from Turkey put the underground mines out of business in 1881, and the Chrome Hotel began a long decline that is nearing an end.

CALVERT, MARYLAND: SOUTH OF MILE 11

In 1701, William Penn and a group of fellow Quakers left New Castle on horseback and rode some thirty miles west into the wilderness. After several days they reached a spot where the soil seemed particularly rich. Penn marked the spot with his own hands and told the others he had "then and there set apart and dedicated forty acres to them and their successors forever, for the combined purpose of public worship, the right of burial ground and the privilege of education."

Not long after, Lord Baltimore fell out of royal favor and the opportunistic Penn pushed south into Maryland territory, laid out thirty-seven lots of 500 acres each, and named the settlement Nottingham. Quaker settlers moved in, bringing their slaves with them, and in 1724 they erected a meeting house on the forty-acre tract selected by Penn. There was a special gallery above the main floor for the slaves. By 1800 most of the slaves had been freed by the Quakers. At first it was called the Nottingham Meeting House, but soon it became known as the Brick Meeting House.

The so-called Nottingham Lots were a focal point of the Penn-Calvert boundary dispute, and when Mason and Dixon drew their line here in 1765, the territory went to Maryland. When the survey was completed in 1767, the surveyors made an elegant, official map of their Line, and the only building depicted on it is the Brick Meeting House.

The village that grew up around it was called Brick Meeting House until 1878, when residents asked the post office for a shorter name. Someone suggested "Calvert," and it was unanimously approved. And thus the spot dedicated by William Penn came to be named after the family of Lord Baltimore.

A sign near the Brick Meeting House proclaims, "DRUG FREE ZONE." I stand on tiptoe, shade my eyes, and peer through the window. There are wooden pews and, above to one side, the slave gallery, with a rail in front. It reminds me of the courtroom gallery in *To Kill a Mockingbird.*

SYLMAR, PENNSYLVANIA: ON MILE 13

Mason-Dixon marker No. 12 is only about three inches above ground, and I can barely make out the "P." Across a field, an Amish farmer (I know he's Amish because there are no electric lines going into his house) in a straw hat is hitching up a team of six mules to plow. I walk about a mile and come into Sylmar, a speck of a place littered with castoff farm machinery. Marker No. 13 should be here somewhere, but I can't find it.

Solomon Northrup, a thirty-year-old free black from Saratoga Springs, New York, and a musician, passed by here in a carriage on the Nottingham Road in 1841 on his way to Washington. He was accompanied by two white men, who had invited him to perform. But soon after reaching the nation's capital, he was drugged by his companions and taken to a cotton plantation in Louisiana, where he worked as a slave until abolitionists secured his freedom in 1853.

RISING SUN, MARYLAND: SOUTH OF MILE 15

It's quiet in the children's room at the Rising Sun Public Library, where some two dozen three-to-five-year-olds—pigtailed girls and cowlicked boys—are listening intently to a volunteer who is reading *There Is Something in My Attic.* The silence is broken only occasionally by the rasp of a telephone or the *nnnch* sound of computer printouts.

Sally Teague is Rising Sun's full-time librarian and forty-dollars-a-month mayor. She issues an admonitory *shhhhh!* to two teenagers, checks out a John Grisham novel, and removes her glasses. She seems to disappear into her own thoughts. Wheels are turning, cogs are meshing.

"Rising Sun has a reputation as a Klan hotbed, and it's always been that way. The Klan applied for a permit to march in the Fourth of July parade in 1993. We turned them down. You still see a Confederate flag flying now and then. When my daughter got married, she invited a black friend from

Elkton, but she wouldn't come because the wedding was in Rising Sun. The American Legion sponsored a softball tournament here a couple of years ago, and one of the teams that came in to play was all black. The Klan rode in on horses with sheets and hoods, and the black team stopped right in the middle of the game, got back on the bus, and left. The longtime grand wizard died last year, and his family has offered his robes and other paraphernalia to a new museum we're opening. I don't know what to do. . . ."

The soil is rich and generative on the Line north of Rising Sun. Measured fields are piled with bales of hay that from a distance resemble golden building blocks. I recognize the old house, even though it's down on its knees ready to collapse. The fields around it are weedy and unplowed, and in the middle is a big sign, surrounded by goldenrod, "BUILDING LOTS FOR SALE." I attended a Ku Klux Klan rally on this spot in 1995.

As part of a magazine assignment to profile Roy Frankhouser, an old-time Klansman from Reading, Pennsylvania, I showed up here on a pleasant October evening wearing a baseball cap with "KKK" and a t-shirt with "White Power" and occasionally mouthing a racial epithet to enhance my deception. Now I stand on the small hillock where they burned the cross, and the memories come rushing back. . . .

Some 200 people were assembled here; they represented klaverns from Pennsylvania, Maryland, and Delaware. The place was crawling with klexters, klokans, klarogos, kleagles, kludds, klokards—a veritable who's who of klandom. They are a sad-sack collection of losers, paranoiacs and dimwits. Towering over the gathering, like a village cathedral, was a 50-foot log cross wrapped in kerosene-soaked rags.

Frankhouser has set up a folding table and is selling Klan paraphernalia—t-shirts, caps, rings, and earrings (dangle or pierced). He does his Jewish merchant impersonation, saying, "Oy, veh, I make you sotch a deal. Reguluh thirty dollas, f'you, t-venty-five."

He's also selling pocket knives that open with a flick to expose a three-inch black blade ("sharp to the tickle"). Stepping from behind the table, he gives two teenagers, a boy and a girl, a demonstration of the proper knife-fighting technique. "You never fight with a knife like this"—he cocks his arm as though he is about to stab them—"the proper method is to never show the blade and slash, like this. . . ." He slashes, expertly.

A swastika-sleeved man, wearing a black Nazi SS uniform and jackboots, greets Frankhouser. He walks with his feet splayed outward, duck-like, and he is fat—a mountainous jello of jowls, chins, and paunch. Beneath a musketeerish moustache, he twitchy-smiles, but his eyes are blank and give nothing away. He begins a tirade about the ACLU, which he calls the UCLA; Frankhouser corrects him. He shrugs and says, "What's the difference? They're all Jewish motherfuckers."

"Lemme tell ya a great story, Roy. You'll appreciate this. We was comin' home one afternoon and passed a bus with a Star of David on it. We couldn't believe it. A kike-mobile! Well, we slowed down and started givin' 'em Heil Hitlers and shouting 'Six million more! Six million more!' and you know what those hook-nosed bastards did? They started crying. Imagine. We cracked up. We couldn't stop laughing. A whole busload of hysterical kikes, screaming, pounding on the windows, tears running down their cheeks. And then the frosting on the cake—the bus driver was a nigger! When the nigger saw our armbands, his eyes bulged out and that bus took off like a rocket. We couldn't stop laughin'. . . ."

Within earshot, three little girls and two little boys, somewhere between the ages of three and five, are catching frogs and lightning bugs in jars. One of the girls has pink ribbons in her hair and wears a black KKK t-shirt; one of the boys has a red t-shirt that says, "Hey, Nigger" and depicts a white hand giving a middle-finger salute.

At sunset, satiny robes rustle as they are slipped from hangers covered by plastic dry cleaning bags. Some reek of kerosene from past nocturnal cross-lightings. The klansmen and klanswomen help each other with their robes, and then peer through the slits of their cone-shaped hoods.

Patrick, eleven years old, is aglow and resplendent, as though he had just donned a new Easter outfit. Frankhouser helps him on with his hood and says, "Always remember as you grow up, Young Man, stick your hand up in the hood to get rid of the stiffness before you put it on." Patrick is rapt with attention, feeding gluttonously on each word.

The aliens are summoned to the sacred altar, which is a waist-high table covered with a Confederate flag, for the ceremony of naturalization. There are nine of them—a young man, a young woman, and seven teenagers— five boys and two girls. In their robes, they look like a choir. For this naturalization ceremony, Frankhouser takes the part of klokard, or teacher. The observing klansmen stamp out their cigarettes and shuffle to attention.

Frankhouser, his face crimsoned by the retreating sun, reads from the Kloran and begins asking a series of questions; each requires an affirmative response from the aliens. "Are you a native-born or naturalized white, Christian American citizen? . . . Do you believe in and will you faithfully strive for the eternal maintenance of white supremacy? . . . Louder! I can't hear you! . . . Do you believe that this is a white man's country, and should so remain, and will you do all in your power to uphold the principles of white supremacy and the purity of white womanhood? . . ."

In a fifteen-minute ceremony, the aliens swear obedience, secrecy, fidelity, and klannishness. They promise secrecy for all fellow klansmen (except in cases of treason, rape, malicious murder, or violation of the Klan oath), and they commit themselves to uphold America's flag, its Constitution, and laws. At the end Frankhouser declares them fit for the Klan. "By virtue of the authority vested in me, I dub thee klansman, the most honored title among men." Each is tapped on the shoulder with the flat blade of the sword. The aliens have passed through the mystic cave to become citizens of the Invisible Empire, gaining access to the Klan's ceremonial language, greetings and responses, avowals and warnings. Each robed figure stands in mysterious oneness with their fellow klansmen.

The sun drops below the horizon and pulls the land into night; on the moon-drenched field the klansmen stand in disordered ranks listening to guest speakers. The first is Barry, pastor of the New Covenant Church of God, wearing camouflage trousers, combat boots, and a black shirt with a clerical collar. " . . . niggers are raping our women with impunity . . . we're sick and tired of it all. Let's go get that filthy kike out of the White House . . . the nigger in this country is a disease . . . a gorilla . . . he has no morals, no principles . . . lives under filthy conditions."

Then Bob, leader of a Delaware klan, huge tattooed arms, goatee beard, black t-shirt, and jeans—he might be central casting's idea of a rebel biker—rants ". . . Clinton, our faggot-loving, Jew-loving president. Those Jews who would like to murder white Christian children. . . . We made America, and now we ride around in old cars while the Jews and kinky-haired faggot niggers ride in Mercedes. . . ."

Frankhouser steps up to the altar. At first he is reserved, reluctant, almost shy, but before long he has turned as mean-looking as a Gestapo thug, and he is ranting like an evangelist with a full tent. ". . . You're damn right I'm a racist, and I'm proud to be a racist. . . ." His voice seems to slip into just the right vitriolic pitch, and his cheeks quiver with rage. "We need to say, 'Niggers, we can't stand this smell anymore. . . .'" The cheering comes in salvos; there is a fusillade of hurrays, damn-rights, and amens.

At Frankhouser's command, the klansmen converge on the cross, each taking up an unlit torch from a pile near the base. Although even klansmen refer to the ceremony as a cross-burning, Klan purists call it a cross-lighting to avoid anything that would even remotely appear to offend Jesus Christ. They form a wide circle and rotate around the cross slowly; as they pass Frankhouser, he lights their torches and says, "I give you the sacred light. Proceed." When all the torches are burning, they stop, and Frankhouser says: "Behold, the fiery cross is still brilliant. All the troubled history has failed to quench its hallowed flame." He ignites the cross. Flames leap up the post and spread over the horizontal bar; the Klan members step forward and place their torches at the base of the cross.

"We light the cross with fire to signify to the world that Jesus Christ is the light of the world. Where the holy light shall shine, there will be dispelled evil, darkness, gloom, and despair. The light of truth dispels ignorance and superstition as fire purifies gold and silver, but destroys wood and stubble; so by the fire of the cross of Calvary we cleanse and purify our virtues by burning out our vices with the fire of his word. . . . Who can look upon this sublime symbol or sit in its sacred light without being inspired with a holy desire and determination to be a better Man?"

"Amazing Grace" plays over a scratchy loudspeaker. ". . . *How sweet the sound. . . .*" The cross continues to burn. The heat of the cross can be felt thirty feet away, and the Klan members sweat under their heavy robes. They spread their arms and legs, Christ-like, and look into the sky filled with acrid smoke, hatred baked on their faces. ". . . *I once was lost but now am found. . . .*" The landscape seems hallucinatory, and the sound of the flames licking at the cross is ghastly. ". . . *Was blind but now I see. . . .*" The air is varnished with the smell of kerosene and burning wood. Large black tatters of burned burlap flap from the cross like vultures haggling over carrion. Up in the evil, miasmic sky, the moon is impaled on a pine tree. ". . . *How precious did that grace appear. . . .*"

Frankhouser asks, "What's the solution?"

"White Revolution!" comes the chorused response.

"White Power," shouts Frankhouser.

"White Power," comes the response.

"White Power! . . .*'Tis grace hath brought me safe thus far . . . .*"

"White Power! . . . *and grace will lead me home.*"

"White Power!"

"White Power!"

They stand silhouetted against the burning cross, dreaming of the day when men will be judged by the color of their skin rather than the content of their character.

MT. ZOAR, MARYLAND: SOUTH OF MILE 20

After emancipation, virulent white racism and Jim Crow laws kept blacks in isolated enclaves in Cecil County, Maryland, in an area known as "the Barrens." Before the white colonists came, the Susquehannock Indians regularly burned huge tracts of forest to flush out game. To white farmers, these rocky, dry, sterile areas, which are on both sides of the Line, were unproductive and worthless, and so they were left to the blacks. One of these enclaves was Mt. Zoar, which was founded in 1869. The few buildings that define Mt. Zoar today include an old Methodist Church.

"My great-grandfather, the Reverend George Black, started this church in 1881," says Franklin Stuart, who's lived in Mt. Zoar for all of his forty-four years. He's setting up tables and chairs outside and women are bringing in large quantities of food. "Bertha Brown passed, and the services are today. She was ninety-five." He invites me into the church. There are little hand fans in every pew. "We have air conditioning, but it still can get hot in here."

I ask if there are any Civil War veterans buried in the cemetery. "Oh, my soul, yes. This cemetery was here before the church." He takes me out to the pine-needled burial ground and points to more than a dozen gravestones: Geo H. Haines, Co C 4 USCT . . . Corp'l J. H. Butler Co H 25 USCT . . . Chas Smith Co D 54th Mass Inf. . . .

Franklin Stuart's great-grandfather founded Mt. Zoar Church in Cecil County, Maryland, in 1881.

He gives me directions to the old Mt. Zoar School, which was built
around 1900 and operated until school desegregation in the 1960s. For a
time it was tavern, but it has been vacant for at least 30 years. Through the
window I can see blackboards and a pot-bellied stove. From the house
across the street, a woman peeks out her door and calls to me. "You know
that used to be our school? I'm 93 years old and I went there. . . ."

Olive Stewart, the granddaughter of a slave, is dressed for Bertha Brown's
funeral in a red dress and red bonnet. She is seated on a sofa between an
indolent cat and framed photographs of three of her great-grandchildren. "I
went through the eighth grade in that school. If you wanted to go further,
you had to go all the way to Elkton, and there wasn't any way for me to get
there. There were two rooms. One had grades one through four, the other
grades five through eight. We had two outhouses, though, one for the boys,
one for the girls. . . ."

MILE 20

Charlie Bitler walks around the marker with an attentive cocking of his
head, the way an AKC judge might appraise a borzoi. Finally, he makes his
judgment. "It's had some rough wear. It's badly chipped. I was here in '76
and took a picture. Since then, it's been turned the wrong way. . . ."

*Olive Stewart, whose grandmother was a slave, attended
the Mt. Zoar School, which operated in Maryland until
school desegregation in the 1960s.*

Charlie Bitler, a retired surveyor and member of the Mason-Dixon Line Preservation Partnership, stands by a crown stone at Mile 20 of the West Line.

Indeed, the Penn coat of arms is facing east, the Calvert coat of arms is pointing west. It's a crownstone. Bitler has brought me here with the instinct of a homing pigeon, climbing over rocks, slashing through thick briars. He is a retired surveyor from Lancaster, Pennsylvania, whose lifelong interest has been the Mason-Dixon Line.

"You've got to remember—it's not a straight line, it's a curved line. The only straight line of latitude is the equator. That's the only one that you can push straight through and just keep on extending your line. Every other parallel of latitude is a concentric circle. Near the North Pole, you can see it very clearly. And down here, around the 40th parallel where we are, the curve is so flat that it appears to be straight.

"After establishing a point on the correct line of latitude, they would orient their instruments toward true north. They would then turn 89 degrees, 55 minutes (five minutes short of 90 degrees). That would form a central angle of 0 degrees, 10 minutes and produce a chord about eleven miles long. According to their computations, they would intersect the curve again at the end of the 11-mile chord.

"At the end of the 11-mile chord, they would set up their observatory and determine how far they had strayed from the correct line of latitude. They would then retrace the surveyed line and make corrections as they transferred points onto the curve at the mile stations.

"Their miles are about twelve feet too long—in other words, 5,292 feet. They mention that in their journal when they surveyed the Tangent Line, which was a very flat section. But remember, they were not too concerned with the distance between the points. They were mainly interested in their position north and south. They wanted to stay on the line between Pennsylvania and Maryland. . . ."

Their principal and indispensable instrument was a six-foot-tall zenith sector, which was pointed directly overhead to study the stars. Just beneath the top of the sector was a telescope that rotated on a pivot. At the bottom was a graduated scale to measure angles. This enabled Mason and Dixon to measure the zenith angle of a star—that is, the angle between the star and the zenith—the point directly overhead. Using charts showing the positions of all the stars at various times of the year, the latitude of any point could be calculated by the zenith angle.

The zenith sector was one of the most sophisticated instruments available at the time, and this particular one was constructed by John Bird, one of the world's leading instrument makers, who had been an early mentor of Dixon. Bird was retained by Thomas Penn to develop a sector specifically for use by Mason and Dixon. The instrument that the two young surveyors brought with them to America was the ultimate in science and craftsmanship.

Once the stellar calibrations were made, they were transferred to the ground and measured with sixty-six-foot iron chains. Each chain had one hundred links, and each link was 7.92 inches long. The ends of the chains were fitted with iron handles so they could be pulled tight. The chains could only be used on level ground. To measure horizontal distances on hills, they used wooden rods, called levels, that were 16.5 feet long.

To facilitate the sighting and marking of the actual line, Mason and Dixon employed teams of axemen who were continually clearing a rough corridor, or visto, about nine yards wide. In the uninhabited areas of the extreme western end of the Line, the visto served as a guide and a trail for new settlers.

Throughout the expedition, beginning on November 15, 1763 ("Arrived in Philadelphia") until September 11, 1768 ("Thus ends my restless progress in America"), Mason kept a journal that occasionally yields interesting insights into the project as well as his personality, but it is mostly taken up by whole pages of arithmetic carried out to seven decimal places and references to zenith angles, azimuths, accessions, precessions, nutations, and other concepts incomprehensible to all but the initiates of geodesy.

The overseers of Mason's and Dixon's work were commissioners from both provinces. There were supposed to be seven from each side, but the number varied from time to time as resignation, illness, or death required new appointments. Not all commissioners attended all meetings. The Maryland contingent included Governor Horatio Sharpe, who was chief executive from 1753 to 1769; John Ridout, an important Sharpe aide; John Leeds, a prominent mathematician and astronomer; John Beale Bordley, a lawyer, large landholder, and probably a slave owner; and Reverend John Barclay, an Anglican minister. Pennsylvania was represented by William Allen, a Philadelphia merchant and confidante of Benjamin Franklin; Edward Shippen, a lawyer who would become the state of Pennsylvania's first chief justice; the aforementioned Chew and Willing; and Rev. John Ewing, a Presbyterian cleric who was also an astronomer. Indeed, Ewing would actively participate in an extension of the Line in 1784.

LANCASTER, PENNSYLVANIA: NORTH OF MILE 23

On January 10, 1765, the off-season for the surveyors, Mason made a thirty-five-mile journey on horseback to Lancaster, explaining in his journal: "What brought me here was my curiosity to see the place where was perpetrated last winter; the Horrid and inhumane murder of 26 Indians: men, Women and Children, leaving none alive to tell."

The incident had occurred some thirteen months earlier on December 14, 1763, at Conestoga, where a surviving remnant of the Conestoga tribe was living under the putative protection of the colonial government. The Conestogas, a branch of the Susquehannocks, had been a large tribe when they were personally visited by William Penn and his son in 1701. But only a handful remained sixty-two years later when a mob of fifty whites from Paxton, Pennsylvania, murdered six of the Indians—two women, three old men, and a young boy—burned their cabins, and paraded their scalps on long sticks. Samuel Smith, the Lancaster County sheriff, locked up the remaining Indians for their own protection.

The so-called Paxton Boys returned to Lancaster on December 27, and, undeterred by the local population, broke into the jail and killed and scalped the remaining members of the Conestoga tribe—three old men, three women, five young boys, and three small girls (Mason had his num-

bers slightly wrong). The terrified prisoners had proclaimed their love for
the English, prostrated themselves, and begged for mercy. The mangled
bodies of the Indians, who were peaceful farmers and had never been at war
with the whites, were buried in Lancaster. None of the Paxton Boys was
ever brought to justice, and the incident highlighted the growing inabili-
ty of the colonial government to protect friendly Indians from what
Benjamin Franklin called "white savages."

Mason's pilgrimage to Lancaster moved him to uncharacteristically emotional prose in his Journal.

> These poor unhappy creatures had always lived under the protection
> of the Pennsylvania Government, and had Lands allotted for them a
> few miles from Lancaster by the late celebrated Wm. Penn, Esq'r,
> Proprietor . . . They had received notice of the intention of some of
> the back inhabitants & fled in to ye Gaol to save themselves.
>
> Strange it was that [Lancaster], Tho' as Large as most market
> Towns in England, never offer'd to oppose them, tho' it's more
> than probable they on request might have been assisted by a com-
> pany of his Majesties Troops who were in the Town.
>
> No Honour to them!

FAIRFIELD, PENNSYLVANIA: NORTH OF MILE 23

More than 500 people assembled on a farm here on June 4, 1924, to witness a Ku Klux Klan initiation ceremony. The principal address was delivered by the Reverend B. Morris Postens of the local Methodist Church.
Several large crosses were burned.

DRUMORE TOWNSHIP, PENNSYLVANIA:
NORTH OF MILE 23

John Neal Russell, a ten-year-old farm boy who lived about eight miles
from the Line, witnessed the abduction of a black woman by a slave dealer
near his house in 1814. The woman was seized in broad daylight, tied up
and gagged, and, as her three young children wailed, tossed into a wagon
for the short trip into slave territory. She was sold into Georgia, and her
three children were raised in the Russell family. The incident left a strong

impression on the boy, and when he grew up and took over the farm, he made it a station on the Underground Railroad. He once moved a group of twenty-two runaways through his home.

Russell's son, Slater B. Russell, remembered that when he was a boy in the 1850s his home was visited by the most prominent abolitionists—Frederick Douglass, Daniel Gibbons, Lucretia Mott, and others. He also recalled an incident involving a farmer named Joseph C. Taylor, who lived about three miles from the Line.

> He was a young farmer. One June morning some one rattled and shook his door furiously, at the same time setting up an unearthly yell that caused him to put his head out of the window in short order. The cause of the noise was that a colored girl had been kidnaped near by, and that the kidnappers were making off with her in a covered wagon at break-neck speed toward the Maryland line. . . . In less time than it can be told, Taylor was mounted on the bare back of a plow-horse that had only a "blind" bridle, and, hatless and boot-less, away he went. He had time to think, going along, and he thought how foolish would be his journey without arms. Just then he came to Jacob Kirk's store. The clerk was taking down the shut-ters. "For God's sake, give me a gun," said Taylor. There happened to be one in the store which he took away. His steed was too fleet for the Marylanders. He overtook them, within, I think, about one hun-dred yards of the line. Riding around the wagon, he wheeled in the road, aimed his old fowling piece at the driver's head in a way that seemed to "mean business," and brought the horses to their haunch-es as he exclaimed: "Stir another foot and I'll blow your brains out!" A part of the sequel is that he marched the party back to a magis-trate's office, had the girl discharged and the kidnappers put in jail. That is not the best part of the sequel, however; that remains to be told. The old gun hadn't the ghost of a load in it! Taylor didn't know this, neither did the kidnappers, of course, but the old gun not loaded served its purpose just as well as though it had been.

MILE 23

I walk along Mason-Dixon Road with some of the world's richest farmland on either side. Windfall apples are mush under my feet. Old churches of stern and ecclesiastic stone cast long morning shadows over their waiting cemeteries. Signs in a cornfield advise of a coming revival meeting and admonish to "Prepare to Meet Thy God." Here, to borrow Thomas Hardy's phrase, a pound of sin weighs twenty ounces. Robotic towers carrying power lines to Philadelphia cut through the landscape like a wound.

A series of ever-narrowing downhill roads leads to the banks of the Susquehanna. Behind me rise the great granite cliffs, fifty feet high, near where Captain John Smith held a powwow with the Susquehannocks in 1608. They brought him gifts of skins, pipes, and beads. "Such great and well proportioned men are seldome seen," Smith wrote, "for they seemed like giants to the English." The Susquehannocks lived along the Susquehanna in Pennsylvania and Maryland. They were destroyed as a nation by the Iroquois in 1675, and then most of them were wiped out by European-borne diseases. A few descendants were among the Conestoga Indians who were massacred in 1763 in Lancaster County.

Across the river in York County, the lopped-off cones that are the cooling towers of the Peach Bottom Nuclear Power Plant yank me back to the present. A speedboat pulls it wake upstream, defying the great urgency and force of the river. A well-maintained Conrail track runs along the bank, and its creosoted ties are pungent in the sun. The tracks go into a tunnel that is spray-painted with the names of lovers and enemies. At the tunnel entrance there is a painted line on the rocks that says "Pa" and "Maryland"

Mason and Dixon arrived here on May 27, 1765, and immediately set about the task of determining the width of the river, which they calculated at sixty-seven chains and sixty-eight links—or about 0.846 mile. They crossed the river to the west bank and placed a stake to mark where they would continue their westward movement. Then they returned to Peach Bottom on the east bank, set up their equipment, and, under the ancient phosphorescence of the stars, observed Leonis emerging from the Moon and Lyrae and Cygni passing the Meridian.

100 ANTIETAM CREEK 95 90 South Mount 85 TOMS CREEK 80 Run Flat MIDDLE CREEK Nay's Cr. Rock Creek 75 Willoway Creek MONOCACY Road 70 Piney Run

Chapter Five

THE WEST LINE
SUSQUEHANNA RIVER TO THE
APPALACHIAN MOUNTAINS — 77 MILES.

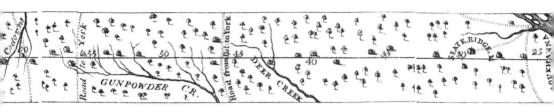

"What, am I to argue that it is wrong to make men brutes, to rob them of their liberty, to work them without wages, to keep them ignorant of their relations to their fellow men, to beat them with sticks, to flay their flesh with the lash, to load their limbs with irons, to hunt them with dogs, to sell them at auction, to sunder their families, to knock out their teeth, to burn their flesh, to starve them into obedience and submission to their masters? Must I argue that a system thus marked with blood, and stained with pollution, is wrong? No! I will not. I have better employments for my time and strength, than such arguments would imply."

—Frederick Douglass, address, "What to the Slave Is the Fourth of July?" Rochester, New York, July 5, 1852.

After reaching the Susquehanna in May 1765, the surveyors retraced their steps and adjusted each of their preliminary mile markers to reflect the corrections to true parallel. They then measured and set permanent boundary stones at the Tangent Point, the Northeast Corner of Maryland, and along part of the New Castle Circle. On June 17 they met at Christiana Bridge with the commissioners, who instructed them to continue running the West Line as far as the land was inhabited.

They were back at the Susquehanna on June 22. A few of the Susquehanna River ferries were propelled by sail, but when the Mason and Dixon party crossed the Susquehanna they probably used a crude raft-like craft poled and rowed by female slaves. From the west bank, they would move steadily westward for ninety-four miles over the next three and a half months, reaching a point about 117 miles west of the Northeast Corner on October 5.

Mason's Journal for this busy period is filled with trigonometrical calculations and zenith distances of stars. His most common daily entry was simply, "continued the line." At twenty-five miles from the Northeast Corner, they went by Daniel Camel's house, which was found to be 264 feet into Maryland; James McKenley's House (twenty-seven miles) turned out to be some 200 feet north into Pennsylvania. James Reed's House (twenty-eight miles), was sixty-six feet into Pennsylvania. Thomas Matson's house (thirty-one miles) was about 300 feet into Pennsylvania.

At the forty-five-mile point, wagons brought up the zenith sector and other instruments and they set up the observatory. It was about midway between the present towns of Stewartstown and New Freedom in York County, Pennsylvania, and not far from the current Interstate 83 highway between York and Baltimore. The summer skies were clear, and for the next nine nights they took their cosmic cues from Capella, Lyrae, and Cygni. On July 23 they calculated their offsets, found they were fifty-six feet south of true parallel, made adjustment to latitude 39° 43' 17.4", and continued west.

In early August they crossed several creeks, including the Codorus, Conewago, Piney, and Monocacy. Some sixty-eight miles from the Northeast Corner, almost directly south of York, they were again out reading the stars. This time they found they were 458 feet off true parallel. With his usual fetish for measurement, Mason recorded a bit of excitement on August 8. "At Noon a great storm of Thunder, Lightning, Hail and Rain. The Hail intermixed with pieces of ice; one piece of an irregular form measured one inch and six tenths in Length, one inch two tenths in breadth and half an inch thick."

They pushed west, passing the homes of border-dwelling settlers, who perhaps learned for the first time whether they were residents of Maryland or Pennsylvania—Stephen Griese (Pennsylvania), Michael Miller (Pennsylvania), Thomas McCewn (Maryland), John Young (Pennsylvania), Matthew Elder (Maryland). . . . By the end of August, they had reached the foot of South Mountain, some 83 miles from the Northeast Corner, just north of what is now Emmitsburg, Maryland. Nothing is recorded of the local reaction to these star-gazing, tree-chopping invaders, but doubtlessly it ranged from hostility to hospitality, from fascination to disdain.

They set up the observatory again on September 9 for nine nights of heavenly reckoning. This was near what is today an underground bunker run by the Pentagon to house the joint chiefs of staff in the event of an enemy attack on Washington.

At Mile 93 they passed the house of Staphel Shockey; some seventy-five years later, the Shockey home would be the first stop in Pennsylvania on the Underground Railroad for fugitives who crossed the Potomac and walked over South Mountain. On Sunday, September 22, Mason visited a large cave some eight miles east of Hagerstown, Maryland. He doesn't indicate whether he was accompanied by Dixon or anyone else, but it made an impression on him. The prose shows Mason's morose nature.

"Went to see a cave (near the Mountain about 6 miles South of Mr. Shockey's). The entrance is an arch about 6 yards in length and four feet in height, when immediately there opens a room 45 yards in length, 40 in breadth and 7 or 8 in height. (Not one pillar to support nature's arch). There divine service is often (according to the Church of England) celebrated in the Winter Season. On the sidewalls are drawn by the Pencil of Time with the tears of the Rocks: The imitation of Organ, Pillar, Columns and Monuments of a Temple; which with the glimmering faint light makes the whole an awful, solemn appearance, Striking its visitants with a strong melancholy reflection, that such is the abode of the Dead. Thy inevitable doom, O Stranger, soon to be numbered as one of them. From this room there is a narrow passage of about 100 yards, at the end of which runs a fine river of water. On the sides of this passage are other rooms, but not so large as the first."

THE WEST BANK OF THE SUSQUEHANNA: 25 MILES FROM THE NORTHEAST CORNER

Pleasure craft—houseboats, speed boats, pontoon boats, rowboats—sit patiently on their reflections in the middle of the river. The Susquehanna was only 0.8 miles wide when Mason and Dixon measured it, but today it is a mile wide because of the backwater created by the construction of the Conowingo Dam in 1928. An island on which the surveyors placed a marker was submerged by the dam. Also inundated was a bridge that spanned the river right at the Line.

From the west bank, the cliffs of Lancaster County, Pennsylvania, and Cecil County, Maryland, are clearly visible. The land rises steeply from the shore, and after about a half mile my feet are dragging like cannonballs. I interrupt my cardiovascular exertions near a new subdivision, Bronwyn Estates, that is going up on the Pennsylvania side, filling a much-needed gap.

DELTA, PENNSYLVANIA & CARDIFF, MARYLAND: MILE 28

A truck with the logo of a septic tank service is parked in front of the Bordertown Restaurant on Main Street just a few feet north of the Line. A waitress looks up from mopping the floor and asks if I want coffee. "Let me finish up here, and I'll take your order." It's a promise, not a request. The place has the feel of a Western cafe, which is enhanced by an Indian motif.

The wall is covered with framed paintings and photographs of Indians in headdresses, and between them hang tomahawks, arrows, tobacco pouches, feathers, and blankets. I ask what it all means. "Nothin'," says the waitress, handing me a steaming cup. "The lady who owned this place before my sister just liked Indians." The coffee is good.

I rig up a conversation with three men who are eating biscuits and gravy at a table with a sign over it that reads, "Official Office of the Delta Fire Police." They tell me about an auto accident a couple of years ago that happened right on the Line. One driver was killed, and his body remained inside the car while Maryland and Pennsylvania State Police tried to determine who had jurisdiction. After eight hours, they decided on Maryland. "It was a borderline case," says one, and gives me a twitchy smile.

Flaharty's Service Feed and Supply Store is right on the Line—most of the merchandise is in Cardiff, Maryland, but the cash register is in Delta, Pennsylvania. A concrete highway obelisk, which looks like an ancient fertility symbol, was placed there about 1937 to mark the Line, but proprietor Marlyn G. Flaharty says it's about fifteen feet too far into Maryland. "The previous owner moved it because it was right in front of the door."

The old Delta High School, built in 1890 some 500 yards north of the Line, has been converted into apartments upstairs and houses the post office on its first floor. When Edith Murray Johnson went to school here, she was one of three blacks in the Delta High Class of 1942. They were all cousins. Edith was a quick learner who frequently stayed after regular school to take advanced courses like calculus and trigonometry. About a week before graduation the three blacks were summoned to the office of the assistant principal, where they were informed that the parents of a white student objected to their child walking in the processional with Negroes. They also did not want Edith to sit on the stage with three white honor students. The official told Edith and her cousins they could still attend their graduation, but they couldn't participate.

"I won't go where I'm not wanted," Edith said. "I want the paper, I don't care about the ceremony." She and her cousins stayed home that night and received their diplomas in the mail.

The Line literally divides the quick and the dead at Slate Ridge Presbyterian Church in Cardiff—the church cemetery is in Delta. Behind the spike fence, the black slate tombstones carry inscriptions like "Er cof Am," which in Welsh means "To the memory of . . ." The discovery of slate in this area in 1734 brought a wave of experienced quarrymen from the

slate regions of Wales. This high-quality Peach Bottom slate was exhibit-
ed at the London Crystal Palace Exposition of 1850, where it won first prize
and designation as the hardest, most durable slate in the world.

These Welsh slaters built villages made up of traditional stone cottages.
Most of them have completely disappeared but one of them, Coulsontown,
has survived. When I walk into the village, it is so authentic that it seems
there must be a pub nearby with Dylan Thomas knocking back pint after
pint. But on this day a black woman is sweeping off the front stoop of one
of the cottages.

She tells me that in the 1920s blacks began working in the quarries, and
a few bought homes in Coulsontown. For the next forty years, the tiny village was an integrated, harmonious community. When the white residents
died off, Coulsontown became all-black. But before integration, before civil
rights activism, people of two races lived together in this tiny enclave less
than a mile from the Mason-Dixon Line.

It was a border town like Delta-Cardiff that Rita Mae Brown must have
had in mind in her 1988 novel, *Bingo*, which is set in the fictional town of
Runnymede and split down the middle, literally and figuratively, by the
Mason-Dixon Line. Brown writes: "Tuesdays the Masons had their regular
meeting. So did the Daughters of the Confederacy. Their rivals, the Sisters of
Gettysburg, held meetings on Wednesday night in the Pennsylvania side's
city hall." Brown herself was born in York County, where she was adopted
from an orphanage. The family moved to Florida when she was eleven, and
in her autobiography she recalled: "The minute we crossed the Mason-Dixon
Line, which was less than fifteen minutes from home, my mother let out a
war whoop that would have made Tecumseh proud. We sang the whole way
to Florida."

FAWN GROVE, PENNSYLVANIA: MILE 35

In 1925 the people of Fawn Grove, Pennsylvania, and Norrisville,
Maryland, formed the Citizens Volunteer Fire Company to fight fires on
both sides of the Mason-Dixon Line. The unusual interstate arrangement
worked well for six decades, but in 1994 a dispute arose over how company funds should be spent. The Maryland firefighters sued their
Pennsylvania comrades, and in an out-of-court settlement the Marylanders
seceded from the company and formed their own.

The Line is a roller coaster in southern York County, rising and falling at the whim of the terrain. Anne Blevins, a retired social studies teacher, lives in a farmhouse about a mile into Pennsylvania. She pours two cups of coffee from an old percolator and tells me about a classroom experiment she conducted in September 1957, while nine black students under the protection of federal troops were integrating public schools in Little Rock, Arkansas.

"The school was just outside Fawn Grove, half a mile from the Mason-Dixon Line. I wanted to do what I could do to dispel the ugliness of prejudice in my little area of the world, the classroom. We discussed the issue of desegregation in my classes, but sometimes talking about an issue needs physical reinforcement. So, one day, during this period of controversy, I announced to my social studies class that everyone who had blue eyes had to sit in the back of the classroom and only those students who had brown eyes could sit in the seats in the front of the room. Asked by a blue-eyed student why I was doing this, I made my point. 'Is it fair, I asked, to judge people on the basis of eye, hair, skin color, where they attend church, in what section of town they live, the amount of money they have or don't have? Suppose, because you have blue eyes, you could only sit in the rear seats in your classes. Would this be fair to you and would you like this?' Of course, my students answered, 'No.'

"A few days later, another social studies teacher, who had also discussed the issue of desegregation in his classes, and I were told by the administration that the school had received complaints from some parents about how we taught this particular issue. One who had complained, a school director, had a blue-eyed child who had had to sit in the back of my social studies class. We were ordered to stop."

LONG CORNER, HARFORD COUNTY, MARYLAND: MILE 36

Quakers hustled fugitive slaves through here and across the Line into Fawn Grove throughout the first half of the nineteenth century. However, at the same time a number of people living in York County, Pennsylvania, owned slaves and, to avoid the laws against it, they leased them to their neighbors in northern Harford County, Maryland. The archives of the Harford County Historical Society have documents relating to the sale of more than 2,000 slaves between 1775 and 1863. The leading slave dealer was Robert T.

Woolfolk, and "Old Woolfolk" became a name that black mothers used to
frighten their children into obedience.
      Mary Bristow, a local Harford County poet, wrote "History" in 1980:

> according to the history books
> no Blacks
> no Jews
> and only one Woman
> ever lived in Harford county
> Maryland
> Yet in the records
> they are alive beings
> blood and brains
> brawn and guts. . .
> and the graveyards
> are full of them
> who never lived
> in history books

Some of the worst border violence that preceded the drawing of the Mason-Dixon Line occurred in the rich farmlands of southern York County, where German farmers—some lured here by the Penns, others by the Calverts—often did not know to whom they should pay their taxes. In pushing across the Susquehanna, Pennsylvania authorities abandoned William Penn's policy of only allowing settlement on lands that had been officially purchased from the Indians.

A major figure was Thomas Cresap, an English-born Calvert ally who would be a colorful frontier figure for most of the eighteenth century. Calvert granted Cresap a 500-acre tract of land near the Susquehanna River on the 40th Parallel—some eighteen miles north of where the Line would later be established. And here, where Calvert claimed with some justification that Maryland began, Cresap built a blockhouse in 1730. He brought with him a dozen followers—rogues who had no moral restraints against murder—and a wife who carried a rifle, two pistols, a tomahawk, a scalping knife, and a small dagger that she concealed in her boot.

For the next twenty years, Cresap and his band harassed and attacked settlers loyal to Penn and called them poachers, squatters, and traitors. He turned the Indians against the Pennsylvanians by claiming they cheated them in trade, and then Cresap sold them goods at less than cost. When he failed to persuade the border settlers to swear allegiance to Calvert, he drove them out by force. In retaliation, Sheriff Samuel Smith of Lancaster County, Pennsylvania, and twenty deputies crossed the Susquehanna at midnight on November 23, 1736, and surrounded Cresap's blockhouse. A warrant for his arrest was read, and when Cresap failed to appear after fourteen hours, they set fire to the house and smoked him out.

Cresap and four of his allies were taken to Philadelphia, where they were paraded through the streets past jeering crowds eager to see the famous "Maryland Monster." Cresap, though manacled and facing the gallows, swaggered insolently, and when someone asked him how he liked Philadelphia, he replied, "Damn it, this is one of the prettiest towns in Maryland!"

Governor Ogle of Maryland demanded Cresap's release, and when the Pennsylvanians refused, four Pennsylvania German settlers were seized and taken to Baltimore. Pennsylvania replied in kind, and the border war heated up. Cresap was held in Philadelphia for nine months and resumed agitating after his release. In London, the King fumed over his unruly colonial subjects.

Some thirty years later, in January 1765, Charles Mason was out for a ride and by chance met Sheriff Smith, who told him of Cresap and the border war that directly led to his and Jeremiah Dixon's mission in America.

STEWARTSTOWN, PENNSYLVANIA: MILE 42

The old Stewartstown fairgrounds has given way to baseball diamonds, soccer fields, and tennis courts, but in 1944 and 1945 it was the site of a POW camp where 2,000 Germans were housed in tents and monitored by armed guards. They worked on local farms and in canneries to ease the wartime manpower shortage. The same ships that carried supplies to Europe for D-Day returned with the prisoners. The distance from home meant escape was not a realistic consideration. By 1946, the POWs were gone.

WEST LIBERTY, MARYLAND : SOUTH OF MILE 43

Day-care children are hee-hawing and seesawing in back of the West Liberty Methodist Church, which was founded here in 1819 and called

West Liberty Church was founded in 1819 as "Meredith's Meeting House."

Meredith's Meeting House. It was built about two and one-half miles from the Line on land donated by Samuel Meredith. The congregation had white and black members, but the latter, whether slave or free, were required to sit in a separate gallery. Blacks took communion after whites and left by a separate door. A list of contributors to the church construction cost is still preserved in church records. It includes a wealthy farmer named David Gorsuch ($142.94) and a slave named Almony's Ben (37 cents). The present church was built in 1898.

MARYLAND LINE, MARYLAND: MILE 46

Motorists are locking horns on the old Susquehanna Trail, which today is a busy commuter road for southern Pennsylvanians who work in the Baltimore area. It was first a Susquehanna Indian path, then a route for Calvert's settlers, then a toll road, and in the pre-interstate era, the main highway between York and Baltimore. Mason and Dixon crossed here for the first time on July 24, 1765.

Many of the farms in this area existed before the Line, and so they are bi-state operations. Larry Malone ignites a Winston. "I can start picking corn in the morning in Maryland, and by the time I'm done I'm in Pennsylvania." Malone owns the one hundred-acre Mason-Dixon Farm, which has seventy-five acres in Pennsylvania, including his house, and twenty-five acres in Maryland, including his barn. Mason-Dixon marker

No. 49 is in the middle of his wheat field, about 200 feet west of Interstate 83, which is now the main route between York and Baltimore. I buy a dozen ears of Pennsylvania corn and a basket of Maryland apples.

"During Prohibition there was a grocery store here where they secretly made moonshine," Malone says, whistling smoke through his lips. "In fact, all of the corn grown on this land went into corn liquor in those days. They used to move the operation back and forth over the Line to confuse the authorities. Then one day the Feds cracked down and closed the store. So they cut the thing in half, put the southern side on logs, and dragged it down the road. That was the start of the Maryland Line Inn. . . ."

I have a tremendous crabcake at the Maryland Line Inn, but they dispute Malone's version of the origin of the establishment and contend it was serving weary travelers before the Civil War. The town was called New Market in those days, and at the United Methodist Church they still have the old name over the door in stained glass. The congregation was organized in 1834, and the present church was built in 1925. A large contingent from the Maryland Line Ku Klux Klan attended the cornerstone laying ceremonies.

John Thompson escaped from his master in Prince Georges County, Maryland, in 1852 at the age of forty. Free blacks guided him north through hostile country at night, but sometimes there was no help available and he wandered off course, once almost going into Baltimore. He reached the Line at the Susquehanna Trail one night just as the first incendiary hints of day were on the eastern horizon.

Thompson was an unusual fugitive because he could read and write, and when he made his way to New York the abolitionist movement capitalized on this by having him write his life story and publishing it in 1856. It was a powerful document and widely read in the North. There are many poignant passages, such as this early account of the sale of his older sister.

> . . . My mother heard of the sale, which was on Saturday, and on
> Sunday took us with her to see our beloved sister, who was then in
> the yard with the trader's drove, preparatory to being removed far
> south, on the Monday following. After traveling six miles, we

arrived at our place of destination. Mother, approaching the door of
the trader's house, fell upon her knees, in tears begging to be permitted to see her imprisoned daughter, who was soon to be dragged
away from her embrace, probably to be seen no more in the flesh.
It was not his custom to admit slaves into his yard to see their
friends; but at this time, his heart seemed to be moved with com-
passion, for he opened the door, telling us to go in, which we did.

Here, the first thing that saluted my ears, was the rattling of
the chains upon the limbs of the poor victims. It seemed to me to
be a hell upon earth, emblematical of that dreadful dungeon
where the wicked are kept, until the day of God's retribution, and
where their torment ascends up forever and ever.

As soon as my sister saw our mother, she ran to her and fell
upon her neck, but was unable to speak a word. There was a scene
which angels witnessed; there were tears which, I believe, were
bottled and placed in God's depository, there to be reserved until
the day when He shall pour His wrath upon this guilty nation.

The trader, becoming uneasy at this exciting scene, and fear-
ing the rest of the drove would become dissatisfied with their sit-
uations, permitted sister to leave the yard for a few moments, to
keep mother's company. He did not watch her, as I thought he
would have done, but permitted her to go about with mother, and
even to accompany us part of our way towards home. He ordered
dinner for us, but not one of us could eat one mouthful. I thought
my heart would break, as the time drew near for our departure. I
dreaded the time when I should bid farewell to my beloved sister,
never more to see her face, never more to meet her in the paternal
circle, never more to hear her fervent prayer to the throne of God.

I watched the sun, as it seemed to descend behind the western
hills; but this did not stop its progress. The time soon arrived
when we must go. When mother was about to bid farewell to my
sister, and reached out her hand to grasp hers, she burst into a
flood of tears, exclaiming aloud. "Lord have mercy upon me!"

The trader, seeing such parental affection, as he stood by, hung
down his head and wiped the tears from his eyes; and to relieve
himself from a scene so affecting, he said, "Mary, you can go some
way with your mother, and return soon."

Turning to mother, he said, "old woman, I will do the best I
can for your daughter; I will sell her to a good master."

We then left the house. After going with us two miles, sister
Mary, in obedience to orders and her promise, could go no farther,
and she said, "Mother, I suppose I must go back."

Here another heart-rending scene took place. I well remember her parting words, "Mother," she said, "don't grieve, for though we are separated in body, our separation is only for a season, and if we are faithful we shall meet again where partings are no more. Mother, will you try to meet me?"

We all promised to do so. We then parted, and have never heard directly from her since. She was, as we afterwards understood, taken to Alabama, and sold at public auction.

William Parker and his brother, Charles, escaped bondage on an Anne Arundel County, Maryland, plantation in 1839, traveled by night along the Susquehanna Trail, and crossed the Line near the present site of Larry Malone's farm. About ten miles into Pennsylvania the pair was stopped and questioned by three whites, who carried with them an advertisement for two runaway slaves that fit the Parkers precisely. One of the whites reached for a pistol, but William Parker struck his arm so hard it appeared to break. Then the Parkers chased the white men until they disappeared southward.

Such boldness and determination would characterize William Parker over the next dozen years in Pennsylvania. The brothers crossed the Susquehanna River at Columbia and stopped in the rural Lancaster County town of Christiana, Pennsylvania, where William became the leader of a self-defense group of free blacks who fought slave catchers. The fear of being abducted and returned to slavery forced blacks together in resistance groups all along the Line following passage of the Fugitive Slave Law in 1850. His courage and leadership made Parker a charismatic figure among Lancaster County's 3,000 blacks, and he was respected and feared by whites.

The entire Chester-Lancaster County border of the 1850s was a battleground. In his 1991 book, *Bloody Dawn*, Thomas P. Slaughter writes: "Lancaster's blacks challenged the slave system by providing a visible alternative to the lives of northern Maryland's slaves. There was constant communication among blacks, slave and free, on either side of the Mason-Dixon Line; the Northerners provided aid and sustenance to those who ran away and engaged in guerilla warfare against slave masters and their agents who dared confront them in pitched battle."

Monkton, Maryland: South of Mile 46

There are eight mailboxes in front of the old Gorsuch Tavern, which stands just a few feet off the Susquehanna Trail. A woman puts a letter in one of them, flips up the red flag, and assures me that this is the original tavern built in 1810. "It's been broken into apartments, but it looks exactly the same on the outside as it did back then. This is where they met to plan the trip into Pennsylvania. . . ."

On November 6, 1849, four slaves—Noah Buley, Nelson Ford, and George and Joshua Hammond—took the Susquehanna Trail north to freedom just as William Parker had ten years before. They ran away from the farm of Edward Gorsuch, which was right across the street from the tavern. Gorsuch was a benevolent master, but the four had helped a free black steal some grain from the farm, and they feared they were about to be discovered.

Two years later Gorsuch received an anonymous letter informing him that his slaves were living in Christiana, Pennsylvania. Gorsuch and several family members met here at the tavern to plan ways to recover their property. The tavern was a popular hostelry on the York to Baltimore Road, and the innkeeper provided cells in the basement where slaves traveling with their masters could be locked up overnight.

On September 8, 1851, Gorsuch and several relatives took a train to Philadelphia, where they obtained four warrants from federal authorities to reclaim Gorsuch's property under the Fugitive Slave Law. The Gorsuch party, accompanied by a federal marshall, then rode to Christiana, where they learned the four runaways were being sheltered by the now famous

*Gorsuch Tavern in
Monkton, Mayland.*

William Parker. But the blacks had been alerted to the situation, and when Gorsuch approached Parker's house a large number of free blacks had gathered there to protect the four fugitives.

The marshall advised Gorsuch to leave because he was outnumbered, but the Marylander insisted on taking his property home with him. There is great confusion over what followed, but Gorsuch was shot and killed and his son severely wounded. The slave-catching party retreated and the fugitives, including Parker, fled to Canada.

The "Christiana Riot" shocked both sides of the Mason-Dixon Line, further polarized thought on the slavery question, and fueled the fires of secession. "No single event before John Brown's Raid contributed more to the decline of confidence in the nation's ability to resolve the controversy over slavery without wholesale resort to arms," said Slaughter.

SHREWSBURY, PENNSYLVANIA: NORTH OF MILE 47

The Shrewsbury playground overlooks the three-steepled village. At a picnic pavilion, a party of large adults are eating like refugees—pitchforking pasta, harpooning cubes of beef, cramming food into their mouths. A coeducational, intergenerational softball game is in progress on the diamond, where in the 1920s members of the Shrewsbury Klan would don their robes and masks and burn crosses after a picnic.

Albright's Church, erected in 1853, is still standing on Park Street and has been renamed the Shrewsbury Gospel Temple. The building has been in almost continuous use, and when it fell vacant in the 1920s the KKK moved from the Odd Fellow's Hall and made it its headquarters. The Klan called it Bryant Hall.

The KKK has always been popular in York County, and in 1923 there were more Klansmen here than in either Philadelphia or Pittsburgh. In the 1980s the Shrewsbury chapter held meetings in an open field east of town at the corner of Plank and Sweitzer Streets. It's still there, but new houses are surrounding it and will soon overtake it.

NEW FREEDOM, PENNSYLVANIA: MILE 48

The tracks of the old Northern Central Railroad, which opened between Baltimore and York in 1838, still run through the center of town, but nearer the Line they have been removed and the roadbed converted to a long trail for hikers and cyclists. There's a picnic bench right on the Line, and I sit down with a large Styrofoam cup of coffee, a copy of Charles Dickens' *American Notes*, and a photocopy of the Gettysburg Address. It's a sweet, green summer morning, still cool because the sun hasn't yet gotten a grip on the day. The trees are alive with bird twitter and cast elongated shadows on the roadbed. A southbound biker with a Buddha smile cruises by and nods.

Dickens passed by this spot heading in the same direction in 1842 as part of his trip to the United States. *American Notes* makes no mention of the Line, but a few miles into Maryland he was distressed by two wooden bridges over the Gunpowder and Little Gunpowder Rivers. "These bridges are of wood, have no parapet, and are only just wide enough for the passage of the trains; which, in the event of the smallest accident, would inevitably be plunged into the river. They are startling contrivances, and are most agreeable when passed."

I skim on in my paperback copy. "We stopped to dine at Baltimore, and being now in Maryland, were waited on, for the first time, by slaves. The sensation of exacting any service from human creatures who are bought and sold, and being, for the time, a party as it were to their condition, is not an enviable one. The institution exists, perhaps, in its least repulsive and most mitigated form in such a town as this; but it is slavery; and though I was, with respect to it, an innocent man, its presence filled me with a sense of shame and self-reproach."

Dickens was not fond of American trains.

> There are no first and second class carriages as with us; but there is a gentlemen's car and a ladies' car: the main distinction between which is, that in the first everybody smokes; and in the second, nobody does. As a black man never travels with a white one, there is also a negro car; which is a great, blundering, clumsy chest, such as Gulliver put to sea in from the kingdom of Brobdingnag. There is a great deal of jolting, a great deal of noise, a great deal of wall, not much window, a locomotive engine, a shriek, and a bell.
>
> The cars are like shabby omnibuses, but larger: holding thirty, forty, fifty people. The seats, instead of stretching from end to end, are placed crosswise. Each seat holds two persons. There is a long row of them on each side of the caravan, a narrow passage up the middle, and a door at both ends. In the centre of the carriage there is usually a stove, fed with charcoal or anthracite coal; which

is for the most part red-hot. It is insufferably close; and you see the hot air fluttering between.

Lincoln passed this same spot on November 18, 1863—one hundred years and three days after Mason and Dixon arrived in America—en route to make a speech at Gettysburg. Shortly after his coach crossed the Line, he arose and told his traveling companions, "Gentlemen, this is all very pleasant, but the people will expect me to say something to them tomorrow, and I must give the matter some thought." He went to a private room at the rear of the car. However, most Lincoln historians believe he had written the speech in Washington, and merely polished it on the train.

The occasion was the dedication of a cemetery for the Union soldiers who had died in the battle and been placed in temporary graves four months earlier. Local authorities contracted to have the reburials done at $1.59 a body, but the job was not completed in time. When Lincoln spoke, there were legs and arms sticking out of shallow graves all over the battlefield. For Lincoln it was also a political trip—he was cranking up for his re-election campaign, and he hoped to mend some fences with the Northern governors who would be there.

Another speaker at Gettysburg, Secretary of State William H. Seward, apparently thought he was in Maryland, because much of his speech was addressed to slave owners, and he said it was the first time he had an audience "on this side of the Mason-Dixon Line."

I count the words in the Gettysburg Address. There are 271. I count the one-syllable words. There are 202.

One year and five months later, on April 21, 1865, a nine-car train carrying Lincoln's body and that of his son, Willie, who had died in 1862, stopped on this spot at 5:30 P.M. An honor guard from Pennsylvania fired a twenty-one-gun salute, and the church bells of New Freedom knelled for America's first assassinated president. Governor Andrew G. Curtin of Pennsylvania boarded the train, where it was ceremonially turned over to his care by Governor Augustus W. Bradford of Maryland. "I propose to take charge of the remains at the line of the State and to accompany them until they leave the State," Curtin intoned.

As the train moved northward through New Freedom and Shrewsbury at twenty miles per hour, the tracks were lined on both sides with mourners, black and white.

YORK, PENNSYLVANIA: NORTH OF MILE 50

One of America's first urban riots began here on February 23, 1803, after a black woman, Margaret Bradley, was convicted of attempting to poison two local white sisters, Sophie and Matilda Bentz, and sentenced to four years in prison. Blacks believed Bradley was innocent, and for the next three weeks they took to the streets and burned buildings. Governor Thomas McKean sent the state militia into the city and order was restored. Some twenty-five blacks were arrested and given long prison terms.

On March 21, the local burgesses published a notice "to the inhabitants of York and its vicinity to a distance of ten miles."

"All white citizens having negro slaves are required to keep them at home under strict discipline and watch, and not allow them to come to town on any pretence whatsoever without a written pass. Such negroes are to leave town one hour at least before sundown on pain of being imprisoned or at risk of their lives. Freemen are required to get a pass from a justice of the peace, in order that they might not be restrained from their daily labor."

LINEBORO, MARYLAND: MILE 56

The sounds and smells are equine and bovine as I walk along a rutted khaki road between York County, Pennsylvania, and Carroll County, Maryland. On either side, bright red barns are set off by complementary green fields. Marker No. 56, chipped and rusted, sits on a concrete platform and is protected by a black iron cage. It was moved here in 1983, some twenty feet west of its original position, because it had become a roadside hazard. Horses with flourishing tails graze in a nearby pasture next to a farm with a lawn jockey in front.

White habitation began here in 1745 when colonists built a grist mill and called the town Plymouth. It was changed to Lineboro soon after the surveyors came through. Lineboro today consists of fifty or so houses lining Main Street. The population is about 200, mostly retired persons, and there are three times as many graves in the Lazarus Church cemetery.

The homes get grander as you move south down Main Street, and near the end they lean towards the mansion end of the housing spectrum. The Lineboro General Store is closed and boarded up, and the sign on the Village Inn says

An iron cage protects Marker No. 56 near Lineboro, Maryland.

it's only open between 10 A.M. and 1 P.M. The marquee at the Lineboro Volunteer Fire Department announces "Bessie Bingo This Weekend."

I peek inside and find a gray-haired man who is alternately polishing a red truck and then standing back to admire his work. I pop the question. "What's Bessie Bingo?" He looks at me as though I'd asked if we are standing on Planet Earth at this moment. He recovers and then answers. "We fence off a big area in back of the firehouse and make squares like a giant bingo card. We number the squares. There are a hundred squares. People bring in their cows and everyone bets on where the cow will poop. It's a lot of fun. The people try to coax the cows into certain square by giving them food. . . ."

HANOVER PIKE: MILE 60

Some Union cavalry units rode nonstop for three straight days to get to Gettysburg, and by the time they reached the Line on July 1, 1863, they were exhausted. Horses were falling dead in the heat, and some of the men were walking and carrying their saddles. The troops in the rear were almost unrecognizable from the dust that covered them.

That same day a diarist with the 188th Pennsylvania wrote: "Rousing cheers, demonstrative shouts, ringing enthusiasm greeted the good old Commonwealth of Pennsylvania. The unfurling of colors and rolling of drums at one o'clock in the afternoon indicated the crossing of the line. There was a firmer step, better closed ranks, more determined countenances. Beyond there had been some cavalry fighting. The fences were down and the bodies of dead horses scattered about." All along the route, people came out to welcome "Mr. Lincoln's Army."

HANOVER, PENNSYLVANIA: NORTH OF MILE 63

The Penn-Calvert dispute flamed white hot over a 10,000-acre tract that was given by the Calverts to John Digges of Prince Georges County, Maryland, in 1727 under unusual circumstances. Digges was allowed to choose the location of the land as long as it was unoccupied. The area he picked near the present borough of Hanover became known as "Digges' Choice." However, it wasn't the Calverts land to give, because it belonged to the Indians—at least until 1736, when it was part of a tract purchased by William Penn from the Iroquois.

Nevertheless, Digges sold lots to German settlers without providing his purchasers with deeds for their holdings. Border tensions grew into rage when Digges' tried to expel some of the settlers who had come to consider themselves to be Pennsylvanians. There were violent confrontations, and in 1752 Martin Kitzmiller, a disgruntled Pennsylvanian, shot and killed Dudley Digges, John's son; Kitzmiller was tried in a Pennsylvania court, which accepted his plea that the shooting was accidental. The uncertain jurisdiction made the area a harbor for criminals, and it became known as the "Rogue's Resort."

UNION MILLS, MARYLAND: SOUTH OF MILE 65

The twenty-three-room Shriver Homestead is on the Littlestown Pike along Big Pipe Creek, where it served six generations of Shrivers, at various times, as a home, inn, store, school, and post office. It is now owned by Carroll County and maintained by a nonprofit group. It is just seventeen miles from Gettysburg, and Confederate General J. E. B. Stuart made his headquarters here on June 29, 1863—just three days before the only major Civil War battle fought north of the Line.

That night, General Robert E. Lee came to dinner and joined with other officers in singing songs like "My Old Kentucky Home" and "Annie Laurie" while Stuart accompanied them on the Shriver family piano.

T. Herbert Shriver was a slave owner and favored the Southern cause, and the next day he accompanied Stuart towards Gettysburg as his personal guide. They stopped at the Line to water their horses and then proceeded north.

The dust from Stuart's cavalry had barely settled when later the same day, the Union Army marched into town, and General James Barnes spent the night here. The next day they pushed off for Gettysburg, and the official history of the 10th Regiment of Cavalry, New York State Volunteers, records:

> After a time, Major Avery said, "I think we must be in Pennsylvania." The means for ascertaining were at hand. A blooming little miss, from a farm-house situated away back from the main road, had ventured down to the gate to look at the passing troops. "Miss, will you please tell us whether we are in Maryland or Pennsylvania?" she was asked. "You are in Maryland yet, but the edge of the woods, just ahead, is the State Line," she replied. "We will cross the line singing 'John Brown,'" says Major Avery. Everybody sang or attempted singing. It was a grand swelling of loyal voices in spontaneous accord—a sublime crossing of the threshold into the grand old Commonwealth whose sons formed so large a part of the command.

WESTMINSTER, MARYLAND: SOUTH OF MILE 65

The Chattel Records of the Carroll County Land Records Office are in the courthouse annex. There are some seventy-five manumission certificates that were executed between 1842 and 1865. The county clerk witnessed and signed the documents to prove the slaves had been freed. Since it was crucial for whites to be able to distinguish free blacks from slaves, these certificates go into great detail describing the former slave—height, age, body build, scars, and mannerisms. Slaves were also freed in their owners' wills—a favored method because it permitted maximum term of service.

The Civil War actually did pit father against son, brother against brother. In June 1863, just before the Battle of Gettysburg, Major William Goldsborough of the Confederate Second Maryland Infantry captured his brother, John Goldsborough, a surgeon with the Union forces, in Winchester.

LITTLESTOWN PIKE: MILE 68

Several Pennsylvania regiments passed here late on the afternoon of July 1, 1863, on the way to Gettysburg. For many of them, it was their first time in their home state in two years, and as they crossed the Line the men of the 93rd Regiment sang "Home Sweet Home." After he passed into Pennsylvania, Colonel Strong Vincent sent back the word, "We are now on the soil of old Pennsylvania. . . . Hang out the banner and let our march be accompanied by the sound of the ear-piercing fife and spirit stirring drum." Captain Amos Judson of E Company saw Sergeant Rogers unfurl the flag of the 83rd Regiment. The Drum Corps struck up "Yankee Doodle." The enthusiasm spread from regiment to regiment, and soon Vincent got his wish.

Victories at Fredericksburg and Chancellorsville had whetted Southern appetites for a big victory beyond the Mason-Dixon Line, and the first sign of the coming battle came in mid-June when large numbers of blacks— men, women, and children—came streaming over the border. Most of them were from seceded states and had been freed by the Emancipation Proclamation. Maryland slaves sought refuge with the Union armies, but when they realized that the proclamation did not apply to slaves from states that had remained with the Union, many returned to their masters.

THE FREDERICK-LITTLESTOWN ROAD: MILE 71

I walk west along the Line between two cultivated fields about 500 feet to Marker No. 68, which is next to a mulberry tree. After 232 years, it's chipped and worn, but the "M" and "P" are still clear. I come out of a corn- field onto the highway, which seems almost liquefied in the noon sun. A mirage shimmers and dances across the road. Two cyclists have removed their helmets, opened their water bottles, and are taking turns photograph- ing each other in front of the big blue "Welcome to Pennsylvania" sign.

All along the Line in the early summer of 1863, Confederate troops poured into Pennsylvania. One Virginia cavalry officer passed here and wrote home in a letter: "I crossed Mason's and Dixon's Line today and am now some five or six miles within the boundaries of the Keystone State, surrounded by enemies and black looks, Dutchmen, and big barns."

The Southerners were surprised by the number of draft-age men in the

North who were still civilians. Every able-bodied Southern white man from sixteen to sixty was serving, and the farm work was left to the slaves.

TANEYTOWN, MARYLAND: SOUTH OF MILE 72

Taneytown is bleached out and baking in the summer sun. Its deserted streets seem struck dumb by the 100-degree heat. The bell at Trinity Lutheran Church is tolling noon. It has a new steeple, but in 1863 the church tower was used by Union forces to signal the Gettysburg battlefield some twelve miles to the northwest. They used flags by day, flares by night. It took about ten minutes to send a message on troop movements, supplies, reinforcements, and other vital information. Union soldiers camped beside the stream that bubbles by "Antrim 1844," a restored antebellum mansion built by Colonel Andrew Ege as a wedding gift for his daughter. The remnants of slave quarters are near the stream.

The town is the namesake of Raphael Taney, who laid it out about two years before Mason and Dixon passed by. He shared a common ancestor with Roger B. Taney, the Supreme Court chief justice. Mason spent the night here on February 24, 1766.

EMMITSBURG ROAD: MILE 80

Another junkyard. Plundered vehicles squatting on their axles surrounded by broken glass and strewn garbage. The states of Pennsylvania and Maryland have posted signs naming their governors, welcoming me on one side and thanking me for coming on the other, and stating their official policies on stopped school buses, seat belts, and littering.

The 284 officers and men of the 13th Massachusetts Regiment crossed here on July 1, 1863, and bivouacked on Marsh Creek. Within twenty-four hours, two thirds of them would be casualties.

EMMITSBURG, MARYLAND: SOUTH OF MILE 81

A Union soldier from Pennsylvania came through here on his way to Gettysburg on June 30, 1863, and wrote in his diary: "Our reception was extremely enthusiastic. Ladies and young girls distributed beautiful bouquets to the officers and soldiers; groups of fair damsels bewitchingly posted in conspicuous places sang patriotic songs as the 'boys in blue' passed by and the citizens turned out en masse. Long after tattoo, groups of ladies and gentlemen promenaded through our camps, actuated by a curiosity to see how soldiers really lived in the tented field."

Just under one mile from the Line, Kathleen Williams lives with her daughter in a townhouse around the block from the old Emmitsburg Public School, where she could never go. Her grandmother lived before the adoption of the Thirteenth Amendment, but she doesn't know if she was a slave.

"My family was Catholic, and I went to Catholic school. It was segregated, too. Only at St. Euphenia's they just put us in separate rooms. The public schools had different buildings. Sister Cecilia was our teacher, and I remember that for some reason she liked to teach black children. We were called coloreds back then. The church school only had eight grades, though, and we couldn't go to the public school."

She is bright, sharp, cheerful, friendly, and eighty-five. She's sitting in a rocking chair crocheting an afghan for her second great-grandchild, who's due in a few months.

"I went to St. Anthony's Church when I was a little girl. They had special pews in the back. Then Father Reilly came along and said, 'I'm gettin' rid of those pews,' and he did. He took 'em out. After that we sat wherever we wanted. Father Reilly also got them to stop burying black people in a separate place in the church cemetery.

"There was a white man, Mr. Rosenstein, who had a taxi. It was an old Cadillac. We'd pay him to take us to Gettysburg so we could sit and have a meal in a restaurant and go to the movies. It was just a few miles away, but things were always better on the other side of the Mason-Dixon Line. . . . "

"Sometimes the white kids were mean to us. They'd call us 'nigger' and all. My sister used to fight back. She'd say, 'Hold my books, Katherine.' And then she'd hit them and they'd run away. . . . " Her eyes go wide with the memory.

AN ADAMS COUNTY ORCHARD: NORTH OF MILE 85

Carlos is standing on a ladder, his head hidden in a tree, picking apples and placing them in a basket with a single, swift motion. He says he's twenty-nine years old and was married six months ago in his hometown of

Manaubo, Puerto Rico. He gets a base pay of six dollars an hour, but he makes up to eleven dollars because he's a fast worker. This is at least six times what he can make back home. He's been coming here for the past ten years in July, August, September, and October. His father worked here for twenty years before him.

FREDERICK, MARYLAND: SOUTH OF MILE 86

Sitting off by itself, its brick painted yellow, Roger Brooke Taney's house seems like an intruder in the black neighborhood of downtown Frederick. A dog tongue-lolls on the step of a rowhouse, but most of the humans are inside, held hostage by the 100-degree heat. Overworked room air conditioners jut from many windows, growling, shrieking, and dripping condensation onto the sidewalk.

The door is locked. I ring the bell. Then I see a sign in the window that says for a tour you have to call the Visitors Center. I find a pay phone and a woman tells me it's impossible to see the house today. "You've got to make an appointment well in advance. Hardly anyone goes there. Occasionally a lawyer will ask to see it. . . ."

I go back to the house and peek through the windows. Taney's law books are on the right side near the entrance, and on the left is the desk where he wrote the majority opinion in the case of *Dred Scott vs. Sandford,* holding that Negroes were "beings of an inferior order, and altogether unfit to associate with the white race, either in social or political relations; and so far inferior that they had no rights that the white man was bound to respect." Robert Bork called it "the worst constitutional decision of the nineteenth century."

Toward the rear of the house is a wing that housed Taney's slaves, and the work area for cooking and sewing are still there. Taney freed his own slaves ten years before he wrote the Dred Scott opinion, but he said that he didn't think he could impose his personal views about slavery on others. Taney was a Jacksonian Democrat and led the court in extending rights and protections to the common man. At least the common white man.

A new duplex home is at 111–113 Ice St., on the site of where the Free Colored Men's Library operated out of the living room of the Rev. Ignatius Snowden. The library was incorporated on March 27, 1913, and bought books after a fundraising drive yielded one hundred dollars. The drive had a campaign song, sung to the tune of the "Battle Hymn of the Republic":

> Books by men like Washington, Dubois and Dunbar
> Kelly, Miller, Norris and Joseph, Gordon, Bryant
> And many other writers too you are sure to find
> At the Free Colored Library.
> Fairy tales for children such as Old Mother Goose
> Who Killed Cock Robin and Little Red Riding Hood
> Tales of a winter night and many more as good
> At the Free Colored Library

The library provided books for Frederick's blacks until the public library was desegregated in the 1960s. In 1995 the Frederick Historic District Commission approved the demolition of the building to make way for the duplex.

Charles Mason passed through here on February 25, 1766, on one of his long, off-season jaunts. He left the Harlan Farm on February 21 "and proceeded for curiosity to the Southward to see the country." He crossed the Susquehanna at Nelson's Ferry, some seven miles north of the Line he had just helped draw, and went on to York, Taneytown, and then Frederick. From here he went into Virginia and then back into Maryland, arriving at Annapolis on March 11. He returned through Frederick on March 17 while making his way back to the West Line.

BLUE RIDGE SUMMIT, PENNSYLVANIA: MILE 89

Right after the Civil War, the Western Maryland Railroad began providing service to Blue Ridge Summit, which is 2,000 feet above sea level and intersected by the Line. It became a premier mountain resort, and some of its first visitors were Confederate veterans who had come here while retreating from

Gettysburg in 1863. They remembered the cool air and dramatic scenery.

The resort wilted in the Depression and train service was halted in 1957. The following year the railroad turned over the station to the Blue Ridge Summit Free Library. The current and longtime librarian is Nancy Bert, a white woman who with her husband raised an adopted black son here in the 1980s.

"The Mason-Dixon Line was more than symbolic for our family. North of it we were accepted. South of it, we drew angry glares. When my son was an adolescent, he was at a party in Frederick that was raided by the police. He and the other blacks went off to jail. The whites got a warning."

PEN MAR, MARYLAND: MILE 91

A century ago thousands of tourists came to the conifered mountains of Pen Mar and its cool, resined air to escape the summer heat of Baltimore and Washington. John Mifflin Hood built a huge amusement park here in 1871 that he hoped would lure travelers and help finance the expansion of his Western Maryland Railroad.

Pen Mar became one of the most popular resorts in the United States. It was fashionable. President Grover Cleveland, Dr. Walter Reed, and Alice Longworth Roosevelt all stayed in one of its first-class hotels. There were trains every day, and ordinary people took day excursions, bringing picnic baskets and blankets. The athletic walked three quarters of a mile to a sixty-foot steel observation tower, where they could get a view of Maryland, Pennsylvania, West Virginia, and Virginia.

For many years, a familiar sight was a blind black man named Otho Jones, who waited near the station and recited passages from the Bible in exchange for donations. He recognized frequent visitors by their steps and greeted them by name. He spent the entire summer in the park.

The automobile ended dependence on the railroads, and Pen Mar went downhill. Today, a quiet county park stands in a cool glade where the dance pavilion and amusement park once drew thousands. The observation tower has been taken over by the Pentagon as part of its communications system. Right below the tower, deep in the mountain, is Site R. . . .

The top of Raven Rock is prickling with antennae about 300 yards south of the Line. I come to a chain-link fence topped by barbed wire. The gate is closed and locked, but standing outside is a man wearing white shoes, white pants, and white shirt. "What the hell is this?" I ask.

He gives me a suspicious sideways squint. "This is a highly classified military installation. I can't go into detail, but don't go up there. They shoot first and ask questions later."

In fact, it's a kind of doomsday bunker built by the Pentagon to shelter the Joint Chiefs of Staff and other military leaders in the event of an enemy attack on Washington. The massive 265,000-square foot facility was buried 650 feet into the mountain and houses computers, communications equipment, water reservoirs, streets, tons of freeze-dried foods, a dining hall, barber shop, dental clinic, sick bay, chapel, convenience store, fitness center, and designated smoking areas. Beginning in 1954, there were some 500 soldiers assigned here, but when the Cold War wound down they were replaced by a skeleton crew.

Nearby is Fort Ritchie, which has been closed, the sign says, since 1 October 1998. During World War II it was used to train American spies, and it housed an entire German village. A special unit impersonated German prisoners of war. The Japanese prisoners were played first by American Indians, then by Japanese-Americans.

Children with tiny day packs strapped to their backs are walking along the Appalachian Trail, that narrow swath of boot-packed earth that runs more than 2,000 miles from Springer Mountain, Georgia, to Mount Katahdin, Maine. For long-distance hikers, the Line has always been a milestone because it's almost exactly at the halfway point. The Line and the trail intersect in a field of orange tiger lilies, and the air is redolent of pine cones baking in the summer heat.

Mason and Dixon set up the zenith sector near here to calculate their probable error on September 6, 1765. After two weeks of stargazing, they found they were about 700 feet too far south and aimed north ever-so-slightly to get back on the proper latitude.

MILE 93

The terrain flattens out after Pen Mar, but ahead about tewnty-five miles I can see the aquamarine hump of North Mountain. I cross the Ringgold Pike and look back at the communications towers atop Raven Rock. Marker No. 93 is in a cornfield on a farm, and here I find Todd Babcock and Steve Long.

Babcock, a surveyor from Fleetwood, Pennsylvania, is a founder of the Mason and Dixon Line Preservation Partnership. He brushes away a bit of lichen from the stone with his hand. "There's a bad gouge here, but otherwise it's in good shape. Most of the stones were set in concrete in 1903. This is a good thing and a bad thing. It keeps people from stealing them, but if it gets hit by something, like a tractor, it can break off. That's happened to several of the stones."

Long is a surveyor, Partnership member, and expert in the use of the Global Positioning System (GPS), which calculates latitude and longitude by retrieving information from military satellites. He is setting up a four-foot-high receiver in the middle of the top of the marker. "If Mason and Dixon had this equipment, they could have set up at the Post Mark'd West and walked all the way to the end without stopping to measure again. . . ."

Long interrupts himself. "Here we are. We're at 39 degrees, 43 minutes, 11-point 9-1-6 seconds latitude; 77 degrees, 32 minutes, 27-point-2-6-3 longitude. Six satellites are sending us information, and this is accurate to one quarter of an inch. Mason and Dixon were off by about five seconds."

One of the missions of Babcock and the Partnership is to "promote the true and factual history" of the Mason-Dixon Line. "The true history of the Line has been muddled through years of folklore and hearsay," Babcock says. "It came to be known as the line which divided the free states from the slave states, or North from South. Others believe that to be from 'way down south in Dixie' stems from the fact that they live south of the Mason and Dixon Line. Conversely, I suppose it could be said that a Vermonter is from 'way up north in Masey.' Our objective is to dispel such folklore."

Perhaps the most enduring myth is that the Line is accurate down to the inch. "It's off by as much as 800 feet to the south near Emmitsburg, and when you get out to Sideling Hill, it's 300 feet too far north. Because of these variations, the actual Line can only be determined by going from one marker to the next. You can't go from the first to the last."

Another goal of the Partnership is to identify, inventory, and record precise positions of all of the markers. "This way, we can preserve the Line long after the original markers are gone. If the original markers are stolen, broken off, or otherwise turn up missing, we can replace them and be right on the dime."

MILE 94

I emerge from an apple orchard and cross the Smithsburg Pike into a cornfield. A boy no older than twelve drives a tractor past me. He is hunched forward so he can see over the steering wheel. The defeated Confederate Army recrossed the Line here in full retreat on July 4 and 5, 1863. It was a seventeen-mile wagon train of ambulances and farm wagons filled with thousands of wounded who it was thought could survive travel. The others were left to die at Gettysburg. From the bouncing wagons, men cried out in agony and asked to be left by the roadside to die. It took nearly two days for the procession to pass.

RINGGOLD, MARYLAND: SOUTH OF MILE 94

Daniel Logan, who lived less than a mile form the Line, was considered a good husband and a good father by his white neighbors. He made his living capturing free blacks and runaway slaves and selling them south. He was frequently seen heading south on horseback leading a group of blacks roped together. When black mothers wanted to terrify their children into obedience, they said, "Dan Logan will get you!"

WAYNESBORO, PENNSYLVANIA: NORTH OF MILE 94

Lisa Welsh Bender, a Waynesboro resident when the Civil War began, recorded that the Line was busy from the moment war was declared. ". . . [A] rumor that the confederates were crossing the Potomac would bring through our town hundreds of refugees from Maryland. Sometimes at night we would be awakened by the rumble of wagons and the clatter of horses' feet on the stony streets. . . . the Negroes bound for the Northern States and freedom and the farmers for some remote and almost inaccessible place on the mountain. In a few weeks the farmers would return to their neglected fields, half-starved and tired out, to find that the enemy had not crossed the river after all. The newly invented verb 'skedaddle' forced itself into our vocabulary at the time and was immediately put to hard usage, as no word in the dictionary expressed half so well this helter-skelter rout of an army of non-combatants."

A venetian blind neatly slices the sunlight on the Formica top in the Waynesboro Restaurant. Steve Waltz smooths his gray moustache and nods affirmatively to the waitress poised to refill his coffee cup. "When I got to the tenth grade, my father told me that he had quit school in the ninth grade, and I should do the same. I told him I wanted to finish high school and maybe even go to college. He said that was fine, but I had to do it on my own. Then he told me to get out of the house. There were nights when I didn't get anything to eat or have any place to sleep, but I got through somehow. A lot of white people helped me out, including Rip and his wife, Sonny, and I guess that's why I'm not really angry about everything else that happened. . . ."

Rip was Rip Engle, who in 1936 was the football coach at Waynesboro High School. He would later go on to fame as Joe Paterno's predecessor and mentor at Penn State. Steve Waltz was one of three blacks on the Waynesboro roster, and whenever the opponent came from south of the Mason-Dixon Line, Waltz and his two teammates were not allowed to play.

"About half our games were against teams south of the Line, like Hagerstown, Cumberland, and Martinsburg. And even if the game was here in Waynesboro, we weren't allowed to play. Rip would call me aside after practice and say, 'Steve, you know we can't play you tomorrow.' Then he'd explain to the team and ask them to give one hundred per cent for the white guy who was replacing me."

Officials at Waynesboro and other schools near the Line would explain they were keeping the blacks out of the game "as a courtesy" to their opponents, and the sports pages of local newspapers would explain that the absent players were "ineligible" for the game.

"I went to the game in Martinsburg, West Virginia, as a spectator dressed in civilian clothes and sat on the bench with the team. The home fans started chanting, 'Get that nigger off the bench,' and the state police came and escorted me away. I watched the game by myself from the bleachers in the colored section."

Not all the racists were south of the Line. "Several times in my senior year the Waynesboro Rotary Club named me Player of the Week, but I couldn't go to the luncheon because it was in the Anthony Wayne Hotel. They'd give me a dollar and tell me to go buy a sandwich for lunch."

After high school Waltz attended North Carolina A&T College, and in World War II he was a pilot with the 332nd Fighter Group, escorting bombers over targets in Germany. The unit was better known as the Tuskegee Airmen, an all-black group of pilots trained at Tuskegee Air Field in Alabama. After the war, the Army became an equal opportunity employer, and Waltz worked as a civilian in a top-secret job for thirty-three years, traveling all over the world.

"I'd rather look back on the good things," he says, staring into the dregs of his cup. "Rip was like a father to me. If he told me to walk over hot coals, I would. We were coming back from a game on Saturday afternoon and stopped at a restaurant for dinner. The owner told Rip I'd have to eat in the kitchen. Rip said, 'Well, in that case, Boys, there's no need to sit down. Let's get out of here. . . .'"

CAVETOWN, MARYLAND: SOUTH OF MILE 95

This town was named after what was the largest cave in Maryland. The town survived, the cave did not. It collapsed in 1925 because of extensive rock quarrying operations. A workman at the Cavetown Planing Mill points out the remnants of the cave across a single set of railroad tracks.

"Did you know Charles Mason was here?" I ask.

"Who?"

"Charles Mason. You know, Mason and Dixon?

"Do they live around here?"

MILE 99

The Line cuts through a farm, separating silo from barn. Mason and Dixon were here on September 24, 1765, when it was owned by "Mr. Samule Irwin." Marker No. 100, a crown stone, is next to a mailbox in front of a house. About one hundred yards further west, the Line slices through a cornfield. Marsh Run is high and muddy, and on the east side cows are grazing in the field where Thomas Cresap put up a stone building in 1733 that served as a home, fortification, and trading post for his campaign of harassing the Pennsylvania settlers. The border wars raged on.

Indeed, there was continuous fighting on this section of the Line for more than two centuries. It was contested ground. First, Indians fought other Indians. Then white colonists fought Indians. Then Pennsylvanians fought Marylanders. Next the British and the colonists fought the French and the Indians. Then the British fought the Americans. And finally, Americans fought Americans.

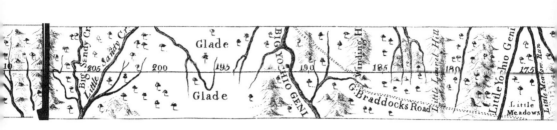

SIDELONG

Line 170 65 ALLEGENY MOUNT. Little Allegeny Jennings's Ru n 160 WILLS CREEK Wills Creek 155 Road to ye Bed: Evits Cr. Evits Mount Plimstong Ridge 150 FLINTSTONE C. The Good Warrior Mo: Little Wa rrior Mo: TOWN CR: 145 Ragged M. 808 m. Fifteen Mile Creek 140 Town Hill

Chapter Six

THE WEST LINE
APPALACHIAN MOUNTAINS TO
DUNKARD CREEK — 130 MILES.

"What we learn about ourselves is that we white Americans are more deeply and tragically human than we tell ourselves in our political and congratulatory rhetoric. Our national pride must be tempered with critical self-knowledge. Our faith in ourselves must incorporate doubt into itself if it is to be lasting, effective faith. The study of our contact with Indians, the envisioning of our dark American selves, can instill such a strengthening doubt."
—Christopher Vecsey, *The American Indian and the Problem of History*

The westward progress continued in 1765 until October 7, when the party set up the observatory at the foot of Cove (North) Mountain, some 114 miles from the Northeast Corner, and five miles south of the present town of Mercersburg, Pennsylvania. They spent nineteen days reviewing their latest headway and, with the help of their old friends Lyrae, Cygni, Capella, et al., carefully calibrating their position, which they found to be 846 feet off the true parallel.

In late October they contacted Captain Evan Shelby, one of the most fascinating characters of the colonial frontier, who had lived on the boundary lands between Pennsylvania and Maryland since he came to America from Wales in 1733. He was a justice of the peace and fur trader who had fought with the British army against the Indians just three years earlier. He was also a surveyor. The two English scientists had a very important purpose for visiting Shelby—they wanted him to escort them to the top of Cove Mountain so they could determine the course of the serpentine Potomac River. The exact course was crucial because if it were to drift north of the Line and then make a turn south, Maryland would effectively be split into two parts by the colony of Virginia.

On their first trip to the summit, the air was too hazy to see far enough, but on the second climb they were reassured, because they saw firsthand that the northernmost bend of the Potomac was still inside Maryland by about two miles. On October 27, Mason recorded: "From here we could see the Allegheny Mountain for many miles and judge by its appearance to be about 50 miles distant from the direction of our Line." Mason and Dixon stored their equipment at Captain Shelby's for the winter and started the long trip back to the Harlan farm. En route, they placed temporary posts to mark each mile until the permanent stones could be set in position the following year.

CHAMBERSBURG, PENNSYLVANIA: NORTH OF MILE 101

James Curry escaped from a North Carolina plantation in 1839 and proceeded to Chambersburg. "I traveled on through Williamsport and Hagerstown, in Maryland, and, on the nineteenth day of July, about two hours before day, I crossed the line into Pennsylvania with a heart full of gratitude to God, believing that I was indeed a free man, and that now, under the protection of law, there was none who could molest me or make me afraid," he said in an interview after the Civil War. But after only a few hours in Chambersburg, he was warned by free blacks that slave catchers were very active in the area and that the local whites supported them. "After finding, to my great disappointment, that I was not a free man, and that I could not send for my wife from here, I determined to go to Canada." Curry returned to North Carolina after the war to find his old family, but he was set upon by whites and beaten badly.

Jacob H. Stoner, the leading historian of Franklin County, Pennsylvania, says Pennsylvania's last slave sale occurred in 1829 on a farm two miles north of here on the road to Hagerstown. Two young blacks were auctioned off—one drew $150, the other $30. The sale was illegal.

GREENCASTLE, PENNSYLVANIA: NORTH OF MILE 102

The Bethel African Methodist Church on Carlisle Street is on the site of the old log church that was built to serve the black community in 1816. It was an emergency harbor for fugitives who had just crossed the Line. They were dispatched to local homes, fed, given a place to sleep, and then guided farther north as soon as possible.

HAGERSTOWN, MARYLAND: SOUTH OF MILE 102

The reassuring, confluent smells of hot dogs, onions, nachos, pizza, and pop-corn seem to fatten the very air around Hagerstown's grand old Municipal Stadium, whose stone gates have been ushering fans into the ballpark since 1930. I buy a four-dollar general admission ticket and head for the bleach-ers. The stadium has the look of a grainy old newsreel, and I half expect to see the Babe doing his spindly legged home run trot. Actually, Ruth's sister lives here, and there's a fifteen-foot mural of the Babe out in right field.

The history of minor league baseball in Hagerstown goes back to 1915, when the Hagerstown Hubs took the field for the first time. Since then there have been years when baseball went away, but it always came back. Tonight about 3,000 people have shown up to watch the ball game—more or less. There are a lot of sideshows going on—young women with baby strollers form tight little gossiping circles, denimed adolescent girls smug-gle giggles to each other, and tow-headed boys in baseball caps run through the stands, bristling with unexpended energy.

The real fans are watching the game in hopes there is some future super-star among the eighteen-, nineteen-, and twenty-year-olds giving their all on the diamond. Many have been here in the past—Brooks Robinson, Robin Roberts, Jim Palmer, Deion Sanders, Albert Belle. . . .

And, on a June night much like this one in 1950, nineteen-year-old Willie Mays made his debut in organized baseball—at least white organ-ized baseball. He had played two years for the Birmingham Barons in the Negro Leagues. Mays had just signed a $4,000 contract with the New York Giants, and he was assigned to the Trenton Giants of the Class B Interstate League. He took a train from Birmingham to Hagerstown to join his new team in a four-game series against the Hagerstown Braves. It was June 23, 1950, and thirty-eight years later Mays remembered it well in his autobi-ography, *Say, Hey!*

> The Trenton Giants were playing a weekend series in Hagerstown, starting on Friday night and ending with a doubleheader on Sunday. I realized that I was a pioneer, for not only was I the first black player on the team—I was the first in the entire league. . . .
> It didn't take me long to realize that Hagerstown was the only city in our league below the Mason-Dixon Line. When I walked

onto the field for the first time, I heard someone shout, "Who's that nigger walking on the field?' But I didn't let it bother me. I was programmed very well from playing with the Barons. I had learned how to be thickskinned.

What I didn't get over was the long train ride that had brought me there. Although I did feel good during batting practice—I hit six or seven balls over the fence—in the game I just didn't feel right. I didn't get a hit that first game or for the rest of the four-game series. I started my organized baseball career oh-for-Maryland, and in a segregated town, to boot. I wondered whether my showing confirmed some of those rednecks' feelings that I wouldn't do well in the big time. What a way to start. And then after the game I found I couldn't stay with the team at their hotel. The club had already made arrangements for me to spend the weekend in a small hotel for blacks.

Marguerite Doleman descends the carpeted stairs slowly, pausing between each step to catch her breath. I reach out for her hand to guide her. It is cool and long-fingered. At the bottom she points to three green oxygen tanks on the floor and says over an emphysematic wheeze, "I might have to put my air on."

But she rallies and asks me to sign the guest book. I note that the last person signed in seven months ago. She started her black history museum in 1975 when she was fifty-five years old. It grew until now it occupies virtually every inch of her downstairs. "I've got to get this place organized. I kept up with it until the arthuritis got me. Now I have emphysema, too, and it's hard to get around."

The word spread through Hagerstown's black community that Marguerite Doleman was starting the museum and would welcome donations. The flood began. Christmas cards with black Santa Clauses. A slave-stitched quilt from 1847. A magnet depicting Henry "Box" Brown. The wallpaper shows slaves working on a plantation. Bills of sale for slaves. Copies of permits given slaves so they could travel. A black G.I. Joe doll. An empty can of "Afro Kola: The Soul Drink." A bandage called "Soul-Aid. . . ."

And a lawn jockey. "A lot of blacks have been offended by this over the years," she says. "But it's actually a tribute to Jocko Graves, a twelve-year-old black boy who was with General George Washington. When he was planning to cross the Delaware River on Christmas Eve, he needed people to go ahead of him, find horses, and wait for the army. Jocko was one of them. When he crossed the river, Washington saw what he thought were horses tied to a tree stump. But when he got there, he found out it was Jocko. He was frozen solid, and his hands still gripped the horses' reins."

She also has an 1882 map displaying cartographic racism. It shows North and South Jonathan Street and East and West Church Street. There was a black section of Hagerstown that included North Jonathan Street. The whites on South Jonathan Street didn't want to be identified with the blacks, so they changed the name of the street to Summit Avenue. In like manner, East Church Street was changed to East Street. The names remain this way today. Such distinctions also were helpful to real estate sales people trying to keep blacks out of white neighborhoods.

Marguerite Doleman was born in Philadelphia, and at the age of ten she and her family moved to Mount Union, Pennsylvania, some forty miles north of the Line in Huntingdon County. "The schools were integrated there, and often I was the only black student in my class. When I was fifteen we moved to Hagerstown, and I was put in the black school. When I crossed that Mason-Dixon Line, it was like night and day. I was way ahead of everyone else in my class. I would have been valedictorian, but they had a rule you had to go to the school for four years. . . . This was in the 1930s."

MILE 102

Dr. George Junkin, president of Washington College (now Washington & Lee University) in Lexington, Virginia, was a Northerner and an abolitionist. A few days after the outbreak of the Civil War, he noticed the Confederate flag flying over the main college building. He ordered it removed, but he was rebuffed by the faculty, which passed a resolution "That the flag be permitted to remain on the building at the discretion of the faculty."

Junkin resigned the next day, purchased a carriage, and came north with one of his three daughters and a niece. When they reached the Line here, he stopped the carriage, carefully washed it, and then crossed the Line. He later explained that he wanted to be sure that no Southern soil crossed into Pennsylvania.

His two older daughters stayed behind because they were married to Confederate officers—one of them to Colonel J. T. L. Preston, the other to General Thomas J. Jackson, who six months later would earn his nickname, "Stonewall" by refusing to budge at the Battle of Bull Run.

STATE LINE, PENNSYLVANIA: MILE 102

Before I began my travels, I wrote letters to small weekly newspapers near the Line explaining my project and inviting contributions and suggestions. Of the dozens I received, one of the best came from Margaret Spangler: "My husband's great-grandparents, Henry and Margaret Ellen Mullen Burger, lived in Jack Wolgamot's house. He made whiskey inside the house, and if the Maryland revenuers raided him, he moved everything to the Pennsylvania side and hid it, and if the Penna authorities raided him, he crossed the line, which ran through the center of the house, into Maryland and hid his whiskey."

Jack Wolgamot was the first white man here, and he was a sheep rustler. The story goes that he built a log home right on the Line and avoided arrest by moving his flock from one state to the other. As other settlers joined nearby, the community came to be called Muttontown.

When Robert E. Lee passed through here on his way to Gettysburg in 1863, the town was called Middleburg. Lee stopped at the farm of David and Mary Martin, a few feet over the Line, where the family's young daughter, Alice Martin, pumped water and gave him a drink.

A Confederate soldier with General George E. Pickett's division wrote these impressions in his diary on June 26:

> We passed the line (Mason-Dixon) this afternoon near a small village named Middletown [*sic*] on the maps but called Muttontown by the natives. It is easy to see, however, that Muttontown is altogether appropriate for the demeanor of many of the inhabitants is sheepish in the extreme. Strange to say we met with a more marked exhibition of welcome at this Pennsylvania town than in any portion of Maryland. I saw fully a dozen miniature Confederate flags waving from windows, while all along the streets were ladies waving handkerchiefs and scarfs from the piazzas and upper windows!
>
> Can it be that these people are sincere? Or, are these demon-

strations merely a part of Dutch cunning to placate the oftpictured, wild, cantankerous, ravenous Reb of whom so many lies are told that simple people believe him a monster of cruelty? Possibly tho', these are Democratic families that have been persecuted and harassed by their abolition neighbors until they really welcome the advent of our army as a relief. Of course, we have little knowledge of the real feelings of the people.

One year earlier a long line of families had come through Middleburg en route to the battlefield at Antietam to pick up the bodies of their dead sons. In late September, a northbound couple stopped their horse-drawn wagon at a farm inside Pennsylvania by a few feet and asked if they could bury their son temporarily because of the stench of the corpse in the summer heat. The couple returned when the cold weather arrived and carried off the remains of their son.

Ludwig Kemmerer, a German immigrant, was warranted land by Lord Baltimore and built a log house here around 1764. Mason and Dixon came through here on September 26, 1765, and noted "Mr. Ludwig Cameron's House 4 chains North." A year later the surveyors placed the 103rd limestone marker near the house. In 1774 Kemmerer built a fortified stone house on the site to ward off Indian attacks, and he called the structure Buck Spring Farm.

Jacob Brumbaugh, another German immigrant, arrived here in 1750 and within a few years was operating a hotel. John Brown, the abolitionist, stayed at the Brumbaugh Hotel with his son in 1859 while he was making his way to Harpers Ferry, Virginia, to raid the federal arsenal. Brumbaugh later remembered the incident. "After breakfast, Brown and his son left, but before departing said that if any person called for them during the day to inform the party that they would be back in the evening. No one called during the day, but in the evening visitors turned up. Two genteel looking men drove up to the house, had their horses put up, got supper, asked for a room with two beds, and very soon after retired. When John Brown returned, he greeted the strangers, one of whom was another of his sons. The whole night the men engaged in animated conversation. My wife and I were interrupted in slumbers by the mumbling, and I am certain that that night the plans were laid for the raid at Harper's Ferry the following Sunday."

Dick Hartle has lived in State Line all of his seventy-seven years. His house is fifteen feet south of the Line, and he was born in the next house north. Jacob Brumbaugh was his great-great-great grandfather. Ludwig Kemmerer's Buck Spring Farm was purchased by his family in 1805 and remained in the Brumbaugh-Hartle family until 1970.

"My parents lived there before I was born," Hartle tells me on the telephone. "It has never been renovated. Everything is just as it was in 1774. The initials L. K. can be seen on the gable. There's a ten-foot fireplace and the walls are two feet thick. There are slave graves nearby and slave quarters in the attic. The house is now on ground owned by the Washington County Economic Development Corporation. They want to tear it down, but we're fighting them. We want to make it headquarters for our new Middleburg/Mason-Dixon Historical Society. . . ."

I get to State Line the following year, look up Hartle, and tell him I want to see Ludwig Kemmerer's Farm. "You're too late," he says. "They tore it down last April."

Marker No. 103 is at the entrance to a business park. "It was right at the lane that led to Buck Spring Farm," says Hartle. "They were widening the road in the 1960s, and the construction crew had it on a dump truck and was going to haul it off to dispose of. My father made them take if off and put it back in place." Inside the park, there's a vacant lot where the old stone farm stood for 225 years.

Hartle shows me a photograph of the pump used to slake the thirst of Robert E. Lee. "It was a working pump until a few years ago. I drank water from it many, many times. They tore everything down about four or five years ago. There's a bank where the Brumbaugh Hotel was. . . ."

Just north of State Line, I come across the Mason-Dixon Auto Auction. They have everything from A to Z in the name of getting from Point A to Point B. They come in all sizes. V-4s, V-6s, V-8s, V-12s. Two-doors, four-doors, five-doors, three-speed, four-speed, five-speed, automatic, sunroofs, moon roofs, no roofs. Dakotas and Comanches. Diplomats and Monarchs. LeSabres and LeBarons. Marquises and Cavaliers. Neptunes and Saturns. A glass-and-metal menagerie. Eagles, Skylarks, Colts, Mustangs, Jaguars, Bobcats, Cougars, Lynxes, Sables, Rabbits, Foxes, Broncos . . . no endangered species here. . . .

Mason-Dixon Road and the Line coincide for several miles. Marker 104 sits askew right at the road's edge, nicked and battered after twenty-three and one-half decades. No. 105, a crown stone, is thirty yards off the road near a picnic table in someone's backyard. I squint into the sun ahead and see the great vertiginous bulges of the Allegheny Mountains. Mason and

Dixon got here on September 29, 1765. It was a Sunday, and Mason took the off-day to travel seven miles south to Potomac, where he forded the river and went to a log fort and tavern on the Virginia side.

On July 4, 1863, George Wardman, a Union scout following the retreating Rebel army, was captured by a party of Confederates at this point. In a flagrant violation of military protocol, Wardman surrendered to the commander by handing him his saber point first. The officer shot and killed Wardman.

MONTPELIER: SOUTH OF MILE 111

Montpelier is an eighteenth century Georgian mansion on a hill overlooking Broadfording Road about three miles south of the Line. I am greeted by Philip Downs, whose family has lived here since before the Civil War. Montpelier was built on the site of the home of Captain Shelby, who escorted Mason and Dixon to the top of North Mountain in 1765 to see the Alleghenies for the first time. The surveyors spent several nights here in the spring of 1766 while working on the Line nearby, and it was here that they stored their instruments from time to time.

"Shelby named the homestead Montpelier, and from here he hunted, farmed, and traded," Downs says. "Mason and Dixon came here and asked him to take them to the top of the mountain so they could see the course of the Potomac. Montpelier itself had about 5,000 acres, but Shelby had additional holdings of about 20,000 acres. It's almost certain that Shelby is buried here." Downs shows me a broken piece of cast iron that he found in the Montpelier graveyard. It says, "e. SH."

The present house was built in the 1770s and owned by Jonathan Thompson Mason, who was a political ally of Thomas Jefferson. The newly elected president came here in 1800 to ask Mason to be his attorney general. Mason declined because of poor health. Downs shows me a page from an account book for Montpelier dated 1804. It is headed "Inventory of Slaves, Stocks and Buildings." It lists each slave by name "Wilson, Ben, Bill, Jerry Leah . . ." There are 187 in all. Downs points out the remains of a small stone house just east of the big house that served as slave quarters.

Just before the Civil War, ownership passed to Samuel Seibert, who was Downs' great-great grandfather. "Seibert was a Democrat, pro-Union, and did not own slaves," says Downs. "The Confederates raided the farm in 1864 and stole 400 head of cattle . . . Now I'll show you something you'll really be interested in." He walks over to the old barn, which was built in 1860. He rips away a piece of ivy that is crawling up the wall and there, about three feet off the ground, is an original limestone Mason-Dixon marker quarried in England and abandoned near Sideling Hill in 1766. It's set in the wall sideways, and the "M" is exposed. Downs takes me to a nearby farmhouse that is even closer to the Line and walks over to the front steps. The first step is an original crown stone, worn smooth by 140 years of use.

MERCERSBURG, PENNSYLVANIA: NORTH OF MILE 112

Before the passage of the Fugitive Slave Law, some runaways crossed the Line and established small communities in the Mercersburg area. A four-block section of downtown Mercersburg was called "Little Africa," and many of the homes were Underground Railroad stations. In 1864, poorly disciplined units of Confederate irregulars made periodic raids into this area, stealing horses, cattle, food, household goods—and blacks. Entire families were seized and taken back to Virginia, where they were sold for personal profit.

Near Mile 114, off Blairs Valley Road, there's a wooden sign that says "Mason and Dixon's Star Gazer's Stone." I follow directions down a wooden fence between a field and a house and find the stone tucked into one of the fence rails. Mason and Dixon stopped at this point in 1766 between October 7 and October 26 to raise the zenith sector and take celestial readings.

Mason and Dixon were back at Captain Shelby's on March 21, 1766, to get their instruments and pick up where they had left off the previous October at the foot of Cove Mountain, some 114 miles from the Northeast Corner. When they reached the summit on April 4, they could see Fort Frederick, seven miles to the south, and Fort Loudon, eleven miles northeast.

They were delayed by snow twice, but on April 23 they had covered another 10 minutes of latitude and stopped just north of Hancock, Maryland, to set up the zenith sector. They were near the narrowest point of Maryland, and they were reassured to see again that the Line would not cut the colony into two parts.

After Hancock, they were in a forest wilderness and there were very few settlers.

This was the wildest of the Wild West at this point in American history, and few Europeans had been here. The surveyors reached the foot of Sideling Hill, which is really a mountain, at Mile 135 on April 29. Their wagons, laden with official stone markers that weighed between 500 and 700 pounds each, couldn't make the climb. From this point on, they began marking the Line with wooden mile posts, about five feet high, around which they heaped earth and stone.

The surveying party left the official stones, about sixty in all, near Licking Creek at Mile 122, and they were later taken to Fort Frederick. During a resurvey in 1903, some of these limestones were placed along the Line west of Sideling Hill. But others turned up over the years as doorstops, steps, and as building blocks in barns and houses.

On April 30, they sent for the zenith sector, which had been left back at Shelby's the year before, set up at Mile 138, and found they were only twenty feet off of 39° 43' 17.4" north latitude. They stopped again atop Great Warrior Mountain at Mile 147, and on June 9 they were near Mile 162—and were as far west as they would get in 1766. They read the stars on clear nights, and on the day of June 14, Mason went to the top of Savage Mountain and wrote: "At present the Allegheny Mountains is the Boundary between the Natives and strangers. . . . From the solitary tops of these Mountains, the Eye gazes round with pleasure; filling the mind with adoration to that pervading spirit that made them."

Here, too, was the Eastern Continental Divide, which separates streams whose basins drain into the Atlantic Ocean from those that go to the Gulf of Mexico. "Beyond the Dividing Mountain (Savage)," Mason wrote, "the Waters all run to the Westward; The first of Note (which our Line would cross if continued) is the little Yochi Geni, running into the Monaungahela, which falls into the Ohio, or Allegany River at Pittsbourgh; about 80 miles West, and 30 or 40 North from hence) call'd by the French Fort Duquene."

On June 18 they began backtracking eastward, marking the Line as they went, with the axemen felling trees for the eight-yard-wide visto between the two provinces. Mason visited Fort Cumberland, Maryland, on Sunday, June 22, and found it "beautifully situated on rising ground" but "in bad repair" with only ten six-pound cannons. On July 6, the surveyors were back atop Sideling Hill, where when they looked back at the just-cut visto they were delighted that they could see the curvature of the earth. "I saw the Line still formed the arch of a lesser circle very beautiful and agreeable to the Laws of a Sphere."

Mason gets terse from here on. "Continued the Line to the 127th, to the 118th, the 73d, the 44th, the 30th, the 21st, the 13th. . . ." They reached the Northeast Corner on Sept. 25.

On November 21, Mason and Dixon met with the commissioners in Christiana Bridge where they were informed that the Iroquois Confederacy was opposed to extending the West Line any further and that Sir William Johnson, the royal agent for Indian Affairs, was working on the problem.

From the day Mason and Dixon stepped onto the streets of Philadelphia, there had been tensions punctuated by violence between whites and Indians. Whatever his ethical shortcomings in the border dispute with Maryland, William Penn was fair and tolerant in his dealings with the Indians. He followed a policy and commitment of peace between the two races, and his treaties are rare examples of racial tolerance and justice in colonial America. After Penn's death in 1718, Quakers carried on his idealism for another generation. But they lost control with the outbreak of the French and Indian War in 1756, and the province became the stage for some of the worst violence between whites and Indians. The Conestoga massacre was the most conspicuous example, but there were many others.

In 1763 the following exchange of letters occurred between General Jeffrey Amherst, commander of all British troops in the colonies, and Col. Henry Bouquet, a commander on the Pennsylvania frontier:

Amherst: "Could it not be contrived to send the smallpox among the disaffected tribes of Indians? We must on this occasion use every stratagem in our power to reduce them."

Bouquet: "I will try to inoculate them with some blankets, and take care not to get the disease myself. As it is a pity to expose good men against them. I wish we could use the Spanish method, to hunt them with English dogs who would, I think, effectually extirpate or remove that vermin."

Amherst: "You will do well to try to inoculate the Indians by means of blankets, as well as to try every other method that can serve to extirpate this exorable race."

There is no direct evidence that this early form of germ warfare was used, but a few months later smallpox cut a deadly swath through the tribes in the region. In addition, the commandant at Fort Pitt reported on a meeting with two Lenni Lenape leaders. "Out of our regard to them, we gave them two blankets and a handkerchief out of the Small-pox Hospital. I hope it will have the desired effect."

On July 7, 1764, while Mason and Dixon moved northward towards the New Castle Circle, Governor John Penn offered white settlers bounties on Indians—130 pieces of eight for the scalps of Indian boys and girls under ten years of age; 134 pieces of eight for the scalps of Indian males over ten; and 50 pieces of eight for the scalps of Indian females above the age of ten. Under this stimulus, peaceful Susquehannas who lived in white towns were hatcheted for profit. Who could tell whether a bloody scalp had been torn from the head of a friendly Indian or a hostile one?

In retaliation, the Indians took to their warpaths and inflicted terrible atrocities on the white settlers—men, women, and children. With their faces and bodies covered with paint, screaming blood-curdling war whoops, the Indians burned and killed.

This was the status of white-Indian relations as Mason and Dixon wintered at the Harlan farm working on a project for the Royal Society to determine the length of a degree of latitude; it was not related to drawing the boundary. On New Year's Day, 1767, Mason recorded a temperature of minus 22 degrees Fahrenheit and said it was difficult to work with the instruments. ". . . {T}he immediate touch of the brass was like patting one's fingers against the points of Pins and Needles; the cold was so intense."

They awaited the results of the negotiations with the Indians, and it wasn't until mid-June, when the temperatures went over 100 degrees, that they were told they could proceed with the West Line. To gain permission, the two colonies had agreed to pay the Indians 500 pounds, which today would be the equivalent of about $57,000. In addition, the Six Nations had demanded that a party of Indians accompany the two Englishmen as "deputies" for the remainder of the survey.

This prompted a written warning from the commissioners dated June 18, 1767: "As the public Peace and your own Security may greatly depend on the good Usage and kind Treatment of those Deputies, we commit them to your particular care, and recommend it to you in the most earnest manner not only to use them well yourselves but to be careful that they receive no Abuse or ill treatment from the Men you may employ in carrying on the said Work, and to do your utmost to protect them from the Insults of all other persons whatsoever." The commissioners' concerns were not overstated. The French and Indian War had been ended just four years earlier, and ever since there had been massacres and white reprisals all along the frontier.

Another letter the same day said: "The Commissioners recommend to Messrs. Mason and Dixon that the Spirituous Liquors to be given to the Indians attending them, be in small quantities mixed with water and delivered to them not more than three times every day." A disbursement sheet for July 25, 1767, indicates that 40 pounds, 10 shillings was paid out for whiskey. That would translate in modern currency to about $4,600, which would buy quite a bit of whiskey. However, by that time the survey party had grown to more than a hundred.

The Mason-Dixon party moved steadily westward, a tented army undeflected by any mountain or stream. They settled into diurnal and nocturnal routines, dictated by the daily dance of earth and sun. They left camp each day with the sun at their backs, and worked until it set in front of them. They journeyed on foot and on horseback. At night the two surveyors would unpack their equipment and get new astral guidance. For hours they would stare into the night sky carbonated with stars that were giving off light that had been on its way to them for many years at the rate of 186,000 miles per second.

Much of their food was obtained from the wilderness, prepared by camp cooks. Berries, fish, and game. But it is also very likely that they brought a flock of sheep with them—these were Englishmen, after all. There were butchers on their staff. One of the supply lists called for "120 gals spirits, 40 gals brandy, 80 gals madeira wine." On May 7, 1765, an expenditure of one shilling, six pence was recorded for "2 wine glasses for the surveyors." Along the way they could pick up barrels of apple brandy—also called applejack, or "essence of lockjaw."

In the daytime, the trees would ring with the sound of axe blows and the squeak and rattle of wagons. Nights would be clamorous with insects and the shouts of crew-men playing cards and shooting dice.

The size of the crew varied from time to time. At any point about half the "hands" would be axemen. Other functionaries were cooks, stewards, guides, chain carriers, instrument bearers, wagoners, shepherds, and pack horse drivers. During the most difficult passage across the mountains in 1767, there were 115 men on the time sheet. This may have been partially due to the increased fears of Indian attacks.

FORT FREDERICK, MARYLAND: SOUTH OF MILE 118

Perched high on the north bank of the Potomac, Fort Frederick's stone walls resonate with the centuries. It was built at the insistence of Thomas Cresap to protect white settlers from Indians. It is the sole surviving fort of the French and Indian War, and just beyond its seventeen-foot stone walls I find a restored log cabin. Inside there is a big chunk of an original lime-stone marker and this sign:

> In 1768 Mason and Dixon wrote a letter to Hugh Hammersley, who had procured from the Isle of Portland the stones to be placed in the line, stating that: "There are now lying at Fort Frederick near the North Mountains Sixty Stones, which were intended to be set this Summer, but we acquainted the Gent. Commissioners that we could not get our Stone to the place designed for it to the west of Sidelong Hill for less than 12 £ per Stone, on which information the Gent. Commissioners thought proper we should desist from setting Stones farther at present.
>
> This is a portion of one such stone.

When it was no longer needed for defense, Fort Frederick was auctioned off in 1791. In 1857 it was purchased by Nathan Williams, an enterprising, strong-willed free black whose grandmother, as a slave, had fled to the fort to escape marauding Indians in the 1760s. Williams moved to the fort with his wife, Amy, a slave girl whose freedom he had purchased for sixty dollars.

Williams paid off the $7,000 mortgage on the fort within ten years by selling farm produce to both Confederate and Union troops, who were camped on opposite sides of the Potomac. He delivered to the Southerners by night, to the Northerners by day. He salved his conscience by giving the Union forces intelligence information on the Confederates.

INDIAN SPRINGS, MARYLAND: SOUTH OF MILE 120

Park Head Church was built in 1833 by the Reverend Jeremiah Mason, a politician and businessman, who made it an unusual union church for worship by any group that believed in the Holy Trinity—Methodists, Presbyterians, Lutherans, Episcopalians, and Catholics. There is a stone under the "V" of the roof inscribed "m1833r"—the letters standing for Mutual Rights.

Mason owned slaves, and he built a gallery in the church so they could attend services. When slavery was abolished in 1865, most of the blacks moved away, but one of them, John Hardy, remained. And each Sunday, he would come to Park Head Church and sit in the gallery alone.

"Uncle," his white co-religionists would tell him, "you are a free man and you can sit down here with us and not up there alone."

"Up in that gallery my people and I found God," he would reply. "They are all gone but God awaits me there each Sunday."

The church door is open. I climb up a ladder to the gallery. It is much warmer up here. Outside, I walk through the cemetery, past fresh flowers and angels with downcast eyes. The granite marker is surrounded by flowers.

A SLAVE
JOHN HARDY
BORN ABOUT 1840
DIED ABOUT 1905

HANCOCK, MARYLAND: MILE 127

I follow the Line down an embankment so steep I feel like I'm on stilts. With relief, I step onto Pennsylvania Avenue in Hancock. The summer heat ricochets off the asphalt. There's a natural gas transmission facility surrounded by a barbwire, chain-link fence. From a tiny house on the west side of the road a man and woman are lugging out a big sofa, which they put on the lawn in their front yard. Next they bring out an overstuffed chair. When they finish, they each sit down and open up a newspaper to read.

About fifty yards into Pennsylvania the Tonoloway Primitive Baptist Church rests on its original, 1751 brownstone foundation. The church still holds services every Sunday. Settlers worshipped in relays to guard against attacks from Indians, who destroyed the church twice. The congregants believed themselves to be in Maryland until Mason and Dixon came through.

Maryland is only two miles wide at this point; Hancock is wedged between two mountain ranges on the east and west, and confined between the Potomac on the south and the Line on the north. This location made it a popular spot for runaways from Virginia to cross Maryland quickly and get to the Line. Newspapers carried numerous ads seeking fugitives, carefully identifying them with phrases like "quick in speech," "bowlegged," "large ears," and "speaks through his nose." There was detailed information on cuts, scars, and birthmarks.

"I drank up all my Scotch last night, so I'm going out to pick up some more," says Ralph Donnelly. "We can stop at one of the markers that's easy to get to. Even so, you'll have to bear with me, when you hit ninety you slow down a bit."

Donnelly spent a career as a surveyor and civil engineer and a lifetime as an aficionado of the Mason-Dixon Line. "It was one hell of job," he says in a deep, resonant, six-o'clock-news voice, "and a very important scientific milestone because it added to our knowledge of the size of the earth." Donnelly has even built a model of the portable field observatory Mason and Dixon used each time they set up the zenith sector. He reconstructed it from written reports made to the Royal Society.

Fifteen minutes later he is pushing aside branches and dodging puddles. Our boots are muddy. "For a long time I wondered why so many markers were near roads, and then I figured out that they deliberately built the roads near the mile markers so they'd know where the jurisdictions changed." Standing knee-deep in grass, he pulls aside thick weeds to show me the "M" and the "P." It's the 128th-mile marker.

Back on the porch of his one-hundred-year-old house, less than two miles from the Line, Donnelly has poured three fingers of Scotch in a tall glass with ice cubes. He chit-chats, filling air time, until his voice slips into just the right pitch, like a needle in a groove.

"So much about the border dispute is confusing. If you just say, 'Lord Baltimore,' in any of this, it really doesn't mean very much because we have five Lord Baltimores involved between the time this starts and the time it finishes. And, similarly with the Penns, we get mixed up with a lot of different Penns.

"The Maryland charter read that the colony went to the 40th parallel. In order to make things a little more confusing, this charter was written in Latin, and it was subject to translation. You know you can get some variations just purely from the translation by people who have the same intent, but when you get somebody hostile translating it, you can get just about the opposite meaning out of it, so at one time the Penns claimed, perhaps conscientiously, that the 40th parallel really began down at the 39th and from there on, you were on the way to the 40th and really the land granted should only extend to the 39th.

"After Penn died, his heirs started a lawsuit in England. This has now gotten to the typical situation we find in most property disputes. The original owners have died; the heirs have inherited something that they're not sure what it was, and the other side doesn't know what they have either, and they are ready to turn the case over to the attorneys. They're going to have a long battle. The practice, of course, was for each one to attempt to lure settlers into the disputed area.

"When the suit started, the question came up of just how this charter did read. In one of the accounts it mentions that somebody was sent out to get an original copy; they didn't want anything else. Ten years later he came back with it, and the suit went on again. They had the exact information and they were able to go ahead. About that time the fourth Lord Baltimore died, so that tied up everything again for another ten years because the heir was in his minority, and they decided to wait until he became of age before going on with the suit. But a decree was finally issued and in it carried the stipulation that the line between Maryland and Pennsylvania, extending east and west, was to be fifteen miles south of the southernmost limits of the city of Philadelphia."

He pauses, reinvigorates his drink, and throws another monologue on the fire.

"Mason and Dixon were furnished with the finest astronomical instruments that were available. There was a very famous instrument maker in England by the name of Bird. It was far different equipment than the colonial surveyors had been using.

"The method they used was to take the direction that it is to the North Pole at one end of a certain length line, and then run in a direction slightly north of west so that at the end of the selected distance the straight line that they were running would cross the arc of latitude that they had to mark on the ground. They decided that they would run ten minutes of longitude and then redetermine their position to see whether they had drifted north or south, correct themselves, and then start off again. Every time that they started off, they would start four minutes and nine seconds north of going due west. So at the end of this distance, they would again cross this curving line. It really didn't make much difference whether they ran this line exactly in the right direction or not, as long as they could accurately determine where they were when they got to the end of ten minutes of longitude, which they took as being a little over twelve miles. If they were too far south, they corrected by a series of offsets that would bring them back onto the line by measuring the offsets to the north; if they were too far north, they computed offsets for every mile that would put them back on the line by measuring them to the south, and that way they could set mile posts which were exactly in the true line even if the baseline was not. They continued running this line for 230 miles.

"Of course, this was an unsettled country, and they were running only at the pleasure of the Indians. They were accompanied by Indian observers, who by the agreement were supposed to be limited to fifteen, but sometimes they had closer to 150. . . .

His voice trails off. His eyes flicker and close, and he tilts his head back like a boxer between rounds.

It's rough going beyond Hancock—steep mountains and a chaos of vines, trees, and brush. Near Mile 131 I come east over a field. There are purple wildflowers growing on the Line, and then I am stopped in my tracks by a dark, frowning forest. Trees stand shoulder to shoulder, rising hundreds of feet from places determined hundreds of years ago by the random dropping of a seed. Ahead, an underground pipeline with its own visto runs just beside the Line on the Pennsylvania side. It was built in 1942 to deliver Gulf Coast crude oil to the eastern seaboard and offset losses of oil tankers to Nazi U-boats.

Directly ahead is Sideling Hill, which originally was called Sidelong Hill because of its length. It was a formidable obstacle to Mason and Dixon—so steep they abandoned the heavy limestone markers. When Interstate 68 was built two centuries later, a V-shaped wedge was blasted out of Sideling Hill that is 850 feet wide and 380 feet deep. This created an instant exhibit of geological history going back 300 million years.

About 600,000 travelers a year stop at the exhibit center to enjoy the panoramic views and study the multicolored veins of newly exposed rock. The volunteer guide on duty today is Walter Dewitt, a retired geologist who says he is the grandson five times removed of Andrew Ellicott, a noted American scientist and surveyor who was a key figure in the project that extended the Mason-Dixon Line to the end of Pennsylvania's southern border in 1784. He points up a 70-degree-steep, rock-strewn hillside. "The Mason-Dixon Line is up there 502 feet. Marker 133 is still there, but don't go. It's rocky and filled with rattlesnakes this time of the year."

I get back on the Line for a time near Mile 135 and behold spectacular mountain scenery. A deer flashes by me in tail-up panic, a marvel of grace and speed. A tractor zippers a field in Pennsylvania. Another mountain looms ahead and seems to lift a white church into the sky.

LITTLE ORLEANS, MARYLAND: SOUTH OF MILE 139

Orleans Road comes down Sideling Hill and flattens out just before it enters town. This area is Piney Plains, and nearby was the place called Darkie Lot by local residents. Slaves would be housed here to be rented out by the hour, day, or week. When someone needed cheap labor, he would drive his wagon to Darkie Lot and pick it up.

CHANEYSVILLE, PENNSYLVANIA: NORTH OF MILE 144

Mel Sonne downshifts his Dodge Dakota and it bounces down a bald, rain-gutted trace of a road. "Even though Mason and Dixon put this area in Pennsylvania," he shouts over the whining engine, "the mountain blocks the way north and these people were essentially southerners. There was no safe place for fugitive slaves to stay here."

Sonne is a retired foreign service officer who had posts in Denmark, Germany, Indochina, Mexico, Italy, and Austria over a thirty-year career. He bought a farm in Chaneysville in 1984, and almost immediately began exploring "the Legend." He stops on a hill. "This was the old Lester Imes farm," he says. We walk over to a field of parched yellow grass. The thirteen stones protrude a few inches from the poor soil.

"I tried to interest the Pennsylvania Historical and Museum Commission in putting a marker on this site, but they turned me down and cited lack of documentation. But it deserves recognition. I am absolutely convinced that something very important happened on this spot. The story is far too well-known, and there's too much circumstantial evidence. How many? How did they die? That's all unanswered. But basically, Bradley is right."

The Legend was passed down from generation to generation. As a child growing up in Bedford, Pennsylvania, David Bradley had heard it from his mother, Harriette Bradley. While working on a Bedford County history, she investigated and concluded that thirteen fugitive slaves had crossed the Line sometime around 1850 only to be cornered by slave catchers near Chaneysville. They managed to get to the farm of Lester Imes, a sympathetic white; they told Imes they would rather die here as free men than be returned alive to slavery. At the blacks' insistence, Imes and some of his neighbors killed the slaves and buried them in the family cemetery.

David Bradley grew up and became a college professor, and in 1981 he published a book, *The Chaneysville Incident*, a fictionalized account of the Legend. Based on ten years of research, he believes that the runaways killed themselves. Imes and his neighbors, Bradley reasons, would not have killed them because they would have been punished under the law. The mass suicide comes in the final pages of the book:

> And then the horror of it struck him. Because her voice was dif-
> ferent, was not the quiet, resigned voice of the woman who had

These stones on a farm near the Line at Chaneysville, Pennsylvania, may mark the graves of runaway slaves.

told of planning and scheming to save her son from slavery. It was a small voice, a frightened voice, a cowered voice. A slave's voice. The rest of them were silent, even the children, waiting for his answer, waiting for him to tell them that there was hope, that there was a scheme, a path, a way. But there was none, and so he looked at the line of torches moving in the south, the line growing thicker and brighter as the men on the flanks joined in when their positions were reached, and he made his estimates and told them: half an hour. . . .

He knew, then, that they were watching him, all of them. Waiting for him to lead them. . . . [H]e took the pistol from his belt and held it high, so they could all see. For a moment he was not sure that he could lead them, was not sure that they would follow, but then he saw Harriette Brewer take her knife from beneath her shawl and hold it high, and then he heard her, heard her singing softly, then louder, heard the others join in, the words of the song growing, rising from the hilltop, floating down the incline, the words sharp and clear against the night: "And before I'll be a slave I'll be buried in my grave, and go home to my God, and be free." For a chorus or two, or three, the song was loud and strong. And then the song grew weaker, the voices that had raised it falling silent one by one. . . .

The old Conrad farm just outside Chaneysville is vacant, slumping into ruin and up for sheriff's sale. Here, in June 1996, the Pennsylvania Ku Klux Klan held a recruiting drive. As they doused the cross with kerosene and set it afire, Grand Dragon C. Edward Foster intoned, "We hail the fiery cross that burns so bright."

South of Chaneysville there's another eyesore near Mile 147 on the Line—discarded appliances, wheel-less trucks with their hoods up, cars flaking rust and sitting in puddles of tire. The sign says, "KEEP PENNSYL-VANIA BEAUTIFUL."

FLINTSTONE, MARYLAND: SOUTH OF MILE 148

In the antebellum days there was a fierce debate among villagers over the moral ramifications of slavery. Soon after the war began, the pro-slavery members of the Flintstone Methodist Church formed their own church, and for the next half-century this tiny town had two Methodist Churches.

Mason and Dixon were back on the Allegheny frontier on July 7, 1767, and on that day they were hosted by Thomas Cresap at his new home, which Mason described as a "beautiful estate," at Oldtown, southwest of Fort Cumberland at a fork in the Potomac River. By this time Cresap was better known as an Indian fighter than a border agitator, and he had become a good friend of George Washington. Thus did the two scientists come face to face with a man who bore considerable responsibility for bringing them to America. However, there is no record of what transpired at this meeting.

On July 13 they were once again atop Mount Savage, where they had stopped thirteen months before. Three days later they were joined by their Indian "deputies"—eleven Mohawks and three Onandagas—plus a white trader, Hugh Crawford, who served as interpreter. One of the Mohawks was a chief named John Green. As the surveyors pushed west, other Indians joined the party from time to time. "Many of the Natives of different Nations came to see us," Mason wrote, "and we were all Brothers in every kind of friendly manner."

On August 9, about 187 miles from the Northeast Corner, the procession crossed Braddock's Road, named for General Edward Braddock, who had blazed the route (actually he widened an old Indian path) just before suffering an ignominious defeat and death by a combined French and Indian force in 1755. Braddock, a mediocre soldier, had misjudged the problems of wilderness fighting. It was one of the worst defeats in the history of the British Army—of Braddock's 1,460 men, 455 were killed and 421 were wounded.

One of the survivors was Colonel George Washington, who ordered that the fallen general's body be buried in the middle of the road at a point that is now about six miles north of the Line. He then had the surface leveled off and concealed to prevent desecration by the Indians. Mason's journal notes the crossing of "General Braddock's Road, which he cut through the mountains to lead the Army under his command to the Westward in the year 1755; but fate, how hard, made through the desert a path, himself to pass and never, never to return."

Mason and Dixon went on through August, stopping to set up John Bird's zenith sector, make their stellar observations, redirect the Line accordingly, and then measure for another 10-minute arc. From time to time, they dispatched axemen eastwards to widen the visto along the just-marked Line.

They reached "Ye Big Yochio Geni"—the Youghiogheny River—on August 12. Five days later, near what is now the border between Maryland and West Virginia, they were visited by thirteen Delaware Indians, including the nephew of Captain Black Jacobs, the famed and feared chief who had been killed at the Battle of Kittanning in 1756. Mason said the nephew "was the tallest Man I ever saw."

This final summer in America found Mason more prolific than he had been at any time since he arrived in the Colonies nearly four years earlier. Some 211 miles from the Northeast Corner, from atop the westernmost ridge of Laurel Hill, Mason beheld "a Wild of Wildes; the Laurel overgrown, the Rocks gaping to swallow you up, over whose deep mouths you may step. The whole a deep melancholy appearance out of nature. . . . there is the most delightful pleasing view of the Western Plains that Eye can behold."

They attained the east bank of the Cheat River on September 12, and they paused, for the next day was Sunday. That evening two of the Mohawks objected to carrying the survey beyond the river. They were overruled by the others, but Indian opposition was growing. No doubt the work of the surveyors, scanning the heavens and staking the earth, was difficult for the Indians to grasp. Samuel T. Wiley, a West Virginia historian, speculated in his 1883 History of Monongalia County: "They could not understand what all this peering into the heavens portended. They looked with especial distrust of those curious little tubes, covered with glass, through which the surveyors stood patiently watching somebody in the far-off heavens. They entertained a suspicion that the surveyors were holding communication with spirits in the skies, who were pointing out the track of their line."

They stopped on September 19 at the 219th mile, and placed the zenith sector on a high bank overlooking the Monongahela River. While they were making their star checks, twenty-six of their hired hands left them because they feared reprisals from the Shawnees and Delawares if they crossed the Monongahela. Both tribes had come *to western Pennsylvania after being displaced from their eastern Pennsylvania hunting grounds by white settlers, and these refugees were strongly opposed to encroachment on their new lands. The Shawnees were particularly defiant and outspokenly contemptuous of white people.*

With only fifteen axemen left, Mason and Dixon kept going at a slower pace. They sent word back to Fort Cumberland that they needed more workers, and on October 7 Mason reported, "We have now our usual complement of Hands." This apparently was about forty and referred only to axemen.

Just two miles west of the Monongahela the geodesists were visited by an influential Lenni Lenape (Mason called him a Delaware) chief, Catfish, who was accompanied by his wife and nephew. All three wore European style clothing. A few years earlier Catfish, whose Indian name was Tongoocque, had established a settlement near the present town of Washington, Pennsylvania. The Mohawks met with Catfish, presented him with strings of wampum—beads, usually white or black, made from seashells. Wampum was sacred—Indians placed their hand on it to take oaths as white men used the Bible. The Mohawks then explained, as best they could, the nature of Mason's and Dixon's work. The chief "seem'd to be very well satisfy'd, and promis'd to send the Strings of Wampum to his Towns, and to come again in 15 days; but he never returned," Mason wrote.

OLDTOWN, MARYLAND: SOUTH OF MILE 150

The grave of Thomas Cresap is marked by a rough fieldstone just off the towpath in the Chesapeake and Ohio Canal National Park. The Cresap Society, an organization of 350 descendants and admirers, maintains the site. Cresap's outpost here became a landmark for Indians and settlers. His hospitality earned him the name "Big Spoon" from the Indians. George Washington, as a sixteen-year-old surveyor's assistant, spent four nights with Cresap in 1748. Cresap traveled into the Ohio country and established trade routes. Andrew Ellicott, the new nation's first surveyor general, wrote in his diary on May 17, 1785: "This evening I spent with the celebrated Colonel Cresap. He is now more than a hundred years old. He lost his eyesight about eighteen months past, but his other faculties are yet unimpaired, his sense strong and manly, and his ideas flow with ease." Cresap died two years later.

CUMBERLAND, MARYLAND: SOUTH OF MILE 157

Emmanuel Episcopal Church is on the site of Fort Cumberland, which Mason found weakly defended and in disrepair on June 22, 1766.

Leontyne Peck is the first professional black employee ever to work for the city of Cumberland. She is also a member of a state commission trying to recapture some of the history of Maryland blacks. "I grew up in Piedmont, West Virginia, about five miles south of here," she says, cruising at twenty miles per hour through the downtown. "We had a black community there. We had a baker, a barber, a club, a picnic ground. We were a black community. There's not that sense of community among the blacks of Cumberland. About 1,800 of the 20,000 people here are black. Virtually nothing has been written down about the history of the African Americans in Cumberland. I'm trying to get it going."

She drives up the ramp onto Interstate 68, which bisects the town. "This used to be Central Avenue, and right about here was Darr's Chicken Palace. Darr was a black guy, but he sold only to whites. He was a businessman, so how else was he going to make money." It is not a question. "Here's the police station. That where Cooper's Tavern was. Cooper's Tavern was where black people stayed when they came to town—Count Basie, Duke Ellington, Nat King Cole, the Globetrotters—they all stayed there. Johnny Cooper ran the tavern, and the rooms were upstairs."

She stops in front of a two-story red brick building with plywood covering the window openings. "This is the Carver School, built in 1922 for black kids. The whites were so upset about the expenditure of money that they didn't dare have an opening ceremony. They just moved the kids in early one morning without fanfare. We're trying to turn it into a combined center with a black history museum. . . ."

Friday is bingo night at Cumberland Aerie #245, Fraternal Order of Eagles. Two rooms hold several hundred people, mostly gray-haired women, who are hunched in front of folding tables. A blue Marlboro haze hangs over the scene. The caller is plucking air-blown alphanumeric ping-pong balls. Electric boards light up the appropriate numbers, and television monitors give a sort of play-by-play from every angle. About twenty-five African Americans are present, and without fail they sit at separate tables from the whites. Nevertheless, there is a steady stream of good-natured repartee between the white and black tables.

ELLERSLIE, PENNSYLVANIA: MILE 159

The Line goes right through Redeemers United Church of Christ. The white clapboard structure is topped by twin pitched roofs—one in Pennsylvania, one in Maryland. The Line is marked by an original crown stone, placed here in 1902, that was among the stones left behind at Sideling Hill by Mason and Dixon.

Mountain ridges stretch diagonally across the landscape, with deep valleys in between. Miles and miles of nothing but miles and miles. The terrain is impassable in many places. Near Mile 168 I come into Pochahontas, Pennsylvania, where St. Mary's Church, a long, gray cinder block building, is having a chicken and ham supper on Sunday night, donation six dollars. Lower New Germany Road is graded gravel that crunches under my feet. Near Mile 174, I come through an old strip mine with slag mounds. A battered, faded sign, barely readable and nailed to a tree, warns that this is a blasting area Monday through Thursday between 8 A.M. and noon. A barn on Route 219 has a "CHEW MAIL POUCH TOBACCO" sign. The pipeline is being repaired and is exposed.

GRANTSVILLE, MARYLAND: SOUTH OF MILE 179

Walking the pipeline visto, I come through a three-silo farm to a road at Mile 179 that leads to Grantsville, Maryland, and Salisbury, Pennsylvania. The farmers market is just opening in Grantsville, and black Amish buggies clip-clop along the side of the road. In Salisbury, there's an American flag on every telephone pole. This is rural America, where a blacksmith, taxidermist, and wheelwright can still make a living—though never on Sunday.

This area of the Line is tableland. The fertile acreage is split among Amish and non-Amish farmers, many of them living on fourth-generation land in century-old houses and barns. I emerge from the woods on a graded dirt road just as a jolly, bearded man, wearing a black, wife-knitted sweater, goes by in an Amish buggy. He waves to me, continues down the road and stops about fifty yards away. He ties the horse to a tree and enters what looks like an outhouse. But when I get closer, I can see "Tela Hut" written on the structure in black paint. He emerges, sees my perplexity, and explains. "Some of the families go together and put this in. We can't have telephones in our houses, but this is all right." A sheepish grin.

He says his name is Yoder. I ask him where the Mason-Dixon Line is. "Oh, it's right next to my farm. There's a marker. Wanna see it?" I climb into the buggy, and he takes me to the marker. It's muddy walking. He points to it with considerable pride. It's an original limestone marker, abandoned by Mason and Dixon at Sideling Hill, that was probably placed here during a resurvey in 1902 at Mile 180.

"I hear one of them, Mason or Dixon, was English?"

"Yeh, they were both English."

"The surveyors around here say they were really accurate. Is that right?

"Yes it is."

Yoder invites me in for a glass of cold, but not iced, tea. It's laced with mint and I stay for a second glass.

Route 40, the old National Road, drops steeply off Meadow Mountain, and where it bottoms out there's a pleasant forest glade that attracted travelers throughout the frontier days. Thomas Cresap, George Washington, and General Braddock all encamped here in the 1750s, and in 1767 the Mason-Dixon party, working just two miles to the north, set up a storehouse here.

The stone-arch Casselman Bridge, built in 1813 and in use until 1933, still spans the Casselman River, which was known to Mason and Dixon as the Little Youghiogheny. The bridge carried the National Road over the river, and the area came to be called Little Crossing. It was one of the best-known points on the frontier. The Red House Tavern was built here in 1760, and it very likely was visited by the surveyors.

In 1818 the Stone House Inn was built on the site by Jesse Tomlinson, a wealthy trader who owned many slaves and was elected to the Maryland Legislature six times. It is still standing on the north side of Route 40 and is a private residence.

The Stone House Inn, now a private home, was built in 1818 along the National Road, now Route 40.

In 1926 a local resident named Ellen Glotfelty, who was eighty-two years old, was interviewed by a weekly newspaper and recalled an incident that had been passed down to her by her mother and father. A party of Indian leaders, en route to Washington to meet with President Jackson around 1835, dined at the Stone House Inn and were served by two slaves named Sarah and Sook.

> While the Indians were delighted with the feast set before them, and could hardly be restrained by the interpreter in charge of them from tearing the roast turkeys to shreds with their fingers in their eagerness to devour them, they nevertheless showed much contempt for the negro slaves and refused to receive any food from their hands. The attitude of the aboriginal Americans peeved Sook and Sarah exceedingly, and they were excused from further duty in serving the Indians. The latter, however, showed due gratitude and friendliness toward the white people for the services rendered them.

The lot of the large slave population in the Little Crossings area was described by Jacob Brown, a local nineteenth century historian. "The slave owners were mostly kind, generous, hospitable and sociable, the colored people happy and contented. . . . No people enjoyed the ten days vacation at winter holiday as the people of color. It was a continuous round of genuine enjoyment and festivity to them, and other people were happy because the colored folks were more so."

Beyond Little Crossing, Route 40 ascends 2,900-foot Negro Mountain, which is wrapped in a robe of clouds. At the summit I'm standing in an oatmeal fog, barely able to see ten feet in front of me. The peak was named in honor of a black slave named Nemesis, who accompanied Michael Cresap, the colonel's son, on an expedition to control Indian raiders and was killed here in 1774.

In 1995, some African Americans objected to the name and petitioned the U.S. Board of Geographic Names to change it to Black Hero Mountain. But at a hearing, the testimony of state officials and private citizens convinced the board that the old name should be retained. Edward Papenfuse, the Maryland state archivist, said the name "reflects an eighteenth century sensitivity to the important contribution African Americans made that is rarely so publicly demonstrated." Also speaking against the change was Marguerite Doleman of Hagerstown.

MILE 187

Route 40 (*née* the National Road, *née* Braddock's road, *née* Nemacolin's Path) dips and ripples like a ribbon as it crosses the Line into Pennsylvania. A crumbling concrete highway obelisk marks the spot. A tractor-trailer rushes past me. The roadside trees tremble in its wake. Its air brakes gasp as it approaches a sharp curve.

I find the remnants of an old National Pike milepost that is rusty and broken in half. But right next to it is a shiny replica that says, "34½ to Cumberland, 96¾ to Wheeling." A few yards into Pennsylvania, the Dixie Fuel Stop offers motorists the chance to "gas up on the Mason-Dixon Line" and the adjacent Dixie Motel invites me to "Sleep on the Mason-Dixon Line" for seventeen dollars a night. It's a single strip of six rooms, each with an identical green plastic chair in front. The gas station, the motel, and the Dixie Snack Shop are all closed, and not just for the day.

Route 40 follows the course of an ancient Indian trail that was widened to accommodate pack horses in 1753 by the ubiquitous Thomas Cresap and a Delaware Indian named Nemacolin. (Nemacolin was the son of the Lenni Lenape chief Chicochinican, who had bargained honorably with William Penn and sold him land in the Brandywine Valley. But after Penn's death Chicochinican was forced out of his village near the Harlan Farm.) Nemacolin's Path, as it came to be called, ran from Cumberland, Maryland, northwest into Pennsylvania where it joined a major artery, Mingo's Path, into Ohio.

It was no more than two feet wide in most places, and when Braddock was planning his campaign in western Pennsylvania he sent a detachment ahead to widen it to twelve feet. They also bridged creeks and laid causeways across swamps. After independence, it became the National Road and was the principal route west. Traffic grew steadily—heavy freighter wagons pulled by six horses and prairie schooners carrying settlers to the ever-expanding western frontier. There were also pedestrians and herds of livestock. In the first half of the nineteenth century, the dust never settled on the National Road.

Part of the commerce involved what was sometimes euphemized as "biped property." In his 1894 history of the National Road, Thomas B. Searight recalls personally seeing slaves "being driven over the road arranged in couples and fastened to a long, thick rope or cable, like horses."

About two miles beyond the National Road, I follow the pipeline visto down to a graded dirt road. On the far side of the road is a shack with loose boards and broken windows. The steps creak under my feet and the porch has a carpet of pine needles. The door is ajar. I look in. Whiskey bottles, wine bottles, magazines are everywhere. There's a filthy mattress and a strong stench that suggests recent habitation. I hear the floorboards squeak upstairs. I move on quickly and get back on the Line. An hour later I'm in a thick forest around Mile 191 when suddenly there's an opening and I see the Youghiogheny River Lake winking in the sunlight. There are hundreds of pleasure boats in the marina. It was only a river when Mason and Dixon got here on August 12, 1767.

OAKLAND, MARYLAND: MILE 190

Slavery was as much an issue in the mountains of western Maryland as it was in the Chesapeake area. Octogenarian Thomas J. Brandt was interviewed in 1900 and recalled: "The first political meeting that was ever held in Oakland was held in a ten-pin alley located a little way north of

Kennedy's grog shop. It was during the Buchanan and Fremont campaign of 1856. Dan Voorhees was the orator. He defended slavery and said 'the tropical sun of the South would broil the brain out of a white man if he tried to do labor there.' The audience was seated on the sides of the alley or stood up as they chose. Mr. Duval led the cheering by stamping his cane on the floor of the temporary rostrum."

As the slaves of western Maryland toiled in the fields, they sometimes sang this:

> The old bee makes de honeycomb,
> The young bee makes de honey;
> Colored folks plant de cotton an' corn,
> An' de white folks gits de money.

FIVE FORKS, WEST VIRGINIA: MILE 199

I pass from Maryland into West Virginia, which was part of Virginia in Mason's and Dixon's day. The Virginia settlers took a dim view of the survey because they claimed this area belonged to them. The issue wouldn't be settled until after the Revolution. Five Forks is no town at all, just a spot where five roads, only three of them paved, converge. Mobile homes and shacks with attendant outhouses speak of disrupted, impoverished households and abandoned hopes. Trash and garbage soil the beautiful landscape. Things have just been allowed to happen here.

UNIONTOWN, PENNSYLVANIA: NORTH OF MILE 210

As they have every year since 1985, Uniontown's blacks are having a reunion this weekend, and they have gathered along Baker Alley just off the main street in the east end of town. Some of them have come from the West Coast. Others have never left, continuing a local family tradition that goes back four and five generations.

A house on Baker Alley was the site of an Underground Railroad station, and the group placed a stone marker here in 1996. "Slave catchers used to come here all the time," a woman in a straw hat tells me. "The runaways would be hidden under the floorboards, and the residents would start dancing, singing, and clapping to muffle any sounds that might give them away."

North of Uniontown, Colonel George Washington owned a large tract of land known as Simpson's that was run with slave labor. The operation was managed by Valentine Crawford, who frequently wrote letters to Washington in which the slaves were called "servants." Some extracts from his letters:

May 7, 1774: "Your servants are all in very good health, and if you should incline selling them, I believe I could sell them for cash out here to different people. My brother, William Crawford, wants two of them, and I would take two myself. . . ."

May 13, 1774: "I write to let you know that all your servants are well, and that none have run away. . . ."

June 8, 1774: "I will go to Simpson's tomorrow morning and consult him farther on the affair, and do everything in my power for your interest. The thoughts of selling your servants alarmed them very much, for they do not want to be sold. The whole of them have had some short spells of sickness, and some of them cut themselves with an axe, causing them to lay by for some time. One of the best of Stephens' [Washington's millwright] men cut himself with an adze the worst I ever say anybody cut in my life. He has not been able to do one stroke for near a month. This happened in digging out the canoes. . . ."

On October 7, about 225 miles from the Northeast Corner, Mason, Dixon, et al., were joined by a Seneca war party of eight braves who were heading south to battle the Cherokees in what is now Tennessee. Mason marveled at their mobility— "These people go 700 Miles thro' these deserts [i.e., wilderness] *to War." Like the Mohawks, the Senecas were one of the Six Nation tribes and so were welcome visitors for the Indians accompanying Mason and Dixon. The Senecas carried guns as well as tomahawks and bows and arrows. The surveying team gave them "a small supply of Powder."*

The Senecas stayed with them for two miles until October 9, when they reached the Catawba War Path; here the war party turned south. The path, also known as the Iroquois Main Path and the Cherokee Path, ran from upper New York State to the Carolinas and was one of the most important Indian highways in North America. With the connections it had at each end, it extended from Canada to Florida and west into the Mississippi Valley. It is the reason that shells from the

Gulf of Mexico have turned up in Canada. It was about eighteen inches wide, and generations of moccasined feet had made it about a foot deep. It followed the higher ground, making travelers less vulnerable to flooding or enemy attack, and it crossed rivers and streams at the narrowest, most easily forded points.

The Catawba War Path also brought the Mason-Dixon expedition to a sudden, permanent halt. The leader of the Mohawks informed the two surveyors that the path, as Mason recounts, "was the extent of his commission from the Chiefs of the Six Nations . . . and that he would not proceed one step farther westward." Thus, on October 9, 1767, the Indians drew their own line.

The assignment to Mason and Dixon from the Penns and Calverts had called for them to go west five degrees of longitude from the shore of Delaware Bay. They were about 35 miles short of that goal.

Shawnee war parties were reported to be active in the area at this time, and the Indians who had been with Mason and Dixon since July 16 did not want to encounter them. The whites were made uneasy by the knowledge that Dunkard Creek, some 3,000 feet beyond the warpath, had been named for a nearby town where settlers had been massacred by Indians in 1755.

The English scientists accepted the ultimatum and prevailed upon the Indians to allow them to go a little farther west to the top of a 300-foot hill. Here—230 miles, 18 chains, and 21 links from the Northeast Corner—they brought out the zenith sector for the last time and used Capella, Lyrae, and Cygni to confirm their position.

While they made their observations, they were visited by Pisquetomen, the brother of the Lenni Lenape chief, Tamaqua, and himself one of the ablest Indians on the frontier. Pisquetomen had been in line to become chief in 1747, but his accession was vetoed by English authorities, who feared they would not be able to control him. In 1755 he had allied with the French and terrorized settlers in Pennsylvania and Maryland.

But now Pisquetomen, who spoke English well, was eighty-six years old. He told Mason and Dixon that he and his brother "had a great mind to go and see the great King over ye Waters and make a perpetual Peace with him; but was afraid he should not be sent back to his own Country."

Mason and Dixon finished their work on October 18 and heaped a five-foot mound of rocks and earth on their final stake. No doubt with some pride, Mason recorded that the mound was "nearly conical." The party turned eastward on October 20 for the long journey back. After cutting vistos, making corrections in the Line, and fighting snowstorms and worker desertions, they were in Christiana Bridge on Christmas Day meeting with the commissioners.

MILE 219

From the bank of the Monongahela, I watch the tow-boat *Michael J. Grainger* push loaded barges up the north-flowing river toward Pittsburgh. To the north and Pennsylvania is the Point Marion lock and dam, which is operated by the U.S. Army Corps of Engineers. To the south and West Virginia are the twin stacks of the Fort Martin Power Plant, an old coal burner. Near the plant Indians massacred Reverend John Corbly, a Baptist minister, and his wife and two children.

I am stopped at Interstate 79 by a deep perpendicular wall of rock near Mile 228. It's a another quarter-mile to Route 19, a winding two-laner displaced by the interstate. Runaway slaves fled down this road, which was on the Underground Railroad leading to Uniontown.

WAYNESBURG, PENNSYLVANIA: NORTHWEST OF MILE 220

At the Waynesburg Public Library, I make a startling discovery. In the Greene County history section, I find a dusty, faded-black, three-volume work entitled, in discreet gold letters, *The Horn Papers: Early Westward Movement on the Monongahela and Upper Ohio, 1765–1795*. It is the work of William Franklin Horn, based on the diaries of his eighteenth century ancestors. It was published in 1945 by the Greene County Historical Society, and it contained information about Mason and Dixon that I had found from no other source.

With mounting excitement, I read that three Mason-Dixon axemen were killed by Indians who feared they were about to chop down a sacred black walnut tree and that the Indians were constantly pilfering from the expedition's supply tents. There is a detailed description of the placing of the final marker at Dunkard Creek. Local people who worked on the survey are named and quoted. It is a trove of hitherto undisclosed information, and I felt afloat on a sea of good luck. It seemed too good to be true.

It was. Some research into the *Horn Papers* themselves turned up a 1947 article in *Time* magazine called, "The Great Hornswoggle." It was one of the great

historic frauds of all time. Horn claimed that he had found documents preserved in a family chest handed down to four generations of Horns since 1795.
Most of them conveniently were written on birch bark and old linen—and so
decayed that he had to destroy them after copying down the information.

Horn persuaded local newspapers to begin running excerpts in 1932.
The stories were riveting, and the information literally rewrote western
Pennsylvania history. A. L. Moredock of the Greene County Historical
Society spent nine years editing them and $23,000 of his own money to
print them. Within two years of their publication, they had been totally
discredited by the academic world. The *Horn Papers* were riddled with
anachronisms, such as an incident where George Washington fell into the
Allegheny River and then couldn't start a fire "because his matches got
wet." There were words not in use at the time they were supposedly
uttered. One Mason-Dixon map, dated 1765, had been treated with ammo-
nia to produce a brown, aged look.

Horn died in 1949 without ever disclosing the motivation for his deception. Moredock spent the last nine years of his life trying to verify the authenticity of the papers, and he died in 1954 a broken man. Many researchers and
genealogists continue to read and believe the *Horn Papers* to this day.

MORGANTOWN, WEST VIRGINIA: SOUTH OF MILE 221

Connie Park Rice is an Appalachian regional history expert at West
Virginia University and has written a book on local black history, *Our
Monongalia*. Her office is right next to Elizabeth More Hall. "In 1943," she
says, "the choir from Monongalia High School, which was the black school,
was invited to sing at the university Christmas program in that hall. The
YWCA wanted to serve refreshments after their performance to get
acquainted with the singers, but the university's dean of women refused to
allow whites and blacks to eat together.

"Back in 1827, there was a slave named Joshua who was arrested for the
rape of a white woman. Joshua was convicted and hanged. He was eighteen
years old. The state reimbursed his owner $250 for his loss. The most bizarre
thing about the case was that it came out at the trial that Joshua had been
aided in the rape by the husband of the victim. Nothing happened to him.

"Morgantown is ringed by hills, and some nights in the 1920s the Klan
would burn crosses up there to remind blacks to stay in their place. The

Klan was big here. . . ."

Indeed, the West Virginia Ku Klux Klan contributed $1,000 toward the construction of Mountaineer Field, the old university football stadium, in 1924. Two years later, on Memorial Day weekend, the KKK held a major rally in the stadium that attracted some 15,000 spectators, who cheered as about 2,500 Klan members marched into the stadium led by the 400 men of Monongalia Klan #59 and its women's auxiliary. They carried crosses illuminated with battery-powered bulbs and waved American flags. There were klaverns from other parts of West Virginia, plus Pennsylvania, Maryland, Ohio, and New Jersey. Spectators contributed by tossing coins and bills into eight-foot-long American flags that were spread open like blankets for this purpose. The main speaker was Imperial Wizard Hiram Wesley Evans, who condemned Catholics, "nigras," and the United States' membership in the World Court; he also called for strict immigration limits. Bishop J. J. Swint of the Wheeling Roman Catholic diocese protested the use of the stadium for the rally, but was ignored by university president F. B. Trotter.

Page 7 of Estate Book 3 at the Monongalia County Courthouse appraises the estate of George Dorsey, a prominent lawyer, who died in 1824. It includes one black mare valued at $20; 2 sows and 11 pigs ($10), 14 head of cattle ($84), one thirteen-year-old Negro boy named Harry ($275), 70 sheep and lambs ($100), one fifteen-year-old Negro girl named Ann ($400), and one sixty-year-old Negro man named Ned ($25).

The last two slaves sold in Monongalia County were auctioned in front of the courthouse on April 11, 1864. They were a brother and sister who brought, respectively, $326 and $71. The low prices were blamed on the proximity to the Mason-Dixon Line, where slaves might easily escape.

A sign marks the Catawba War Path, where Mason and Dixon were stopped by the Mohawks.

MILE 233

A vintage black pickup truck is squatting on its axles along the Catawba Path, where the Seneca war party left Mason and Dixon and where the Mohawks told the English geodesists they had gone as far as they were going to go. There's no sign of the ancient trail, not even an indentation, but the state of West Virginia has marked the spot appropriately with a historic sign.

At the Mason-Dixon Historical Park, a joint venture of Greene County, Pennsylvania, and Monongalia County, West Virginia, the annual Mason-Dixon Festival is running full throttle on a bright September afternoon. There's a Civil War encampment, kiddie rides, and demonstrations of forgotten pioneer skills like candle making and quilting.

But the major portion of the festival is devoted to Native Americans. Costumed dancers are taking cues from drumbeats and chanting. A noisy maelstrom of buckskin-clad kids are standing in line to get their faces painted and shooting each other with pretend bows and arrows. Women dressed like squaws with little bells around their ankles tend food stands offering buffalo burgers, Indian fry bread, Indian corn soup, and bison chili. Men in ponytails under feathered headdresses sit in front of tables tottering with moccasins, bright blankets, beads, pottery, Lakota dictionaries, and CDs by Native American stars like Joanee Shenandoah and Judy Trejo.

One of the tables offers photocopies of a 1995 newspaper article by Jack Anderson calling for a reopening of the case of Leonard Peltier, the Native American serving a life sentence for the murder of two FBI agents on a South Dakota reservation in 1975. Anderson claimed the FBI doctored evi-

The Mason-Dixon Festival is held annually near the stopping point.

dence in building a case against Peltier, but the case has not been reopened.

Near the park, there's a state historical sign that says: "BORDER HEROINE: DURING THE INDIAN RAIDS IN 1779 UPON THE SETTLEMENTS OF DUNKARD CREEK, SAVAGES ATTACKED THE CABIN OF JOHN BOZARTH. ARMED ONLY WITH AN AXE, MRS. BOZARTH KILLED THREE OF THE RED MEN."

I approach a man in a buckskin shirt, jeans, and moccasins and ask him if he finds the sign offensive. He smiles indulgently. "Those signs are from a period before the awakening of our people. It was the good guys and the bad guys back then. We know better than that now."

He says he's part Shawnee and his Indian name is Dreaming Spirit Owl. I ask him why there are so many Native Americans here. "This is sacred land. The land this park is on was occupied for hundreds of years by Native Americans. The Shawnees were here when Mason and Dixon were here. When farmers plow new fields around here, they find the soil is discolored by campfires."

He puts a finger to his mouth contemplatively. "There are many people living in this area who have Indian blood. In fact, if you go back four generations, it's almost a guarantee that you're part Indian because of intermarriage with the settlers. People tried to hide it until fairly recently. . . ."

Hours later the park is bathed in sunset orange, and as the musicians and vendors are packing it in for the day, I begin the long walk up Brown's Hill. It takes about twenty minutes to reach the top, and the stone that marks the end of the line for Mason and Dixon is silhouetted in purply twilight. I shine my flashlight on the stone, which was placed here in 1883 during a resurvey. It's surrounded by gravel to hold down vegetation, and it's leaning slightly towards West Virginia. The night deepens. One by one the stars begin colonizing the sky. The insects begin their nocturne, filling the night with questions.

A stone atop Brown's Hill marks the end of the Mason-Dixon Line.

EPILOGUE

"We shall not cease from exploration
And the end of all our exploring
Will be to arrive where we started
And know the place for the first time"
    —T. S. Eliot, from "Four Quartets," 1943

On September 11, 1768, four years and ten months after they came to America, Mason and Dixon sailed from New York for Falmouth. "Thus ends my restless progress in America," Mason wrote in his journal's final entry.

The commissioners issued a report on November 9, 1768, describing the survey step by step. The names of Mason and Dixon are not mentioned— for they were merely the instruments by which the commissioners achieved their work on behalf of the Calverts and the Penns.

Mason and Dixon parted when they got to England, and there is no evidence that they had any communication afterwards. Interestingly, they both worked for the Royal Society in observing another Transit of Venus in 1769—but Mason went to Ireland, Dixon to Norway. In later years, Dixon busied himself with occasional projects for the Royal Society and routine surveying in Durham. He was visited at Cockfield by Captain James Cook, the famed Royal Navy navigator whom Dixon had met in 1761 on his return journey from the Cape of Good Hope. Dixon died a bachelor on January 22, 1779, at the age of forty-five.

Mason continued his astronomical career with the Royal Society, often working with Nevil Maskelyne, the royal astronomer, on significant projects. He was elected to membership in the American Philosophical Society, probably with the help of Benjamin Franklin, with whom he seems to have had some relationship. He also married for a second time and raised a large family.

Apparently it was too large to support on his scholarly income—for sometime in 1786 Mason returned to Philadelphia with his wife, seven sons, and one daughter. On September 27, he wrote to Franklin informing him of his arrival and that he was ill and confined to bed. In early November, Philadelphia newspapers announced that Mason had died on October 25 at the age of fifty-eight. He was buried in an unmarked grave in Christ Church Burial Ground, which would later be the final resting place for Franklin.

Border troubles continued sporadically along the Line. John Penn complained in a 1774 letter: "The people living between the ancient temporary line of jurisdiction, and that lately settled and marked by the commissioners, were in a lawless state. Murders, and the most outrageous transgressions of law and order, were committed with impunity in those places. In vain did persons injured apply to the government of Maryland for protection and redress." Two years later, Revolution divested the Penns and the Calverts of their colonial holdings.

The Mason-and-Dixon visto accelerated westward migration by providing a quick, well-marked route to the Ohio Valley. This avenue through the wilderness was advertised by the tales of axemen and other Mason and Dixon "hands." It also provided cleared land for the settlers to plant their first vital crops.

The western terminus of the Pennsylvania boundary was determined in 1784 by a team that included several advisers to Mason and Dixon. There were resurveys of all or parts of the Line in 1849–50, 1883, 1892, 1901–03, 1961, and 1977–78. No serious error was found.

George Washington used the term "Mason and Dixon Line" in a letter written in 1774. Thomas Jefferson used "Mason's & Dixon's Line" in a 1776 letter. The phrase "Mason and Dixon's Line" was used several times in 1782 in a Continental Congress debate over the Connecticut border. Almost imperceptibly, it took on its powerful, symbolic meaning in the first half of the nineteenth century. And, in a speech to the Historical Society of Pennsylvania on November 8, 1854, Historian John H. B. Latrobe said:

> There is, perhaps no line, real or imaginary, on the surface of the earth—not excepting even the equator and the equinoctial—whose

name has been oftener in men's mouths during the last fifty years. In the halls of legislation, in the courts of justice, in the assemblages of the people, it has been as familiar as a household word. Not that any particular interest was taken in the line itself; but the mention of it was always expressive of the fact, that the States of the Union were divided into slaveholding and non-slaveholding—into Northern and Southern; that those who lived on opposite sides of the line of separation, were antagonistic in opinion upon an all-engrossing question, whose solution, and its Consequences, involved the gravest considerations, and had been supposed to threaten the integrity of the Republic. Its geographical, thus became lost in its political, significance; and men cared little, when they referred to it, where it ran or what was its history. . . .

Mason or his descendants either lost or discarded the journal, but in 1860 it mysteriously turned up in Halifax, Nova Scotia, among a pile of papers consigned to a trash heap. It was rescued by Judge Alexander James of the Supreme Court of Nova Scotia, who sent it as part of the Canadian exhibits at the Philadelphia Centennial in 1876. Here it came to the attention of Secretary of State Hamilton Fish, who purchased it from James in 1877 for $500. Charles Mason's journal is now on file in the National Archives. Both Mason and Dixon were instructed to maintain field records, but it is not known if Dixon kept a journal.

T. Robert Bechtol, a member of the Mason and Dixon Line Preservation Partnership, has estimated the cost of the survey. Using figures supplied by the Franklin Institute and the National Park Service for the costs of basic commodities, such as leather, flour, and lamp oil, in the 1760s, the Penns and the Calverts each paid about $1.5 million in year-2000 dollars to draw the Line between 1760 and 1769. For their nearly five years of work in the New World, Mason and Dixon each received the modern equivalent of about $200,000 each. The relatively low total is indicative that both were journeymen in their profession.

The zenith sector built for Mason and Dixon by John Bird was stored in Philadelphia, and after the Revolution it was brought to the state capitol at Harrisburg. It was lost in a fire that destroyed the capitol in 1897.

In 1859, Dan D. Hammett composed the song, "I Wish I Was in Dixie's Land," for use in a minstrel show. These performances featured whites who had their faces painted black and loudly sang of their love of the South and slavery. Later the title was shortened to "Dixie" and it became the

Confederacy's unofficial national anthem. Etymologists credit Hammett with coining the word, but they are uncertain what he had in mind when he did. One theory is that the word refers to the Mason-Dixon Line. But another is that is comes from a ten-dollar bill that circulated in the South marked with the French word for ten—"dix." Neither seems totally plausible, and the mystery is not likely to be solved.

George Wayman Dixon drives decisively and confidently, like an RAF fighter pilot, which he once was. He roars into Cockfield village, which stands atop a ridge overlooking mine-scarred land. Slag heaps overgrown with grass give the land an undulating look. There are narrow, stone walled pieces of land called strip fields, which were given to the serfs by the baron in the fifteenth century for their own use. Off in the distance, grazing sheep are white dots on the green hills of Durham. A steady wind is turning up the pale underside of the leaves.

He looks at the two-chimneyed stone house. "It was built in 1751 by Jeremiah's father, who left it to Jeremiah's brother, George. Jeremiah came here whenever he returned to England. He probably lived here from the time he was eighteen. He used this house as his base to travel all over the world. I grew up in this house. . . ."

George Dixon—pilot, retired school principal, local magistrate, amateur boxer, amateur historian, amateur actor, amateur composer, cricketeer, and organist at his local church—is the nephew, five generations removed, of Jeremiah Dixon. When he was twelve years old, a great uncle kindled an interest in his ancestor that has stayed with him.

He leans against a lichened stone wall in front of the Cockfield house and points to a spot about fifty yards away. "The bomb was dropped just where that tree is. My mother hid me under the staircase. The German bombers came in 1940. They came over right after they occupied Norway. They dropped all their bombs but they didn't hit a single building because they were running east and west when they should have been going north and south. It was August 15th."

In the town of Cockfield there's a small, rectangular stone trough that just now is filled with a ganglia of weeds and debris rather than flowers. It is inscribed:

Dixon Garden
Given by the
Children of the School
to Commemorate
the Silver Jubilee of
Queen Elizabeth II
1977.

George looks at it sadly. "It was supposed to be a memorial to Jeremiah, but no one's terribly interested in him in his own land."

The Raby Moor Inn pub is crowded with regulars, whose voices rub cheerfully against each other. The barman downshifts a lager and sets it in front of George, who nods appreciatively. "They must have been incredibly brave, those two, going off all over the world when it was a very difficult and dangerous thing to do.

"There's a lot of erroneous information out there about Jeremiah. Some historians associate him with the army because he wore a red coat. But the truth is he went to the Royal Woolwich Academy in London, and he liked its paramilitary red tunic and cocked hat so much that he wore nothing else for the rest of his life."

He winks. "Jeremiah, you know, was a bit of a rogue. The Quakers kicked him out for his use of strong drink." He ponders the glass in front of him for a few seconds, then continues. "There's also very strong evidence that he was close to a certain widow around here and maybe even sired a few children." He reaches into his vest pocket and emerges with a piece of paper. "I read to you now from the last will and testament of Jeremiah Dixon. 'I leave all houses, gardens, dye houses and premises in the manor of Bondgate in Bishop Auckland, in trust and for the benefit of Margaret Bland, the income of the same to go to the maintenance of the two daughters of the said Margaret.'" He looks at me, smiling triumphantly, like a skater who'd just won Olympic gold. "I rest my case."

In 1995, George Dixon was invited to America by a group of Mason-Dixon devotees. "It was one of my life's ambitions. I got to the place at Dunkard Creek where they stopped, where they were turned back by the Indians. I stood next to the marker . . . the first of Jeremiah's descendants to return to that place since he had left. This was a very emotional and moving experience for me to complete the circle of reunion."

The old Quaker Meeting House at Staindrop, built about 1769, is now a private home, and the old burial ground is a garden. The current owner is an obliging man, and he lets us look around. He says he's only owned the house for two years and is still restoring it. "Just when you get one thing done, another comes up. There will be an end, though." Dixon stands in the middle of the garden, which is surrounded by a stone wall. "I figure he's about here." He points to the ground near the far side of the wall. "It's not marked because early Quakers didn't use headstones." Overhead the sun is playing hide-and-seek with the clouds. The garden is ablaze with lavender, poppies, roses, fuchsia, apple trees, and sweet peas.

As I'm leaving the next day, Dixon hands me a typewritten sheet. It's an extract from a local regional newspaper, the *Newcastle Chronicle,* dated February 14, 1914.

> In the course of that memorable survey in Dixie Land, Jeremiah Dixon one day saw a burly planter unmercifully flogging a poor slave woman with a heavy whip, and he went up to him and said, "Thou must not be so cruel as to do that."
>
> "You be d-----" was the answer of the slave-driver, "I'll do what I like with my own."
>
> Quaker though he was, he suited the action to the word, seized the whip from the planter's hand and thrashed him with it. Dixon brought the whip home to England as a trophy, and I am told that it was to be seen in the North of England up to some years ago. The name of the gentleman to whom it was handed down was Solomon Chapman, a Quaker, who lived at Sunderland or at Whitby, or had associations with these places.
>
> It would be interesting to know what has become of the whip and into whose hands it has ultimately fallen. I was told the whip was taken to the Wilberforce Museum in Hull.

A month later, I receive a letter from Jayne Tyler, Keeper of Social History at Wilberforce House: "Thank you for your enquiry. Wilberforce House had a number of whips on display prior to 1983, many of which were taken off display as their provenance was not clear and the curator at the time could not guarantee their authenticity. . . . I will do a few investigations to see if there is any firm background to the one on display and let you know if I find out anything. If the whip was known to be in Hull Museums before 1939 it could well have been damaged in a bombing attack in the 1940s at the Albion Street museum where lots of items were damaged or destroyed. I will contact you again if I find out more."

There was no further communication.

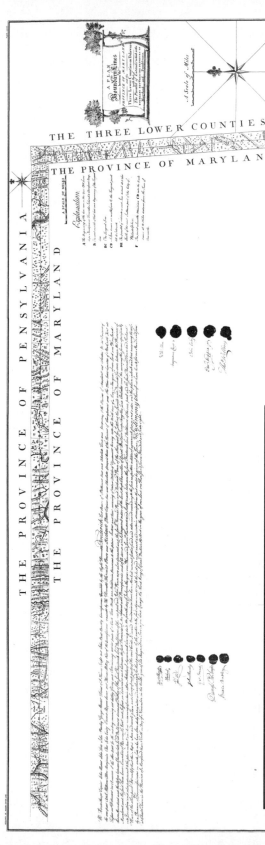

Mason and Dixon's surveying resulted in the above map of the Line, which can be seen in more detail preceding each chapter. The explanation of points given on the map reads as follows:

A   The beginning of the line run in the year 1751 from Cape Henlopen on Fenwicks Island to Chesapeak Bay.

B   The exact middle of that line and the Beginning of the Tangent Line

BC   The Tangent Line

CD   A Line drawn north from C the Tangent Point till it Intersects

DE   The parallel of Latitude or west Line distant 15 Miles South of the most Southern part of the City of Philadelphia

F   The point where the Meridian CD cuts the Circle drawn at 12 Miles distance from the Town of Newcastle.

The map to the left is part of the Benjamin Eastburn map of 1740, showing the boundary line of the New Castle Circle.

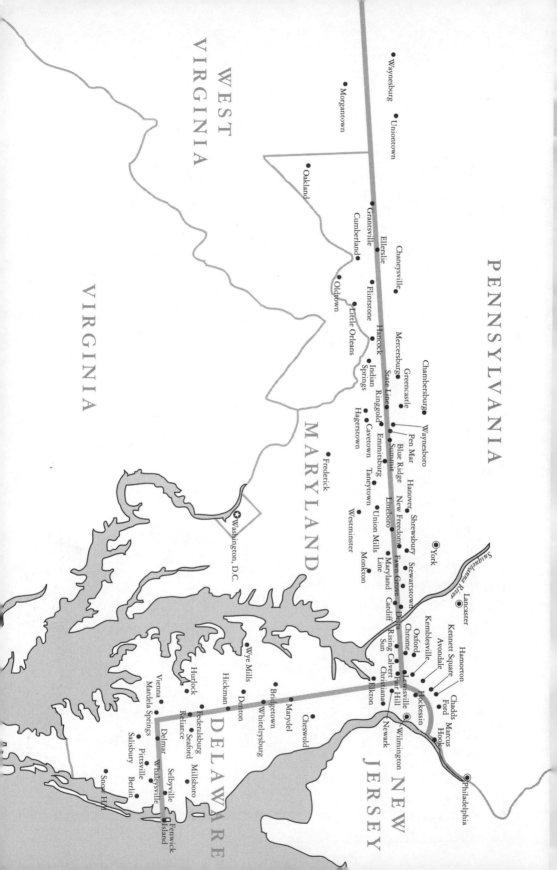